INTRODUCTION TO PHILOSOPHY
A Case Method Approach

EXPERIENCE AND REFLECTION: CASE METHOD SERIES
Series Editors: *Robert A. Evans and Louis B. Weeks*

CHRISTIAN THEOLOGY   *Robert A. Evans and Thomas D. Parker*
FULL VALUE   *Oliver F. Williams and John M. Houck*
INTRODUCTION TO PHILOSOPHY   *Jack B. Rogers and Forrest E. Baird*

INTRODUCTION TO PHILOSOPHY

A Case Method Approach

Jack B. Rogers and Forrest E. Baird

Consulting Editor: Robert A. Evans

National Advisory Council: Charles Hartshorne,
John Smith, Stephen Davis, Alvin Plantinga

1817

HARPER & ROW, PUBLISHERS, SAN FRANCISCO

Cambridge, Hagerstown, New York, Philadelphia,
London, Mexico City, São Paulo, Sydney

FIRST EDITION

Designed by Jim Mennick

Library of Congress Cataloging in Publication Data

Rogers, Jack Bartlett.
 INTRODUCTION TO PHILOSOPHY.

 (Experience and reflection)
 Bibliography: p. 217.
 Includes index.
 1. Philosophy—Introductions. 2. Philosophers.
I. Baird, Forrest E. II. Title.
BD21.R63 1981   190   80-8344
ISBN 0-06-066997-7

81 82 83 84 85 10 9 8 7 6 5 4 3 2

To Ruth E. Rogers, my mother,
who taught me always to think for myself
—JACK

To Joy, for her assistance and continued patience and love
—FORREST

Contents

Acknowledgments

SOME BOOKS are researched and written as a relatively compact and continuous activity by the author(s). Others evolve over a long period of time, arising out of developing experience with materials in a life context. This book is of the second kind. It has grown piece by piece, and has developed and changed as the data has been tested in class by students and colleagues.

Jack Rogers was trained at the Case Study Institute in Cambridge, Massachusetts, in connection with Harvard Business School and the Boston Theological Institute in the summer of 1973. He has written and taught cases in a number of areas, including the history of Christian thought in which he published *Case Studies in Christ and Salvation* with Ross Mackenzie and Louis Weeks in 1977.

In 1975 Forrest Baird, while a candidate for a doctorate in philosophy at the Claremont Graduate School, was acting as a teaching assistant to Jack Rogers in Rogers's basic course in philosophical theology at Fuller Theological Seminary. Rogers and Baird together faced the task of introducing the Western philosophical tradition to students from a wide variety of backgrounds, most of whom had never studied philosophy. In addition to lectures and discussions, they began to use some case studies, written for other disciplines but with philosophical dimensions. Then they decided to experiment with producing cases about major philosophers in the Western tradition. The collaboration continued as Forrest began his own teaching career. Each year a few more cases were added. Previous cases were rewritten after being tested in class. Students were encouraged to write cases as class projects. Sometimes these student cases contributed elements to developing cases. Colleagues gave helpful suggestions, some of which were incorporated at various stages.

The authors are grateful, therefore, to successive years of students in TH500, Philosophical Theology, at Fuller Seminary and to the students and faculty colleagues—Dr. Shirley Richner, Dr. Duncan Ferguson, Dr. Ronald C. White, Jr., and the Core 250 team—at Whitworth College in Spokane, Washington. Both Rogers and Baird have additionally tested the cases with adults in midcareer through courses in Fuller's Extension Education Program in Seattle, San Jose, Santa Barbara, Hollywood, and Boulder. Colleagues at other institutions around the country have used some of the cases and provided valuable insights.

Out of all those who have contributed to this process, the following students and colleagues deserve special mention for their help on particular cases: Socrates—Dr. James Hunt, Dr. David Downing, Dr. Charles Young; Aristotle—Dr. Bruce Murphy, Dr. David Downing, Dr. Charles Young; Augustine—Brett Lamberty; Anselm and Aquinas, and Descartes—Leonard Oakland; Kant— Bruce Boyer and Dr. Norman Krebbs; Kierkegaard—Dr. Ron Kernaghan (who laid the basis for the final draft), Dr. Stan Slade, Richard Farley, Richard Israel, Mark Wiedenmann; Marx—Dr. William Benz; Whitehead—Dr. John Cobb; and Wittgenstein—Dr. Ronald Hustwit and Dr. David Downing.

The authors have been helped immeasurably by the critical interaction with each case by the living philosopher who has written a contemporary response to it. These respondents are, of course, not responsible for remaining flaws, but they have helped to assure us that we are on the right track and reasonably within the center of the interpretative tradition regarding each philosopher. Special recognition and thanks to these leading contemporary philosophers and especially to the philosophers on our National Advisory Council is expressed for all of us by the series editor, Robert A. Evans, in his introduction. The names of these living shapers of the Western philosophical tradition are found in the table of contents.

Our Series Editor has been much more than that to us in this project. Robert A. Evans studied philosophy at Yale University and has a doctorate in philosophical theology from Union Theological Seminary, New York. He is the author of *Intelligible and Responsible Talk About God* and editor of *The Future of Philosophical Theology*. He shared with us the concept of having living scholars write "briefs" in response to cases, a concept he and Thomas Parker used so successfully in *Christian Theology: A Case Method Approach*, the first in the Harper & Row Case Study Series. Evans joined us in inviting members of the National Advisory Council to participate and did significant editing of the manuscript at several stages. His friendship and insight provided us with support and creative vision over a period of several years as this project developed.

In two instances, the authors turned to friends who were both students and colleagues and asked them to write cases that appear in an edited form in the book. We drew on their expertise regarding the philosopher involved and their skill as case writers. And we asked their help to meet deadlines on short notice. The inclusion of the cases on Karl Marx and William James add depth and balance to the array of philosophical emphases presented.

Stanley David Slade wrote the case of Karl Marx. He is presently assistant professor of philosophy at Jamestown College in North Dakota. He studied philosophy at Stanford University and has a doctorate in philosophical theology from Fuller Theological Seminary. He has published articles and reviews on biblical interpretation and liberation theology.

Julie Hastings wrote the case of William James. She has earned three bachelor degrees: in English literature at the University of Redlands; in humanities at Cal State, Dominguez Hills; and in philosophy at Cambridge University in England. She has studied drama at the University of London, has done graduate work in psychology at Claremont and currently is pursuing a master's degree in theology at Fuller Theological Seminary. She has published numerous newspaper and magazine articles.

The authors wish to give signal recognition and thanks to those teachers who first introduced them to the joys of philosophy. For Forrest Baird, they were Dr. Robert Wennberg and Dr. Stanley Obitts at Westmont College; for Jack Rogers, the late Dr. O. K. Bousma at the University of Nebraska.

Forrest Baird remains grateful to the philosophy faculty of the Claremont Graduate School for their encouragement and patience while he worked on this book and taught at the same time that he was completing his dissertation. Jack Rogers acknowledges with thanks the assistance of two institutions and many people who have supported this project. The work was carried out and finally completed during two sabbatical leaves granted by the board of trustees and the administration of Fuller Theological Seminary. During a sabbatical year in 1977–78, this manuscript was one of several projects Jack pursued while in residence as a fellow of the Institute for Ecumenical and Cultural Research in connection with St. John's University in Collegeville, Minnesota. A sabbatical for the spring quarter, 1980, at Fuller Theological Seminary gave opportunity for the final editing. Dolores Loeding and Barbara Ann Shore each typed earlier drafts of the cases. The final version was typed on a Diablo 1650 Word Processor by Margo Houts and Karen Johnson. It is somehow appropriate that ancient wisdom should be communicated through the contemporary technology of the computer age.

Finally, the deepest thanks go to those who have accepted us as we are and who loved and supported us in the most important ways: our wives, Joy Baird and Sharee Rogers; and our children, Whitney Jaye Baird and Matthew, John, and Toby Rogers.

An Introduction to the Case Method for Students and Teachers

ROBERT A. EVANS

> When a person is ready and willing to taste every kind of knowledge, and
> addresses himself joyfully to his studies with an appetite which never can
> be satiated, we shall justly call such a person a philosopher, shall we not?[1]

SOCRATES provides in this declaration a simple and basic way to understand philosophy. It is the love of learning. The Greek word *philosophia,* many scholars think, was coined by Pythagoras (about 570–490 B.C.) and means the love of wisdom. Numerous ways of understanding and defining philosophy have developed over the centuries since Socrates. The reader will encounter several examples in the cases and commentaries that follow. These cases are drawn from the life experiences of twelve pursuers of wisdom who have shaped the Western tradition of philosophy.

What is fascinating about Socrates' insight is not only its simplicity but its emphasis on the joy and the almost irresistible attraction of tasting every form of knowledge. Such a love affair with learning usually serves as the foundation for more technical definitions of philosophy sometimes required by thinkers in special times or circumstances. Like the authors of the cases and commentaries, I have been both a student and teacher of philosophy. The excitement and transforming power that a genuine love of wisdom provides has often but unfortunately not always been present in courses in philosophy that I have taken or offered.

The philosophical tradition has sought to nurture not only critical and comprehensive thinking but also forms or methods of seeking knowledge that are persuasive and arresting. The Platonic dialogues are an example of a form of communication that is so engaging it has proved threatening to established persons and perspectives in society from the 5th century B.C. to the present.

Experience with the Method

The case study approach evidences promise as a method that may assist in renewing intellectual vitality and personal application to the classroom teaching of philosophy. The cases in this book have been tested in philosophy classes at the undergraduate and graduate levels. The evaluations of students and teachers who have used cases as a supplementary methodology have been extraordinarily positive. The discussion of cases induces involvement, demands a decision, and requires the articulation of the philosophical grounds on which a position is taken. The method was originally introduced as a catalyst for further reflection and as a means to evaluate the integration and application of philosophical learning. Since its introduction there have been requests from teachers and students alike for more cases to be employed regularly throughout courses.

Assumptions, goals, and limitations for a particular educational approach will vary according to the design of the course and the aims of the instructor. From extensive experience with cases, several basic assumptions and consistent goals have emerged, however. These are shared not because they are believed normative but because they may function as illustrations of assumptions and goals that may be shared by teachers and learners alike during the first years of employing this teaching approach.

Assumptions

A completed philosophical case could be compared to a well-written but condensed mystery story. All the appropriate clues are present. The primary limitations on information are only the same natural ones that operated for the actual participants in the case determined by the limitations of their humanity or historical circumstances. The aim of the case-oriented teaching style, and one of the most distinctive elements in this approach, is to foster and facilitate the student's analytic and creative skills in the area of philosophical reflection. Accomplishment of this goal is based not only on the skill and sensitivity of the case teacher but also on the following working assumptions about the pedagogical style as related to philosophy.

Skill Facilitating

The initial assumption is that the case method actually does facilitate analytical and creative skills. Many teaching methods demonstrate or point to the skills or capabilities that one is to develop. The case method assumes that a person will actually grow in the ability to analyze carefully and to create perceptive, imaginative alternatives for the participants in the case and for him-/or herself. This working assumption has been confirmed by students and teachers who have experimented with cases. The accompanying implication discovered in this skill development is that both analysis and creativity are dependent on and enriched by others. Perhaps this is best illustrated by the experience of many case teachers who find that a case they teach regularly is constantly changing and coming alive in new ways through the insights and perspectives of different students. So a teaching plan employed by case instructors will always demand revision as the instructor draws on and incorporates the philosophical discernment of students as well as his or her own research and reflection. The philosophical community, whether the one present in Plato's Academy or in your classroom, can be an important resource in finding authentic, humane, and imaginative alternatives to a human predicament as set forth in a case.

Self-Involving and Affirming

The second working assumption is that the case discussion, more than many other methods, will rely on the resources of the student in analyzing the problem, selecting a creative alternative, and developing a philosophical rationale for the form of action or understanding that he or she comes to own. Experience in schools of law, business, and theology with the case method approach affirms the working assumption that this is one of the most self-involving pedagogical styles presently available. Participants find themselves drawn into a discussion of the case precisely because it seems to make contact with similar elements in their own experience. Also, a case provides a nonthreatening point of entry into controversial discussion, because one begins by sharing views about Socrates, Kant, or Wittgenstein and what they ought to do. After one is involved in the case discussion, a shift frequently occurs, and participants share their own judgments and convictions about their response in a comparable situation. The responsibility for a decision frequently becomes an element of such involvement.

Another side of this working assumption shared by many case teachers and students is that a genuine trust is communicated, not only for the mutual contributions of student and teacher, but also for the personal integrity of other people's thoughts and commitments as they participate in this dialogue form of education. The case approach to teaching tends to confirm in its pedagogical style a philosophical stance that honors the human rights and freedom of each person. A type of personal affirmation can take place through the support and critique that emerge from the instructor as well as from the students' reciprocal responsiveness to judgments, insights, and feelings. From a graduate school seminar to a college classroom setting, the case method assumes the mutual respect and critical appreciation of one another's humanity. This method bears the promise and potential of a self-involving and self-affirming reciprocal process that may call participants to be accountable to one another and to the variety and richness of their Western heritage in philosophy.

Goals

Whether or not they are specifically articulated, both learning and teaching goals for what is hoped to occur in the interaction of students, teachers, and data exist in most educational experiments. Goals vary, of course, depending on the particular context of the course of study. Personally, I have developed the pattern of sharing my goals for a specific course with my students in the same way I convey course requirements. As instructor I thus become accountable to my students for teaching both in context and method. Students are invited to share in and take responsibility for these educational expectations.

Wisdom

The term *wisdom* has a rich and multifaceted meaning in the philosophical tradition, but a common goal for those seeking wisdom seems to be integration—the integration of knowledge, discernment, and action. The model employed here seeks a "bringing together" of resources from philosophical traditions with actual decisions about, and understandings of, the realities of human life in the world. Cases function in at least two ways as bridges to wisdom. First, they function as "catalysts" for philosophical thinking by posing concrete issues in such a penetrating and demanding form that students will often emerge from a discussion of the meaning of the good or happiness in Plato and Aristotle newly sensitized to seek the philosophical sources that shaped the use of the term *good* in Immanuel Kant or informed William James as he contemplated whether life was worth living. The contemporary responses to the cases by living philosophers contribute to this quest for wisdom by providing illustrations of their integrative processes of philosophical reflection.

Second, for those seeking wisdom, the case may also function as an evaluative instrument for testing the degree to which their own integration has progressed. The case of Augustine deals with the problem of evil. This offers an opportunity to explore the degree of a student's personal integration and application of learning in an introductory course on philosophy. I would ask the students to pose a problem of evil—in their personal life or in society—that they can describe briefly. Then they can be asked to present their own commentary on their "lived case." Students could be required to choose between the approach to good and evil articulated and illustrated by Socrates, Aristotle, or Augustine. Or, alternately, they could be urged to draw on assigned readings, case discussions, class lectures, and on personal experience to define and defend their own position. Specific recommendations for action can be pressed for in class discussion of students' commentaries, along with philosophical reasons for the decisions they have made.

Maturity

The philosophical tradition has often sought maturity in thought and action as a measure of philosophical training. One dimension of maturity is the ability to make decisions guided by reason and experience and to take responsibility for the consequences of those decisions. Preliminary data seem to affirm that the case method both forces and facilitates this "owning" process. It encourages participants to be more critical of their own philosophical assumptions and more open to hearing with critical appreciation the positions taken by others from different perspectives. The cases and the commentaries help to test the adequacy of philosophical interpretations against human experience. The method encourages interdisciplinary dialogue. Students and teachers together seek understanding that is mature enough to comprehend the philosophical pluralism in our midst and yet demanding enough to insist that one's own position be clearly articulated. The resultant commitments can then be tested in the community of interpretation that is constituted by the wider human society.

Discernment

Philosophical discernment can be understood as a special kind of perception that depends on the development of certain skills or capacities within the context of a thinking community. Discernment is the keen judgment or insight that is the basis for integrating wisdom and responsible maturity. This insight is more than knowledge, because discernment requires both intuition and sensitivity to discriminate between alternatives and their implications for an authentic response. Discernment demands skills in analysis, critique, and creativity. The eye of reason seeks to analyze the crucial issues and options, to criticize constructively positions taken and the assumptions that underlie them, and to propose creative and compassionate alternatives for problems encountered. Discernment, like wisdom and maturity, is a skill developed in community. Students and teachers depend on and learn from each other as they strive toward these goals. The cases provide an opportunity to develop discernment and to build community as we experience and learn to trust one another's insights. The case method can become a means to and a measure of the goals of wisdom, maturity, and discernment.

Limitations

Investment in any experiment in education involves commitment to and advocacy of the project. However, one cannot ignore the problems that also exist, or one is no longer conducting an experiment. The editors of this text, with other professors and students, have been struggling to employ and improve the case method for the last eight years. Lest one give the impression that a case method is a panacea for teaching, I must identify some limitations of the method, particularly because this project was in part conceived to address these limitations.

Lacks Depth

The case method can lack the dimension of critical depth if employed exclusively. Some courses in given institutions use the case method almost exclusively. It is often assumed by representatives of these institutions that the student will acquire on his or her own initiative the information or skills needed to address the cases. This view tends to favor a pragmatic stress on the decision-making task of the future professional. The focus is on a style of leadership, a particular approach to decision making, and on certain criteria for evaluation that are perhaps appropriate for the future business executive but are not necessarily appropriate in the same way for the student of philosophy. The exclusive use of the case method in philosophy can lack critical depth in addressing specific issues and problems and may give insufficient attention to the philosophical tradition as it informs the discussion and decisions that surround a case.

In view of this limitation, the use of cases needs to be coordinated, in my judgment, with assigned reading and research and with lectures and exercises in philosophical reflection. A significant danger of the case method is that one may get so absorbed in the variety of issues posed and so excited about the degree of involvement in a case that the level of focused reflection and thus of genuinely new insights may be overlooked and/or underestimated. If the method is going to have a dimension of critical depth, both instructors and students after their reflection on the case must assume responsibility for investigating other materials that will lead them further.

Hides Assumptions

The method may hide implicit value judgments. Unless the case teacher is open and aware of this danger in the method, it bears the potential of being manipulative. Other methods, of course, sometimes exert overt control over students. Control may be less evident in the case method because it affirms student involvement and contribution as well as focuses on the concerns, interests, and insights of the class. However, case teachers and students often operate under basic philosophical assumptions and criteria that influence their recommendations. Instructors and students experienced in the method urge that ways be sought to make these assumptions explicit either through an introductory lecture by the instructor or opportunities for students and instructor to share during the case discussion.

The point can be illustrated by an interchange between one of the instructors at Harvard Business School and a student who inquired about the criteria employed for evaluating a proposed program to solve a dilemma in a business case. The instructor's response was that there were no predetermined criteria for an acceptable solution apart from the content and boundaries of the particular case. My own experience in the Harvard Business School sessions, however, has suggested another factor. There appeared to be an assumed business "trinity" that was implicitly operative in almost every business case this editor observed: profitability, efficiency, and growth. These criteria are not necessarily objectionable if they are made explicit and critically examined. If assumptions are not open to examination, the case study method has a potential for being a subtle and powerful form of indoctrination just as lecture and discussion methods can be.

For the method to be an effective educational instrument, care must be taken by both student and instructor to examine the presuppositions involved in their analysis of a case. Case teaching experience suggests that at least a working definition of what is meant by terms such as *good, being,* or *evil* is crucial in guarding against implicit value judgments that shape learning from a case. Suggested questions for study are provided at the end of each case. Use of these questions, either in class or in small study groups that meet prior to the general discussion, can draw attention to central concepts and terms. The philosophical commentaries in this volume also seek to expose some of these implicit value judgments in order that they may be critically and appreciatively considered. The limitations of implicit value judgments (not unique to the case method) can never be completely overcome, but they may be modified through the process of self-conscious and consistent exposure.

Hints for Teaching and Learning

In accord with the concern of the American Philosophical Association in their "Newsletter on Teaching Philosophy" and the program of the American

Association of Philosophy Teachers, a few suggestions for using the method are certainly in order.

The cases can be used for reflection by individual readers comparing their own response to that of the contemporary philosopher whose commentary follows each case. The cases are primarily designed, however, as instruments for class discussion in which an informed instructor "teaches" the case. The cases and the contemporary responses to them could be used in such courses as an introduction to philosophy and the history of philosophy or in some topically oriented courses such as the philosophy of religion or ethics. Individual cases could be employed in courses dealing with specific people, periods or issues. Each case treats the basic metaphysics and epistemology of the philosopher presented. In one or more of the cases, other traditional problems of philosophy are treated, such as ethics, esthetics, philosophy of science, and political philosophy. Each case also treats philosophy of religion and can provide a platform for discussion of the integration of personal beliefs and rational reflection about them.

Role of the Instructor

The dilemmas evident in the life situations of these philosophers do not, in the opinion of the case authors, have only one applicable solution nor a single philosophically appropriate response. However, some responses are usually discovered to be more adequate than others. The excitement and power of cases as learning tools is in allowing and assisting participants in the discussion to discover for themselves not only what decision they might make in a similar situation but also what other decisions the person depicted in the case might have responsibly made, and why, in the view of others.

Consider the earlier comparison between a case and a mystery story. A mystery has clues to be discovered and assembled in order to discover the solution. The difference is that there is not just one "right" solution to the case. The case has clues that, evaluated by the participants' criteria and values, pose various "solutions" or alternative types of response. The case teacher in this situation is not usually seen as a dispenser of information or knowledge. Rather, he or she is a co-learner along with the students in analyzing the case and proposing responsible and creative alternatives of understanding and action. The first function of the case teacher is to foster a meaningful dialogue among the students, to highlight verbally or on the blackboard the issues and insights they mutually discover, and, finally, to assist by employing his or her own resources in the summary and clarification of the insights that arise from the discussion of the case. This is the role of a facilitator in the learning process. The responsibility for clear goals and objectives for a given discussion session, of course, rests with the instructor. The case teacher does not relinquish appropriate authority for guiding the discussion in this approach; rather, the instructor's resources and skills are reflected in the quality and rhythm of the discussion.

If the instructor allows the class to speculate far beyond the data in the case or get caught up in arguing about a minor issue, this may add to the excitement but impede real progress. One role of the teacher may be periodically to remind the class to be responsible to the material in the case, even if students' interests quite properly move beyond the situation in the case. Some instructors find that simply to ask, "What evidence do you have that your suggestion might work?" keeps everyone honest. The participant is then free to call on the case or personal experience to interpret his or her view.

Some case teachers report that a useful means of guiding a discussion is to record on the blackboard or on newsprint the essence of what a student has contributed to the conversation. The role of interpreting and organizing a participant's remarks and showing the relation to other points of view is crucially important for the instructor. One case-teaching style involves probing the student to clarify what was said, or, alternatively, for rephrasing it and then checking out the rewording with the student. The participatory style of the case method can be unusually effective in drawing out a personal response from students. Experience indicates the case teacher needs to be constantly alert for vulnerable forms of self-disclosure not foreseen by the participant and to provide a context in which the student will feel supported.

Preparation for Case Discussion

Learners and teachers alike have parallel responsibility to master the case facts and comprehend the situation. Experienced case teachers usually prepare a teaching note or discussion plan that lists the central issues, the principal characters and their positions in each drama, a time line of the major events and dates in the case, and the philosophical resources available to the characters as well as to the participants. Thinking through the various paths the case principals might take, not to supply an answer, but to enable better learning in the form of clear questions or additional data, tends to sharpen the discussion. The suggested teaching note is seen by many only as an aid to the teacher's own creative imagination based on experience with each case. Students should be encouraged to read the case several times and, ideally, to discuss it with a small group of peers before plenary discussion in class.

Teaching the Case

There are different styles of initiating a case. Some instructors recommend beginning with a survey-type question: "What is the situation in the case? What does the problem seem to be?" Such a question provides a wide range of entry points into the dialogue. The second step is to ask for a deeper analysis of the problem or situation. On other occasions, the instructor may wish to ask for a conclusion immediately: "What would you do if you were David Hume, and why?" The reasons and rationale for the decision emerge during the discussion. Conflict of opinion and controversy are characteristic of and constructive in a lively case discussion. Honest conflict is a great learning tool *if* the reasons for the differences of opinion are made clear. The case teacher may wish to highlight the conflict by putting respondents into a "minidebate" with one another.

Especially as a session nears its conclusion, the instructor may encourage the group to build on the suggestions of one another, sketch concrete alternative solutions, and then critically compare these alternatives and their consequences. One value of using the case method with some regularity is that participants and teacher develop skills in analysis and presentation. Experience indicates that the benefits and quality of discussion increase as all participants become comfortable with the method.

Additional Teaching Tools

Further instructional tools that have been employed by other case teachers are listed here to suggest a variety of ways in which cases can be taught.

Role Play

An exciting way to heighten existential involvement with a case and to introduce an affective dimension is to ask participants to assume imaginatively the roles of the people in the case for a specified period in the discussion. In a group role play or simulation experience, the instructor might, for instance, invite the entire class to be the group of philosophical colleagues surrounding Socrates in his jail cell in Athens. What advice would they give Phaedo? In the controlled use of individual role play, the experience of many teachers is that, rather than asking for volunteers, or assigning roles, it is better to seek participation from students who give evidence in the discussion that they understand the issues and can identify with certain characters in the case. Asking permission of the students before propelling them into a role play is carried through in the "de-roling" process following—for example, a five-minute role play. In this way the participants' personal integrity is guarded by checking with them first: "How did *you* feel about the conversation? Were you comfortable with what you said?" When they have shared their feelings, the instructor may turn to the other members of the class to discover what they learned from the role play or how they might have played the role differently.

Voting

The dialogue may sometimes be focused or brought alive by the call for a vote on a controversial issue: for example, should Aristotle decide to flee and save Athens from committing another crime against philosophy or should he stay? The students are then asked, "How did you vote and why?" Most instructors record the vote on the board. When students are reluctant to take a position, a category of "undecided" provides a possible opportunity to test the impact of discussion by taking a second vote later. The dynamics of case teaching reveals that the issues may be clarified by pushing people to decide and to defend their choice. Many instructors also use the vote to probe for implicit reasons and assumptions that stand behind a given decision. A second vote and a discussion of any switches made may illustrate how the group discussion has really informed and persuaded the participants.

Concluding the Case

In providing a "wrap-up," some case instructors find it constructive on occasion to ask participants what they learned from the case and from one another and then to list these learnings as a communal summary. On the other occasions, however, the instructor may appropriately have important insights or an integrative way of understanding the case or issue that he or she has a responsibility to share. The pattern of identifying these contributions as concerns of the instructor and thus distinguishing them from any suggestion that this is *the* solution, most case teachers find is an important element in the learning experience. Some instructors introduce their own summary with a style that says, "This way of thinking about the case interests me, and so I share it with you." The follow-up on the case can take the form of additional readings, lectures, or asking students to prepare their own commentary.

Additional Resources

For further information on additional cases or training in the method or for information on a case newsletter, one may contact the professional society—Association for Case Teaching (ACT), c/o Hartford Seminary Foundation, 77 Sherman Street, Hartford, CT 06105. The Intercollegiate Case Clearing House (ICCH), Soldiers Field, Boston, MA 02163, provides bibliographies of cases in several fields and distributes cases at cost. A bibliography of recent case books and articles on case writing and teaching is available from ACT on request.

Background of This Project

James Bryant Conant estimates the introduction in the 1870s of the case method at Harvard Law School by Dean Christopher Columbus Langdell as so innovative that "Langdell is to be placed among the great American inventors of the nineteenth century."[2] Conant declares that the uniquely American contribution to education by Langdell "was as revolutionary in its impact on the United States as, say, the McCormick reaper."[3] Various branches of medicine and social work have used different forms of the case method. Most recently, in the 1970s theological education seriously began to explore this technique in a systematic way by establishing the Case Method Institute. Its founding director, Keith R. Bridston, has more fully described the institute's genesis, which also occurred in Cambridge, Massachusetts.[4] The Case Method Institute has stimulated the production of over a thousand cases and six case textbooks in theological disciplines, in addition to its primary function of training some 250 faculty members in the use of the method. A book of cases, *Christian Theology: A Case Method Approach,* prepared with the support of the Association of Theological Schools and the Lilly Endowment as a supplementary textbook for teaching systematic theology, provided a pattern for this experimental project in philosophy.[5] Nine theological cases were accompanied by critical commentary from established theologians.

Several teachers of philosophy expressed interest in developing a similar volume for use as a supplementary introductory text in the history of philosophy or in the philosophy of religion. As director of the earlier project on theology and the case method, and as a philosophical theologian regularly called on to teach philosophy, I feel the design for the present project is clearly in response to needs and interests expressed by teachers of philosophy. Jack Rogers and Forrest Baird have collaborated in preparing case studies on a number of philosophers and have tested and refined these cases through classroom teaching at the undergraduate and graduate school level. Their pioneering work has provided the core of this educational endeavor to enhance the quality of teaching in philosophy.

Project Development

A National Advisory Council was formed to assist the case authors and editors in the selection of cases and of those philosophers asked to be contemporary respondents to the cases. The authors and editors are enormously grateful to the following people for their counsel, critique, and participation as members of the National advisory Council for this project: Stephen Davis, Claremont Men's College; Charles Hartshorne, University of Texas; Alvin Plantinga, Calvin College; and John E. Smith, Yale University.

The historical approach is only one of several formats that might have been selected for this initial experiment. However, some form of the history of philosophy in the West is a component in almost every program in philosophy. Although there was obviously some disagreement about which figures should be included, the final list was shaped both by the availability of cases and general agreement among members of the council that this was a basic and representative selection of philosophers. Because the entire thought of a particular philosopher could not be comprehensively covered by a single case of any length, some focus was required. The formation of each case involved an attempt to deal with certain central issues in the thought of the philosopher and to provide limited but essential background material. Each case was one that engaged a critical human issue that affected both students and teachers: for example, death, goodness, integrity, evil, freedom, love, and duty. A balance of issues focused on was sought in the selection of the twelve cases.

It is obvious that the Western tradition is only one dimension of a rich philosophical heritage that includes philosophical systems from India, China, Islamic nations, and Latin cultures as well as approaches to wisdom with more focus on an oral tradition, such as those from the Near East, Africa, and Pacific Islands. This work concentrates on a significant but small slice of the Western philosophical tradition that serves only as one entry point to the love of wisdom.

The choice of commentators was shaped by invitations to people who knew the thought of the philosopher well and thus could make suggestions to the author of the case concerning the accuracy of the material and any necessary revisions. The final group of contemporary respondents include women and men, in the United States and Canada, teaching in two-year community colleges, church-related and private liberal arts colleges, state and private universities, and theological seminaries: Marilyn McCord Adams, University of California at Los Angeles; Stephen T. Davis, Claremont Men's College; Jerry H. Gill, Eastern College; Arthur F. Holmes, Wheaton College; Robert C. Levis, Pasa-

dena City College; George I. Mavrodes, University of Michigan; Ralph McInerny, University of Notre Dame; Harry A. Nielsen, Windsor University; Alvin
Plantinga, Calvin College; John K. Roth, Claremont Graduate School; Marjorie Suchocki, Pittsburgh Theological Seminary; Robert Williams, Vanderbilt
University. Some philosophers who were supportive of the project were unable
to contribute but recommended colleagues for consideration. The mandate to
those preparing commentaries was to prepare a brief statement that would reflect three factors: (1) simple, nontechnical language that could be understood
by a college freshman; (2) an example of how philosophy deals with basic human concerns in contemporary society; and (3) a personal answer to the questions posed at the end of the case, asking what would be an appropriate response
to the problems faced by the philosopher in the case. Our respondents supplied
commentaries with all the mix of perspectives and styles that could be anticipat-
ed. To these commentators as well as to the National Advisory Council, the authors and editors express their deep appreciation for the philosophical talents,
interest in the project, and time carved out of busy academic schedules and even
sabbatical leaves by these outstanding contemporary philosophers. Any comments from readers about the cases or commentaries would be welcome in the
authors' evaluation of the experiment and their consideration of future directions in the area of philosophy and the case method.

Bibliographies have been included at the end of each case to encourage
further study. These bibliographies include (1) one or two primary sources, (2)
one biography (except in the Anselm and Aquinas case, where two biographies
are cited), (3) several of the most important secondary sources used in preparing
the case, including some of introductory nature. In addition, at the end of the
book there is a brief general bibliography of reference books and histories of
philosophy.

NOTES

1. Plato, *The Republic of Plato*, bk. 5, trans. John Llewelyn Davies and David James Vaughan
   (London: Macmillan, 1895), cited in Robert N. Beck, ed., *Perspectives in Philosophy*, 2nd ed.
   (New York: Holt, Rinehart and Winston, 1969), p. 45.
2. James Bryant Conant, *Two Modes of Thought: My Encounter with Science and Education*
   (New York: Simon & Schuster, 1964), p. 45.
3. Conant, p. 33.
4. In the preface to R. Evans and T. Parker, eds., *Christian Theology: A Case Method Approach*
   (New York: Harper & Row, 1975), pp. xi–xv.
5. Evans and Parker, introduction by Robert A. Evans.

INTRODUCTION
TO PHILOSOPHY
A Case Method Approach

Part One

THE CLASSICAL CATEGORIES

OUR WORD *civilization* grows out of the notion that the inhabitants of cities are those who enjoy the rights and privileges of citizens—free people. Cities probably began to form around 2500 B.C., when there was enough agricultural surplus that not everyone had to raise food. Specialization became possible. People could group together and trade their goods and services.

Segregation and subordination often accompanied specialization. Women, who had been equal with men and who even sometimes dominated an agrarian economy, now were restricted to tasks in the home. With specialization, some men became full-time warriors, and others were suppressed and enslaved. The early civilizations of the Tigris-Euphrates Valley boasted large cities ruled by powerful kings. The power of the ruler determined the fate of the masses. Each city had its own myths—stories of this people's heroic past, which defined the inhabitants' view of the world and how it worked. These myths served to enforce conformity to tradition and custom.

The Greek Setting

The civilization of Greece, however, beginning in about 1000 B.C., developed significant differences. Geography helped: Greece was an area of peninsulas and islands. The total land area was less than that of the state of Florida. It never was able to support more than a few million people. Each region was sharply separated from all others by mountains or seas. The Greeks developed small, democratic city-states. The people lived by trading with others, which produced a constant flow of new ideas. They had no great natural resources or wealth. Personal, human values thus came to be prized.

For the Greeks, knowledge was power. The world was knowable by the human mind and so controllable in part by the human person. Myths were replaced by principles learned through speculation or investigation. Rational principles were thought to be universal, common to all people. Greeks created the concept of philosophy (literally, "love of wisdom"). The earliest philosophers whose writings survived thought about the character of being—what constituted all that existed. They wondered about the nature of matter, the idea of number, the problem of identity and change. Later they turned to the question of the nature, purpose, and function of human being itself.

Socrates and Plato

Socrates, whose case we encounter first, was born in the mid-fifth century B.C. What disturbed some and delighted others about Socrates was his total commitment to the life of reason. He spent his life in a search for truth through the relentless questioning of people's accepted ideas. His teaching through asking questions has given us the term "the Socratic method."

The Hellenic period of glory, when Greek values flourished, was in decline as Socrates grew older and his most brilliant pupil, Plato, reached adulthood. Plato was in his late twenties when Socrates was executed. Plato came from an aristocratic family. He had been born just two years after the death of Pericles, Athens' greatest democratic leader. He grew up during the civil strife and protest occasioned by the dreary war with Sparta. As a student of Socrates for eight years, he had been engaged in public debate and been encouraged in private deliberation.

Plato had hopes of a political career. But when the man he considered the wisest and most just, the best man he had ever known, was unjustly accused and executed, Plato gave up on politics. He ceased to trust the public process, whether dictators or democrats were in charge. Only if the philosophers, the people with integrity and intelligence, could be the kings would there be hopeful possibilities through government.

Plato committed himself to carrying on the work of Socrates. He wrote dialogues, often with Socrates as the chief character, that developed ideas about fundamental human issues. At the age of forty he founded a school, the Academy, to train mathematicians, philosophers, and statesmen. That college lasted for 900 years, until the Roman emperor Justinian embezzled its funds and closed it down.

Classical Realism

Plato, along with his greatest pupil and colleague, Aristotle, stimulated what is now regarded as the golden age of Greek philosophy in the fifth and fourth centuries B.C. We call their kind of thinking *classical realism*. Classical refers to its origins in Greek thought. Realism indicates that such thinkers believed that there was a real world that existed whether anyone knew it or not. But they firmly believed that this reality could be known by the human mind. Plato and Aristotle differed on what that reality was and how it was known. But they shared a commitment to the value of two fundamental philosophical problems: metaphysics, which asks the question "What is real?"; and epistemology, which asks the question "How do you know?" Other questions necessarily spun off from these two—"What is valuable?" (axiology), "How should I live?" (ethics),

"What is beauty?" (esthetics), and a whole host of others—as society, humanity, science, religion, indeed every aspect of life, was brought under philosophical scrutiny. The way in which Plato and Aristotle asked those questions has influenced our lives. They provided many of the basic categories of thought still employed in Western civilization.

Platonism

The case of Socrates, Plato's teacher, introduces one of the distinctively Western ways of thinking. It is sometimes called *idealism* because, metaphysically, reality is ideas or ideals. It is also called *rationalism* because we know, epistemologically, by rational deduction from these abstract ideas.

What is the relevance for us of this mode of thought? Earlier Greeks (as well as those in many other cultures) did not distinguish the abstract from the concrete. In our culture, especially in higher education, we properly criticize teaching that is too abstract, that never gets its feet on the ground. But Plato's problem was just the opposite. In his culture, people confused particular beautiful objects with beauty as such and became attached to the objects. They needed to distinguish between justice as it was practiced by their governments and the ideal of justice that could be thought and hoped for. Concepts such as *abstract* and *concrete* had not yet been developed. Plato was probing these problems and trying to clarify them.

Aristotelianism

Plato's greatest pupil was Aristotle. Aristotle was famous in his own time for his published writings on popular themes. They were in the style of dialogues, as was Plato's writing. The Roman orator Cicero praised their "golden style." These writings are lost. We know of them only at second- or third-hand through quotations or summaries in the writings of others. Boethius, a Roman statesman and philosopher, translated Aristotle's logical works into Latin. These became the only works of Aristotle known in Europe before A.D. 1100.

Logic was not a science for Aristotle. It was an instrument, or tool. It was to be used for clarifying terms and analyzing problems before one went to work on them. The syllogism was the center of Aristotle's logical system. Three statements are arranged in the form of an "if-then" proposition. *If* A is true *and* B is true, *then* C is true of necessity and tells you something new. The most famous example of deduction as it has been formed by tradition is

> All men are mortal.
> Socrates is a man.
> Socrates is mortal.

People had, of course, reasoned logically before Aristotle. But he was the first to define the formal principles involved. He is considered the "founder of logic," and all formal logic until the twentieth century was based on his teaching.

Aristotle is equally famous for induction. Just as Plato's philosophy laid the foundations for rationalism, Aristotle opened the way for empiricism, knowing based on experience. His method was to observe and draw generalizations on the basis of patterns perceived in many particulars. He did not experiment in the modern sense, but his work was a forerunner of what we call the *scientific method.* Aristotle is considered the father of the science of biology, and especially of its subdiscipline zoology. He gathered the first scientific collection of plant and animal specimens. He invented the basic terms for description of animals— *species, genus,* etc. Biological writings comprise a third of all Aristotle's published work.

The philosophical term *metaphysics* probably comes to us from an editor of Aristotle's works. Some think that this title for his philosophy of reality originated because a first-century B.C. editor placed it *meta* ("after," in Greek) his works on physics. Some commentators understood *meta* as "after" to imply that philosophical knowledge was arrived at after knowledge of the physical world. Others interpreted *meta* as "beyond," meaning that philosophical knowledge referred to objects beyond the world of physics, or nature. In any case, the thinking of Plato and Aristotle has focused the Western philosophical tradition on metaphysics—the attempt to say what is fundamentally real, after or beyond or behind what appears to the senses.

Plato and Aristotle: Similarities and Differences

The problem Plato and Aristotle inherited from the pre-Socratic philosophers was that of permanence and change. Although they shared much in common, they saw this problem somewhat differently. For Plato, everything in the physical world was in the process of change. There was no stability or permanence. For Aristotle, there were patterns of continuity within changing things. He had observed those orderly patterns in, for example, animal and plant reproduction.

Plato's and Aristotle's metaphysical views were responses to their differing visions of the problem. The real for Plato was not to be found in this world. Reality was in abstract, absolute ideas or ideals that existed as "Forms" in heaven. Aristotle found reality in the particular things in this world. Each object was a substance composed of both matter (stuff) and form (structure).

The epistemologies of these founding fathers of Western philosophy necessarily matched their differing metaphysics. Plato did not trust his senses. They told us only how things appeared in this world and could deceive us. The mind, however, held dim memories of the great ideas we had known in heaven before our birth. Those innate ideas gave us general principles from which we could rationally deduce the truth about particulars. Aristotle grew up in a physician's home. He was aware of the human body and knew that the human senses could aid in diagnosing the body's difficulties. He continued to train his senses and through them learned secrets of plant and animal behavior. Aristotle's logic builds on the deductions of Socrates and Plato. But his science introduced induction. Beginning with the data of our five senses, we can amass material. Then we can draw valid general conclusions based on enough individual instances.

It was in the period of decline in Greek civilization, the Hellenistic period, that Plato and Aristotle developed their philosophies. Continual questioning and open-ended answers, as used by Socrates, were no longer considered appropriate. Philosophers now attempted to build systems of thought that would provide answers to the basic questions human beings could ask in every area of life.

Plato and Aristotle constructed comprehensive systems of thought that have influenced our lives. They formed foundations of Western tradition from which the civilizations of Europe and America grew. There is some justification for declaring, as the twentieth-century philosopher Alfred North Whitehead did, that the Western philosophical tradition "consists of a series of footnotes to Plato." If we also take seriously the differences between Plato and Aristotle, we can see themes from one or the other of them being replayed in most of our modern controversies.

Augustine

One of the initial applications of Greek philosophy was in the religious realm. The Christian church came into being in a world whose rulers were Roman and whose language and culture were Greek. Christians adapted to this Hellenistic culture in order to survive and in the effort to win converts. A form of Platonism was dominant in the culture of the first century A.D. and continued down until the rediscovery of Aristotle's writings in the eleventh century. Thus the philosophical categories of Platonism were used by the theologians of the early church in developing Christian thought and culture. The case of Augustine gives us an example of the use of Platonism as a framework to approach religious problems. In the Middle Ages, the reintroduction of Aristotle's scientific works prompted a rethinking of the way in which Christianity related to life. The case of Anselm and Thomas Aquinas focuses on the transition from the use of Platonic categories to the dominance of Aristotelian thought as the chief means of formulating and communicating religious meaning in the West.

Augustine's conversion to Christianity was preceded by a conversion to Neoplatonism. Augustine became disillusioned with the Manichaean religion, of which he was an adherent. Moving from North Africa to Rome and thence to Milan, Augustine sought employment as a professor of rhetoric. In Milan, Augustine joined a group of young intellectuals who were Neoplatonists. With his new friends, Augustine listened to the preaching of Bishop Ambrose, whose sermons were usually a synthesis of Scripture and Neoplatonic ideas. Augustine began to read the Neoplatonists Plotinus and Porphyry. Their thought provided him with insights that he felt emancipated him from Manichaean philosophy and opened him to Christian faith. Augustine experienced a dramatic conversion to Christianity and was baptized by Bishop Ambrose. He was later ordained a priest and then became bishop of Hippo, a city in his native North Africa.

Many Neoplatonic concepts became central in the Christian philosophy of

Augustine. As a Manichee, Augustine had found it impossible to think of God as both present in the world and at the same time separate from it. Plotinus provided philosophical arguments for a spiritual world that was related to the world of time and space and yet distinct from it. The integration of biblical and Platonic thought can be seen especially in the maxim of Augustine's theological method: "I believe in order that I may understand." This used the Platonic notion of great ideas, implanted in the mind, that enabled persons to understand particular things in this world. For Augustine, the truly important realities—the knowledge of God, of virtue, and of eternal principles—were implanted in the mind by God from our birth. These realities were known by intellectual vision, contemplation, and memory. The knowledge of these eternal realities preceded and illumined the realm of temporal things. Knowledge from the eternal realm was accepted in faith and led to understanding of the temporal realm. According to Augustine, all understanding was finally possible because of this inner illumination provided by the "Uncreated Light of God."

Thomas Aquinas

The Crusades of the eleventh and twelfth centuries, designed to wrest the Holy Land (Palestine) from the Moslems, brought Europe into contact with Islamic culture. Through the Arabs, the complete philosophical works of Aristotle arrived in western Europe in the thirteenth century. It was this infusion of a fresh philosophical perspective that made possible the development of classical scholasticism (from the Latin word for *school*). This term came to designate a distinctive method of teaching in the medieval schools. Ancient texts from Scripture and the early church theologians were introduced and commented on. Arguments were presented in a dialectic, or yes and no, form that attempted to balance diverse opinions. Questions were asked, answers given, objections lodged, and finally a definitive conclusion reached. The final literary form of scholasticism was Aquinas's *Summa Theologica*, which attempted to give an objective exposition of God's truth in a humanly reasonable form.

Thomas Aquinas became the chief exponent of the scholastic method in the thirteenth century. He created a monumental synthesis of the philosophy of Aristotle with Christian revelation, attempting to show their ultimate harmony. Thomas assumed, with Aristotle, that the human mind has no God-given content at birth. We are born with reliable senses and the capacity to reason. He developed five ways by which the existence of God could be proved by human reason beginning from sense experience. Scripture and divine illumination were necessary only to establish such Christian distinctives as the Trinity that were beyond reason. The Thomistic system proclaimed a harmony of what could be known through nature (Aristotle) and grace (revelation).

There were, of course, opposing intellectual forces throughout the medieval period. Neoplatonism continued even after the rise of Aristotelianism to dominance. In its more extreme forms, Platonism led to mysticism in systems like those of Bonaventure (1217/18–1274), who taught in Paris with Thomas Aquinas, and of Meister Eckhart (1260–1327), who laid the foundations of German mysticism. Other anti-Aristotelians laid stress on the primacy of the will and were skeptical about the abilities of human reason. Duns Scotus (1265–1308) and William of Occam (1285–1347) provided impetus for later voluntarist and skeptical philosophies.

After the peak of classical scholasticism in the thirteenth century, medieval civilization experienced a gradual decline for about two hundred years. New forces were already rising that eventually led to the restructuring of society and the renewal of thought through those movements we know as the Renaissance and the Reformation. We will look at those forces when we come to the matrix of modern thought. However, many values and attitudes that we cherish today were formulated during the earlier periods. In the first four cases, we will attempt to understand something of what we have inherited from these formative Western thinkers in our ancient and medieval past.

CHAPTER 1

The Case of Socrates[1]

What Is the Meaning of Life and Death?

IN 399 B.C., Phaedo sat in Socrates' jail cell and listened to the condemned man's words. Many of Socrates' friends had come for one final conversation. Apollodorus sat in the corner sobbing uncontrollably. Xanthippe, Socrates' wife, had had to be removed because she was so emotionally distraught. A dozen other friends fought to control their emotions as they listened to Socrates' words. Simmias and Cebes were questioning Socrates about the immortality of the soul. Socrates was about to die as an enemy of the city-state of Athens. They wanted to know what he thought and how he felt.

As the afternoon wore on and the time for Socrates' death came closer, the questioning became more intense. Was the philosophy by which Socrates had lived really worth dying for, as he apparently believed? Was his theory of "Forms," by which he proved the immortality of the soul, true?

Heraclitus

"What is the world made of? Is it something solid and unchanging? Or can it change its shape and character? How do we account for the unity and the diversity that we experience?"

These questions had troubled thoughtful people for centuries. Some studied and speculated, trying to make sense of it all. They were called "philosophers," lovers of wisdom. Some specialized in "metaphysics," the effort to understand all that exists, and attempted to come up with a theory that would explain all of reality. One such thoughtful person was a Greek named Heraclitus who lived in the Greek colony of Ephesus, on Asia Minor, in 500 B.C.

Heraclitus looked around and saw that the world seemed to be constantly changing. He began to search for some underlying unity that held it all together. Earlier philosophers had claimed that the apparently diverse reality could be reduced to some material thing, such as water (Thales) or air (Anaximenes). Others found unity in some structural principles such as pairs of opposites (Anaximander) or numbers (the Pythagorians). But these explanations seemed inadequate in everyday life. How did one thing change into another? If water, for example, was the basic stuff of the universe, then where did dirt come from?

Heraclitus held that the basic stuff of the world was neither air, nor water, nor some fusion of opposites. It was fire. He proclaimed, "This world-order . . . was always and is and shall be: an everlasting fire."[2]

At first, this position appeared to be just another unitary "oneness" to which the "many" apparent diversities of the world could be reduced. His position seemed similiar to those claiming that reality was ultimately united in earth or air or water. But actually Heraclitus had come up with a totally new concept. When he said "fire," he meant the process of change. It was change according to "the measures."[3] Heraclitus also talked about fire, water, and earth, but it was the way in which these three things were constantly changing into one another that provided the clue to the "oneness" or unity of all reality. For Heraclitus, all was flux. He declared that one could not step into the same river twice.

Parmenides

While Heraclitus was working out his theory of ordered change, a young man named Parmenides was putting together a completely different conception of the world. Parmenides lived in Elea, a Greek colony in southern Italy. He saw the same change and diversity in the universe. But he did not form his opinion from what he encountered with his physical senses. Beginning with the idea that all of reality is one, he pointed to what his reason held to be two obvious ideas: "What is not, is not," because it could not be thought, and "Whatever is, is."[4] These seemed on the surface like truisms that no one would deny. But for Parmenides they had a deeper meaning.

The first premise, "Whatever is not, is not," meant that there could be no such thing as nothing. The word *nothing* did not name anything. According to Parmenides, "you cannot know or utter what is not—that is impossible."[5] To say that "nothing exists" was unthinkable, because there was no "nothing" that could be said to exist. Yet when he asserted that "Whatever is, is," he included both objects in the world and ideas in people's minds. Anything that could be thought of existed. To say of what is that it is not would be untrue. What is could not fail to exist. "What can be spoken and thought must be," Parmenides wrote, "for it is possible for it to be, but impossible for nothing to be."[6] Thus, one single, unchangeable reality existed.

As the Greeks of Parmenides' time came to see, these premises led to staggering conclusions. It followed from Parmenides' thesis that whatever is is *uncreated*. He argued that if it had been created it would have to have been created out of nothing. But what did not exist was unthinkable. Or it would have had to be created out of something else. But there was no something else—only what is. Similarly, what is, is *indestructible*. The destruction of a thing meant its change into nothing. Because there was no *nothing* to change into, the destruction of a thing was unthinkable. Hence, whatever is, is *eternal* (uncreated and indestructible). Furthermore, whatever is is unchangable. Nothing could change, because change required that the present state of affairs be destroyed and a new state of affairs be created. So all of reality was of the same kind—unitary and indivisible. There were no degrees of being—all is one. Whereas Heraclitus had described all reality in terms of orderly change, Parmenides considered all change to be an illusion.

Sophists

In the years following Heraclitus and Parmenides, the political and social situation in Greece began to deteriorate. Athens engaged in an ill-conceived and poorly executed war with Sparta. The reaction to the Peloponnesian War was basically negative. Civil war almost broke out in Athens. Athenians became reactionary and cynical. They trusted power rather than principle and followed expediency rather than ethics. People who had been open to new ideas became deeply suspicious of nonconformity.

Among philosophers, the views of Parmenides dominated. Several new schools of thought had developed. But all accepted Parmenides' method of beginning with reason and analysis rather than observation and experience. This along with the political changes led many people to distrust reason. If reason could deny change that seemed so obvious to most people, then perhaps reason was not the tool with which to discover reality.

In this atmosphere of moral decay and distrust of reason, a new group of thinkers arose. The Sophists were itinerant teachers. They taught the skill of *arete* ("excellence," in the sense of bettering oneself and getting ahead). They offered different styles of success depending on the teacher. But generally they tended to deny that there was an objectively knowable world beyond the world of experience. They were either not interested in metaphysics or only interested enough to help people construct theories by which to counter their opponents.

Socrates

In this reactionary period of suspicion and cynicism, the presence of a man such as Socrates was not appreciated by many. He had fought with courage in the Peloponnesian War and lived through the strife that followed in Athens. Like the Sophists, he was dedicated to *arete* (excellence). His interest in words and arguments was notorious. But, unlike the Sophists, he took no fees for his teaching. His intellectual standards and his commitment to metaphysical truth and moral purposes also set him apart from them.

It was the way in which Socrates' teaching differed from the Sophists that annoyed the authorities. Socrates felt that he had a "divine mission." A friend of Socrates had asked the oracle at Delphi "whether any man was wiser than Socrates." The oracle had replied "None." Socrates knew that he was not a wise man. So he set out to find a wiser one as "an excuse for going back and cross-examining the Oracle." Socrates later described the method and the results of his mission:

> Accordingly I went to one who had the reputation of wisdom, and observed him—his name I need not mention; he was a politician whom I selected for examination—and the result was as follows: When I began to talk with him, I could not help thinking that he was not really wise, although he was thought wise by many, and still wiser by himself; and thereupon I tried to explain to him that he thought himself wise, but was not really wise; and the consequence was that he hated me, and his enmity was shared by several who were present and heard me. So I left him, saying to myself, as I went away; well, although I do not suppose that either of us knows anything really beautiful and good, I am better off then he is—for he knows nothing, and thinks that he knows; I neither know nor think that I know. In this latter particular then, I seem to have slightly the advantage of him.[7]

Socrates continued his mission by interviewing the politicians, poets, and artisans of Athens. Using a method known as "dialectic," he would enter into conversation with a person who claimed to know the meaning of equality, justice, or some other concept. Through intense questioning, Socrates would make it clear that neither he nor the person he interviewed really knew the meaning of the concept. Socrates would then invite the other person to join him in a search for true knowledge of the given quality. Socrates would pose questions that could be accepted or rejected by his fellow searcher. Invariably, they would fail to discover precisely what the quality was. Some, now aware of their lack of knowledge, were eager to continue their search in the future.

Socrates' style of questioning reflected his theory of knowledge. He felt that knowledge was gained through constant self-examination. "The life not tested by criticism is not worth living," he said.[8] Knowledge could not be sold like a book. It had to be discovered. Philosophy was not learning a set of answers, but the process of search for them.

This approach was not popular among those Athenians who thought themselves well informed. Being proved less than wise angered many powerful people. In 399 B.C., Socrates was brought to trial in the court of King Archon and convicted. The charges were impiety and corrupting the youth. Many felt that the real reasons for his condemnation were the questioning of his culture's "sacred cows," his friendship with political outcasts, his unwillingness to go along with accepted practices, and his constant criticism of the powerful.

The Theory of Forms: Metaphysics and Epistemology

Like philosophers before him, Socrates was interested in the relationship between permanence and change. Heraclitus had seen the problems in permanence and so explained everything in terms of change. But, if everything was always changing, how could anything maintain its identity? How could one ever say that one's horse, home, or even one's friend would be the same horse, home or friends next week?

Parmenides, on the other hand, had been intent on maintaining the identity of objects and ideas. This led him to assert that nothing ever changed. In fact, some of his followers were convinced that motion from one place to another was impossible.

Socrates contemplated the conflicts surrounding permanence and change. He realized that if reason was to be saved from the cynicism of the Sophists some reconciliation was needed.

It occurred to Socrates that Heraclitus, Parmenides, and the Sophists had all assumed they were dealing with the same world. But what if there were really two worlds? If there were two worlds, one could be in constant flux, as Heraclitus claimed, while the other was eternally stable, as Parmenides asserted. For Socrates, the changing world that Heraclitus saw was the world one knew with the senses—sight, hearing, smell, taste, and touch. It was a world where things grew, changed, and decayed. But beyond this world of flux there was a world of permanence, as Parmenides had reasoned there must be. This was the world of ideas or ideals called "Forms."

As Socrates developed this position, some serious questions were raised. First, what exactly were Forms? Second, how could these unchanging Forms be related to the world of flux that people experienced with their senses? Third, how were these Forms related to each other? Fourth, if the Forms existed beyond the world of flux that people experienced with their senses, then how could they be known?

To the first question, Socrates replied that Forms were concepts, *objects* of thought. One might *see* or *touch* a couch one was about to sit on. But one *thought* about the idea or concept of a couch. The qualities or properties that made a thing a couch made up the Form "couchness." A particular couch might break and be thrown away. It was part of the world of change. But the concept of what it was to be a couch remained the same. It was part of the world of permanence. It was a Form, and Forms never changed.

This theory of Forms applied more clearly to abstract concepts than to concrete things. A triangle was the concept of a plane figure formed by three straight lines intersecting by twos at three points and so forming three angles. A drawn triangle's lines would not be perfectly straight. But the concept "triangle" would always be perfect and available to the reason. So also any particular just act was an imperfect copy of the concept of justice.

But this did not mean that people invented the concepts of "couchness," "triangle," or "justice." The properties of each of these three concepts were eternal and universal, quite independent of any particular mind. A particular couch, for instance, only had reality as it represented (or "participated in") the universal Form, "couchness." A particular couch was only an imperfect copy of the universal Form of "couchness." In some way, the Form "couchness" controlled the essence (or basic nature) of a given couch. Similarly, the Forms of "triangle" and "justice" determined the essence of particular triangles and just acts.

Having defined Forms as abstract ideas or concepts, Socrates could answer the second question. Forms, which belonged to the world of permanence, were related to the world of flux in three ways. Particulars in the world of flux "participated in" the universal Forms. Particulars were imperfect copies of the universal Forms. Forms caused the essence of particulars.

In response to the third question, Socrates stated that all the forms were arranged in a hierarchy. At the bottom were the Forms of things in the world of flux, such as couches. Above these were the Forms of abstract concepts, such as triangle. Higher yet were the valued qualities, such as Truth, Beauty, and Justice. At the pinnacle of the hierarchy was the "Form of the Good."

Finally, Socrates responded to the fourth question. If one never saw the Forms, in the world of flux and change how could one ever come to know the Forms? In other words, if the knowledge of the Forms did not come through the senses, then how did the reason acquire such knowledge? According to Socrates, the reason, which was a part of the soul, always had the knowledge of the Forms. Before a person was born, his or her soul existed in the realm of eternal Forms. At birth a person retained a dim memory of the Forms. Thus, whenever a person learned something about the Forms, he or she was really just recollecting or remembering what he or she always "knew." For Socrates, this meant that the soul, which was able to know the eternal Forms, must be immortal. The soul came from the world of eternal Forms, and it would return there.

This theory about the immortality of the soul led Socrates to a more detailed explanation of ethics and politics.

Theory of the Soul: Ethics and Politics

According to Socrates, the soul was an immaterial principle of life and movement. Each soul was divided into three parts. The first, and most important, part of the soul was the reason. The reason was the thinking part of the soul—the part that could have knowledge of the Forms. The next part of the soul was the spirit. The spirit was the acting part of the soul. Finally there was the appetite. The appetite was the physical needs part of the soul.

Each of these parts of the soul had a virtue or good that corresponded to it. Wisdom, or exercising its power, was the virtue of reason. Courage, or exercising its power, was the virtue of the spirit. Temperance, or *not* exercising its power, was the virtue of the appetite.

If the Form of the Good could be known, and if the good for each part of the soul consisted of pursuing the appropriate virtue, then where did evil come from? According to Socrates, evil was nothing more than the spirit and the appetite overwhelming the reason. Evil, therefore, was closely associated with the needs of the body. The reason did not cause evil—only those parts of the soul associated with the body caused evil. In fact, if a person really understood the situation—that is, had the virtue of wisdom—he or she would never choose to do wrong. Evil, then, was not a problem of a misdirected will, but of an unrestrained body and a weak reason. The proper way to avoid evil was for each part of the soul to fulfill its proper function in harmony and balance with the other parts of the soul. This harmony and balance would promote the Good.

The state, according to Socrates, was simply the "soul writ large." The ideal state was similar, in its proper make up, to the soul. Just as there was a three-part division of the soul, so also there had to be a three-part division of the state. Corresponding to the rational part of the soul would be a class or people known as "guardians." These "guardians" would be the rulers of the people, using their virtue of reason. They would be few in number. As befits their emphasis on reason, these "guardians" would deny their bodies and own nothing other than the bare essentials of life. Corresponding to the spirit part of the soul would be a class of people known as "auxiliaries." These "auxiliaries" would comprise the military forces and, with courage as their virtue, would defend the state. Like the "guardians," the "auxiliaries" would be few in number and would not be allowed many material possessions. Corresponding to the appetitive part of the soul would be the "craftsmen." These "craftsmen" would make up the bulk of the state and could be allowed to accumulate private property. Just as the individual soul promoted the Good by harmony and balance among its parts, so also the state would promote the Good as the different classes of people worked together harmoniously.

The Final Hours

Socrates' friends had arrived early that morning. They knew this would be the last time they would see their beloved teacher. All of the local people who followed Socrates were there: Phaedo, Critobulus and his father, Hermagenes, Epigenes, Aeschines, Antisthenes, Cresippus, Menexenus, Crito, and others. Apollodorus, who always had a difficult time controlling himself, was also there. Only Plato, who was ill at the time, was missing. Simmias and Cebes, whose foreign accents betrayed them as visitors, added to the conversation. There were also a few other out-of-towners, such as Euclides and Terpsion, and several servants.

While Apollodorus sat in a corner weeping and moaning about the injustice of it all, Socrates discussed the future of his own soul. Addressing Simmias and Cebes, Socrates said,

> But I wish now to explain to you . . . why it seems to be that a man who has really spent his life in philosophy has reason to be of good cheer when he is about to die, and may well hope after death to gain in the other world the greatest good. I will try to show you, Simmias and Cebes, how this may be.
>
> The world, perhaps, does not see that those who rightly engage in philosophy study only dying and death. And, if this is true, it would be surely strange for a man all through his life to desire only death, and then, when death comes to him, to be vexed at it, when it has been his study and his desire for so long.[9]

Then Socrates introduced the idea that the soul was immortal because it could perceive and have a share in Truth, Goodness, and Beauty, which are eternal. As Socrates discussed this idea with his friends, he defended his confidence in immortality by employing his theory of Forms.

Plato later recounted Phaedo's description of the discussion.

> "We admit," said Socrates, "that there is such a thing as equality—not the equality of stick to stick and stone to stone, and so on, but something beyond all that and distinct from it—absolute equality. Are we to admit this or not?"
>
> "Yes, indeed," said Simmias, "most emphatically."

"And do we know what it is?"

"Certainly."

"Where did we get our knowledge? ... Was it not from seeing equal sticks or stones or other equal objects that we got the notion of equality, although it is something quite distinct from them? Look at it in this way. Is it not true that equal stones or sticks sometimes, without changing in themselves, appear equal to one person and unequal to another?"

"Certainly."

"Well, now, have you ever thought that things which were absolutely equal were unequal, or that equality was inequality?"

"No, never, Socrates."

"Then these equal things are not the same as absolute equality."

"Not in the least, as I see it, Socrates."

"And yet it is these equal things that have suggested and conveyed to you your knowledge of absolute equality. . . . So long as the sight of one thing suggests another to you, it must be a cause of the recollection, whether the two things are alike or not."

"Quite so."

"Well, now," he said. "What do we find in the case of the equal sticks? ... Do they seem to us to be equal in the sense of absolute equality, or do they fall short of it in so far as they only approximate to equality? Or don't they fall short at all?"

"They do," said Simmias, "a long way."

"Suppose then when you see something you say to yourself, 'This thing which I can see has a tendency to be like something else, but it falls short and cannot be really like it, only a poor imitation.' Don't you agree with me that anyone who receives that impression must in fact have previous knowledge of that thing which he says that the other resembles, but inadequately?"

"Certainly he must."

". . . Then we must have some previous knowledge of equality before the time when we first saw equal things and realized that they were striving after equality, but fell short of it."

"That is so."

"And at the same time we are agreed also upon this point, that . . . it must be through the senses that we obtained the notion that all sensible equals are striving after absolute equality but fall short of it. Is that correct?"

"Yes, it is."

"So before we began to see and hear and use our other senses we must somewhere have acquired the knowledge that there is such a thing as absolute equality. Otherwise we could never have realized, by using it as a standard for comparison, that all equal objects of sense are desirous of being like it, but are only imperfect copies."

"That is the logical conclusion, Socrates." [10]

Phaedo

Phaedo listened to the discussion intently. Was all this talk simply the wishful thinking of a man about to die? Or was there an immortal soul that participated in the heavenly Forms? Did this theory really account for the diversity and unity of the world? Did his theory of the soul really provide an adequate account of ethics and politics? Phaedo wondered if this were an adequate philosophy, by which one could live and die.

NOTES

To make it easier to find a particular passage in various editions of translations of a work, we have adopted throughout this book the custom of identifying passages from standard works of philosophy by number and/or letter rather than by the page on which they appear in a specific edition. See, for example, note 8, below.

1. It should be noted that many of the ideas the authors have attributed to Socrates may actually have been developed by Plato and put in the mouth of Socrates. For our purposes, however, we will credit all of the ideas to Socrates.
2. Heraclitus, frag. 30, quoted in W. K. C. Guthrie, *The History of Greek Philosophy* (Cambridge, England: Cambridge University Press, 1962), vol. 1, p. 454.
3. See Ibid., pp. 464–469.
4. Parmenides, frag. 2, quoted in Guthrie, vol. 2, pp. 13–14.
5. Ibid.
6. Parmenides, frag. 6, quoted in Guthrie, vol. 1, p. 20.
7. Plato, *Apology*, quoted in Robert F. Davidson, ed., *The Search for Meaning in Life: Readings in Philosophy* (New York: Holt, Rinehart & Winston, 1962), p. 19.
8. Plato, *Apology*, 38A, quoted in *The Encyclopedia of Philosophy*, *s.v.* "Socrates."
9. Plato, *Phaedo*, quoted in Romano Guardini, *The Death of Socrates* (New York: Sheed and Ward, 1948), p. 102.
10. Plato, *Phaedo*, trans. Hugh Tredennick, in *Plato: The Collected Dialogues*, edited by Edith Hamilton and Huntington Cairns (Princeton, N.J.: Princeton University Press, 1961), 74A–75B (pp. 57–58).

BIBLIOGRAPHY

Primary Source

Plato. *The Collected Dialogues of Plato*. Edited by Edith Hamilton and Huntington Cairns. Princeton, N.J.: Princeton University Press, 1961.

Biography

Field, G. C. *Plato and His Contemporaries*. London: Methuen, 1930.

Interpretative Works

Brumbaugh, R. S. *Plato for the Modern Age*. New York: Macmillan, 1964.
Friedlander, Paul. *Plato*. New York: Harper & Row, 1958.
Guardini, Romano. *The Death of Socrates. An Interpretation of the Platonic Dialogues: Euthyphro, Apology, Crito, and Phaedo*. New York: Sheed and Ward, 1948.
Guthrie, W. K. L. *The History of Greek Philosophy*. Cambridge, England: Cambridge University Press, 1962–1978. Five vols.
Shorey, P. *What Plato Said*. Chicago: University of Chicago Press, 1933.
Taylor, A. E. *Plato, the Man and His Work*. New York: Barnes and Noble, 1966.

QUESTIONS FOR STUDY

1. What are the metaphysical (theory of reality) positions of
  a. The earliest pre-Socratic philosophers?
  b. Heraclitus?
  c. Parmenides?
  d. Socrates?

2. How is Socrates' epistemology (theory of knowledge) similar to and different from that of
  a. Heraclitus?
  b. Parmenides?
  c. The Sophists?

3. Describe the "Socratic method" of teaching. Debate the pros and cons of that method for contemporary education.

4. Outline Socrates' theory of Forms. Discuss the following questions:
  a. To what extent are the Forms objective, and to what extent are they subjective?
  b. To what extent are the Forms abstract, and to what extent are they concrete?
  c. What is their hierarchical arrangement?
  d. How does the mind grasp them?

5. Define the soul as Socrates does. Then
  a. Outline the three parts of the soul and the virtue that belongs to each part.
  b. Compare the three offices in the state and the manner of life of those who occupy them with the three parts of the soul.
  c. Explain the origin and character of evil.

6. What argument does Socrates advance for the immortality of the soul? Criticize his view and offer your own argument in class discussion.

A Contemporary Response

STEPHEN T. DAVIS

Is THERE anything you can think of that might be worth dying for? Is there anything—a person, an organization, an idea, a belief—that *you* would be willing to die for?

These are odd questions. But, as Socrates shows us, they are some of the fundamental questions of philosophy. Perhaps for you the answer is no—there is nothing for which you would willingly sacrifice your life. Perhaps you even think the whole idea ridiculous. But some people—including Socrates—have had to decide. It was not ridiculous to them. On the contrary, it was the most important question they ever faced.

Plato's dialogue *Crito* tells of a conversation between Socrates and his beloved friend Crito shortly before Socrates' death. Socrates had been condemned by the Athenian court for impiety and for corrupting the youth of Athens. The real problem, of course, was that he asked too many tough and embarrassing questions. He exposed too many of the elite of Athens for the pompous fools they were. By Athenian law, his execution should have followed soon after his condemnation. But a ceremonial complication delayed matters for about a month. A state galley had been sent on an annual religious mission to Delos, and custom dictated that no prisoner be executed until the ship returned.

Socrates' friends wanted him to escape from prison and flee the city. They used the delay to make plans. Guards were bribed; things were arranged. There was even some feeling in Athens that the authorities would be relieved if Socrates simply disappeared from sight.

As the *Crito* opens, the sail of the galley had just been sighted at Cape Sunium in Attica and will soon appear at the Piraeus (Athens' port). The moment of truth fast approaching, Crito makes one last attempt to convince his old friend to flee. The dialogue is Plato's professed report of the conversation between the two friends. This is Socrates' last chance—if he does not flee now, he will have to drink the hemlock.

In a sense, then, Socrates' life is in his own hands. He can flee and live—or stay and die. It is up to him. What should he do? Should he flee, as Crito urges—indeed, begs and beseeches—him to do? Or should he allow the sentence of the court to be carried out? What do you think? Is there anything here that, as far as you can tell, is worth Socrates' dying for?

Suppose you were in Crito's shoes? What arguments would you use? I suspect that you would remind Socrates that if he flees his life and work can continue, that his wife, children, and friends can continue to enjoy him, that his death might make his friends look cowardly and disloyal for not rescuing him, that he should not die just because a biased jury so sentenced him.

But Socrates refuses to listen to all such considerations. To him, they pale into insignificance beside the main principle of his life: "The really important thing is not to live, but to live well."[1] What he means by "living well" is living honorably, rightly. And, because this principle means that one should do what is morally right rather than what is merely expedient (where the two conflict), Socrates chooses to stay in Athens and die.

It is true that the Athenians had wronged him, Socrates admits, but disobeying the lawful decision of a lawful court—misguided though it was—would amount to committing another wrong. And one should never defend oneself against an evil by doing another evil. As he says to Crito, "It is never right to do a wrong or defend oneself against injury by retaliation."[2] Furthermore, says Socrates, no state can survive if its citizens disobey its lawful commands. "Do you imagine," he says, "that a city can continue to exist and not be turned upside down, if the legal judgments which are pronounced in it have no force but are nullified and destroyed by private persons."[3] In other words, civil disobedience (intentional disobedience of the law or of lawful authority for a moral purpose) is never morally justified.

Socrates, then, was quite prepared to die for the sake of his philosophy, his deepest convictions, his integrity. So I again ask, "Is there anything *you* would be willing to die for?" Probably not for the sake of your possessions—clothing, money, home, car. But how about for the sake of your parents or your best friend? Would you be willing to die for your country? (Many have been asked to do this very thing.) Would you, like Socrates, be willing to die for your deepest convictions? Would you be willing to die if your death were the only way to preserve your integrity? Why or why not?

But of course these are questions that cannot be answered in a vacuum. The answer you will give to them will be decisively influenced by your opinion on other questions: for example, "What is death?" and "What happens after death?" In other words, a person's willingness or unwillingness to give up his or her life may well depend on whether or not he or she believes that we survive death.

It has often been said that death is the most awesome and frightening reality human beings face. And this is doubtless true. But exactly *why* is death so frightening to us? What is it about death that is so threatening? Let me suggest five reasons we fear death.

1. We know that death is inevitable, but in the case of most of us we never know when we will die. We therefore live constantly under death's threat.
2. Death is unknown. Because death is apparently not something we experience but rather the end of experience, there are many opinions but few or no certain truths about death and what (if anything) happens after death.
3. We have to face death alone. Perhaps if we could all hold hands and leap together into the void, so to speak, death would not be so frightening. Sadly, we can't.
4. In death we will be separated from our loved ones and our future personal hopes and aims will not be realized.
5. There is the real and frightening possibility that death is total annihilation, that "death ends all." After my death, I will simply no longer exist.

Why was Socrates so calm in the face of death? Perhaps if we ask this question in relation to these five reasons to fear death we can see the answer. First, unlike most of us Socrates knew when and how he would die. He would die by drinking the hemlock on the appointed day. Second, while of course Socrates would admit to being ignorant of much of death, he was convinced his fate after death would be a happy one.[4] Third, Socrates knew he had to face death all alone, but facing difficult tasks by himself was something that never daunted Socrates. Fourth, Socrates knew he would be separated from his loved ones and that many of his earthly goals would remain unrealized, but he believed this was worth the price. Retaining his own integrity was far more important. Fifth, Socrates had an argument—based on the theory of Forms—that convinced him that people do indeed survive death.

Although Plato lists several other arguments for the immortality of the soul besides this one (see his dialogues *Phaedo* and *Republic*), let us look at it. Is it a good argument? Should it comfort people like you and me today who fear that "death ends all"? Should it convince us that we survive death?

The argument appears to run as follows: We can all be shown to possess knowledge of certain *a priori* truths or ideal concepts that we have not learned in this life. For example, we all have the idea of "perfect equality," but in fact we have never experienced two perfectly equal things. Where, then, did we learn the idea?

Another example: Unlearned children can be shown to "know" certain fairly difficult concepts in geometry despite the fact that they have never studied geometry. Socrates proves this in Plato's dialogue *Meno*.[5] Merely by asking Meno's slave boy some pointed questions, Socrates shows that the boy "knows" certain concepts in geometry, which he has never studied. It follows from this, Plato says, that these facts and concepts were learned in a prior existence and that our soul is therefore indestructible, that is, immortal. Accordingly, our souls survive death.

Is this a good reason for you and me not to fear death? Sadly, I think not. Let me explain why.

In the first place, even if the argument's main claim is correct (that is, that we know certain things because we recall them from a previous existence), this is not a proof of the immortality of the soul. It only shows that the soul existed before death, not that it will also exist after death. We do not have here a proof that the soul is indestructible. In the second place, even if the soul is indestructible (that is, survives death) that will be of no interest to me unless it can also be shown that my soul is me. As Antony Flew says, "Unless I am my soul the immortality of my soul will not be my immortality; and the news of the immortality of my soul would be of no more concern to me than the news that my appendix would be preserved eternally in a bottle." And, in the third place, the main claim of the argument may well be wrong. Instead of saying that we know *a priori* truths and ideal concepts because we recall them from a prior life, why not simply say that memory is not involved in our coming to know such things? Surely there are other simpler ways of explaining the achievement of Meno's slave boy than by positing that he studied geometry in a prior life.

Do you fear death? Are you vitally interested in the question whether you will survive death? If so, the conclusion seems to be that you will have to look elsewhere for evidence or a proof that you will survive death. It also appears to follow that if Socrates took the hemlock at least in part because of his acceptance of the argument we have been discussing he was to that degree sadly misguided. This is not to say he should have followed Crito's advice and escaped. Perhaps Socrates did the correct thing after all. But if he did the correct thing because of the preceding argument he did it for the wrong reason.

"What?"—you might be saying to yourself at this point—"Could Socrates have been wrong? Wasn't he supposed to be one of the wisest thinkers who ever lived? Could such a man have believed in life after death because of an invalid argument? And if Socrates could have been mistaken on such an important point, what hope have I, a beginning student of philosophy, of ever finding the truth?"

There is a lesson to be learned here: Yes, Socrates, Aristotle, Kant, and James are knowledgeable and wise people, *but they are not infallible*. To properly study the discipline known as *philosophy*, it is not enough just to learn what great thinkers believed. You must also learn to think for yourself. Don't accept anything merely because Plato or Aquinas or Descartes or Whitehead said so. Criticize what you read. Learn to think carefully. Accept something only if, after you have thought about it, it seems correct to you. Then you will be *doing* and not just *learning about* philosophy; you will *be* a philosopher.

Yes, Socrates might have been wrong. In fact, I believe he was. I happen to agree with him that there is life after death, but his argument for it just isn't convincing. But more importantly, what do *you* think? Is there any good reason to believe that we survive death?

NOTES

1. Plato, *Crito,* trans. Hugh Tredennick, in *Plato: The Collected Dialogues,* ed. Edith Hamilton and Huntington Cairns (Princeton, N.J.: Princeton University Press, 1961), 48B (p. 33).
2. Ibid., 49D (pp. 34–35).
3. Ibid., 50B (p. 35).
4. Plato, *Phaedo,* trans. Hugh Tredennick, in *Plato: The Collected Dialogues,* 63C (p. 46).
5. Plato, *Meno,* trans. W. K. C. Guthrie, in *Plato: The Collected Dialogues,* 81B–86B (pp. 364–371).

CHAPTER 2

The Case of Aristotle

Can We Be Happy in an Unjust World?

Mobs were forming everywhere. Athenians were celebrating the death of the emperor, Alexander the Great. Filled with hatred for all who had been associated with Alexander, some citizens brought accusations of impiety against his former tutor, Aristotle. At that very moment in 323 B.C., the courts were handing down an indictment against Aristotle. He had gotten word of the forthcoming indictment, and now he wondered what to do. Should he flee the city? How could he best live out his philosophy? Aristotle had to decide quickly.

Aristotle's Early Life

Aristotle was born in the "neutral" town of Stagira in Thrace in 384 B.C. Had he stayed there, he might never have gotten involved in the struggle between the neighboring country of Macedonia and the city-state of Athens. But when Aristotle's father became the court physician to the king of Macedonia, the family's life was inextricably linked to politics.

Macedonia and Athens had been engaged in power plays and intrigue long before Aristotle's time. They had a common enemy in the Persians, but cultural differences made them suspicious of each other. Many Athenians viewed the Macedonians as uncultured, mindless brutes. Many Macedonians, in turn, saw the Athenians as weak, pampered snobs. Fortunately for Aristotle, Macedonia was strong enough to force an alliance on Athens. That made it possible for this bright, well-connected seventeen-year-old to go to Athens and study at the famous Academy of Plato.

The Academy and Plato

Sometime between 380 and 370 B.C., Plato had founded a school dedicated to developing Socrates' philosophy. Among Plato's philosophical tenets were the theory of Forms, the centrality of mathematical or deductive reasoning, and the importance of political philosophy.

Plato had long held that politics should rightly come under the province of philosophy. In the *Republic,* he declared,

> Until philosophers are kings, or the kings and princes of this world have the spirit and power of philosophy, and political greatness and wisdom meet in one . . . cities will never have rest from their evils, no, nor the human race.[1]

For Plato, political philosophy was to be deductive. One should reason from universal principles to particular instances. For example, if one wanted to know what to include in a city's constitution, one would first try to grasp the idea or Form of "Goodness." Then that universal principle would be applied to the particular section of the constitution being considered. This would mean that the one writing the constitution would have to be able to "grasp the Forms." The person would have to be a philosopher.

Plato did more than simply theorize about the relationship between philosophy and politics. About the time that the seventeen-year-old Aristotle arrived, the Academy became involved in political experiments in Sicily. This involvement led to a close identification of the philosophical interests of the Academy with the political interests of Athens.

During the two decades that Aristotle was associated with the Academy, he was deeply influenced by Plato. His earliest writings, intended for a popular audience, were in the style of Platonic dialogues.

Involvement with Alexander

Plato died in 347 B.C. Aristotle left Athens and accepted the patronage of a former fellow student, Hermias, who had gathered a group of philosophers on the island of Assos, which he ruled. Using the resources of Hermias' court, Aristotle recorded his observations of the sea life around the small island. Following Hermias' betrayal and murder, Aristotle fled to the island of Lesbos. For three years, he continued his scientific studies there.

In 342 B.C., Aristotle moved back to Macedonia. This time he came as tutor to the king's thirteen-year-old son, Alexander. It was a different Macedonia from that which Aristotle had left as a boy twenty-five years before. The king, Philip, had created a powerful military machine. Macedonia now ruled the Hellenic League and was poised to invade Persia.

Philip saw Aristotle not only as an excellent tutor but also as a valuable political ally with connections in the Greek cities and colonies. When Alexander reached adulthood, Aristotle accepted a political appointment in his hometown of Stagira, now under Philip's rule. The town had been destroyed, but as a favor to Aristotle Philip allowed him to supervise the rebuilding of the town. After five years as a successful administrator, Aristotle was ready to return to Athens and philosophy.

The Lyceum

When he arrived in Athens, Aristotle was disappointed. He discovered that Xenocrates, whom he considered a second-rate philosopher, now headed the Academy. Aristotle disagreed with this man's extreme emphasis on mathematics. With the goodwill and financial backing of the Macedonian court, Aristotle had no difficulty in establishing his own institution. He acquired the best available school property in Athens and named it the Lyceum. Aristotle brought with him enough teaching materials (maps, books, models, records of observations, and so on) and assistants to attract significant attention. This public awareness quickly translated into new students, and the Lyceum was an immediate success. It tended to attract the youth of the aspiring middle class. The Academy continued to be the stronghold of the more conservative aristocracy.

During the next eleven years, Aristotle concerned himself with teaching, writing, and organizing all the observations he had made in Assos, Lesbos, and Macedonia. Because of Aristotle's relationship with Alexander, the Lyceum enjoyed a privileged status. Alexander even sent records of his observations of nature and specimens of plants and animal life from the distant battlefields back to the Lyceum. As the years passed, Aristotle was able to develop his own philosophy in distinction from his mentor, Plato.

Continuity and Change

Aristotle felt dissatisfied with Plato's theory of Forms. Like Plato, he, too, wanted to discover what was real. He, too, wanted to find a solution to the problem of change as presented by Heraclitus and Parmenides. But, unlike Plato, Aristotle did not believe that reality was only to be found in heaven, or in the mind. It was not only immaterial, eternal ideas that were real. Particular things in this world were real. Things changed. But Aristotle's observations at the seashore had convinced him that there were patterns of continuity and stability within the changing world. Sea animals could be grouped by similar structures and functions. They reproduced their own kind with remarkable uniformity.

Actuality and Potentiality

For Aristotle, one way of understanding the continuity within change was to think of a thing's actuality and its potentiality. Xenocrates changed during his lifetime, but he always remained Xenocrates. The baby was potentially the adult. At each stage of change from infant to child to youth to adult to aged, one could recognize the continuity of the person, Xenocrates. This, for Aristotle, was not because one could discern the origin from which Xenocrates came, but rather because one could recognize the goal toward which he was moving.

Nature was a realm of purpose, according to Aristotle. Each thing was developing its potential toward the actuality it could become. When Xenocrates was a baby, he had in him all of the potential to become the adult Xenocrates. That potential was provided by his parents. Thus, for Aristotle, actuality preceded and governed potentiality. There could be no potential adults (babies) if there were not actual adults (parents) first. There could be no acorns if there were not oaks first. All things grew toward the goal for which they were designed. Each entity developed according to its characteristic structure. Human babies became human adults, not donkeys. Acorns became oak trees, not orchids. Actuality and potentiality were principles that helped Aristotle understand organic change within particular things.

Form and Matter

Aristotle also needed to understand what things themselves were and how they could change into something else without destroying all continuity. Aristotle had observed that each particular thing had a certain structure or function that determined its identity. This structure was its "form." Forms were not heavenly realities, as Plato had thought, in which earthly things only partially participated. Forms were embedded in particular things. The characteristic structure of a chair was its form. This structure was intimately related to the function that the chair performed; namely, to support a partly reclining human body. But to accomplish that purpose a chair had to be made out of some stuff; for example, wood. This stuff was the chair's "matter." Reality was a particular thing called a "substance," which was composed of both form and matter. Reality was not the concept of "chair-in-general." Reality, or substance, was the particular chair on which Aristotle was sitting as he wrote. That particular chair embodied the structure or form of chairness, *and* it was made of a particular matter, wood.

According to Aristotle, form and matter were not separate things. They were paired principles by which substances—real, particular things in this world—could be understood. These principles enabled Aristotle to understand the problem of permanence and change. All things passed through changes. But patterns of continuity could be observed. A chair could be broken into pieces to burn in a fire. The form of the substance then changed from chair to kindling. But a continuity with the former chair could be observed. The new form, kindling, had as its matter, chair. When the kindling was burned in the fire, it took on the form, ash. The matter, kindling, then provided the continuity between the new form of the substance and what it had been. Thus, for Aristotle, particular substances could take on new forms. What had been the form now became the matter or principle of continuity carried on in a new form.

Four Causes

To understand how a thing came to be what it was, Aristotle took into account four kinds of causes. The first cause was the stuff or matter of which something was made. This was its *material* cause. The second cause was the thing's characteristic structure or form. This was its *formal* cause. The third cause was the agent who acted on or affected the matter to bring it into its present form. This was the *efficient* cause. Lastly, and most importantly for Aristotle, was the purpose for which something was created. This purpose determined all of the other steps in the process. Aristotle called this purpose the *final* cause. For example, the mast on a Greek sailing ship was made from a tree trunk. Its material cause, then, was the tree from which it was made. Its formal cause was the shipbuilder's design or drawing of a straight pole of a given height and shape. The efficient cause was the work of the laborers who trimmed and smoothed the trunk according to the shipbuilder's design. The final cause, the cause which determined all of the others, was the goal or purpose of the mast, that of supporting a sail capable of carrying the ship forward in the wind.

Aristotle's Theology

Aristotle argued that actuality preceded potentiality. There had to be something already actualized for the potential to move toward. It followed that there had to be something that was ultimately actualized. Aristotle concluded that there was an Unmoved Mover who actualized all of the potential movements in the universe. But, Aristotle assumed, this Unmoved Mover could not itself change. It was eternal form without matter. He identified this Unmoved Mover with divine thought or mind and did not hesitate to call it God. This God was not the creator of the material world. Matter was eternal. God was rather the energizing form of the world. God moved the world not from behind but as its goal. God moved the world as a beloved moved the lover. All things moved toward the actualization of their potential, drawn by the energy of the supremely actual one, God.

This God was not personal. It did not exercise any providential oversight of human affairs. Aristotle did not recommend praying to it. What did God do? Aristotle said, "Thought thinks itself as object in virtue of its participation in what is thought."[2] The quality of thought depended on the nature of its object. God, therefore, thought about that which was highest: the unchangeable. God was a mind, thinking about its unchangeable self.

According to Aristotle, the highest function of humanity, as of God, was to think. The rational part of humanity was the divine element that separated humankind from the rest of creation. The highest kind of thought was of unchangeable ideas. Thus, like Plato, Aristotle held that theoretical wisdom was to be prized over practical. Only the active reason in humans was considered separable from the body and immortal.

But unlike Plato, in most human affairs Aristotle preferred to move from the sensible, practical, and experiential. Politics, for Aristotle, was a matter of practical knowledge. It represented the expression of another part of human nature, the desire to form groups. Aristotle contended that the human being was a social or political animal. The best kind of *polis*, or group, could be discovered by observations of human experiments with government.

Political Theory

Aristotle's disagreements with Plato regarding politics were rooted in his different understanding of the nature of reality (metaphysics) and how it was known (epistemology). Plato's epistemology was based on innate, abstract ideas or Forms from which conclusions could be derived. He believed that one first had to grasp the universal Form and then apply it to a specific situation. He used deductive reasoning, from the universals to the particulars. Aristotle's theory of knowledge was rooted in his boyhood experience as the son of a medical doctor. His epistemology had been confirmed by his careful observations of plant and animal life. For Aristotle, most knowledge began with the observation of particular things in this world. People encountered these objects with their five senses. Then, as they gathered a mass of evidence, they could reason from the particulars to generalizations that applied to them. This inductive reasoning moved from particulars to universals.

Aristotle applied his general theory of knowledge to politics. Plato had assumed that one could begin with the nature of the soul and an abstract idea about what was "good" and then embody that idea in a particular form of government. Aristotle, instead, believed that the "good" was that which persons sought by nature. In order to find out what people did in fact aim for, one had to begin by observing actual governments and how they worked. Then general conclusions were drawn as to which forms of government proved to be "good" for human beings. Aristotle asserted, referring to Plato,

> Now our predecessors have left the subject of legislation to us unexamined; it is perhaps best, therefore, that we should ourselves study it, and in general study the question of the constitution, in order to complete to the best of our ability our philosophy of human nature. First, then, if anything has been said well in detail by earlier thinkers, let us try to review it; then in the light of the constitutions we have collected let us study what sorts of influence preserve and destroy states, and what sorts preserve or destroy the particular kinds of constitution, and to what cause it is due that some are well and others ill administered. When these have been studied we shall perhaps be more likely to see with a comprehensive view, which constitution is best, and how each must be ordered, and what laws and customs it must use, if it is to be at its best.[3]

Aristotle acted on his theory by gathering the constitutions of 158 Greek city-states. Using these constitutions as the basis, he distinguished between three types of states: the rule of the one, the rule of the few, and the rule of the many. In each of these types of governments, Aristotle pointed out that there could be either a true or a perverted kind of rule. Aristotle did not say specifically which of these types he thought best. Instead, he pointed out that one must observe each type of state to see how well it worked. Aristotle aimed at a practical, workable state that would take into account human nature. He sought to mediate between what was desirable and what was reasonably attainable.

Happiness

According to Aristotle, human beings by nature sought happiness. Happiness was the end or goal toward which all people were striving. Aristotle stated, "Everything we choose we choose for the sake of something else—except happiness, which is an end."[4]

Happiness, for Aristotle, was not simply trivial amusement or bodily pleasure. "Happiness . . . does not lie in amusement."[5] Rather, happiness was "activity in accordance with virtue."[6] When a person was acting virtuously, he or she would be happy. Virtue consisted in avoiding extremes, in finding the middle ground or mean. For example, the moral virtue of courage was the mean between the vices of fear and foolhardiness. Courage, was a balance or harmony between two extremes.

Although Aristotle held that happiness is more than amusement and was in fact found in virtuous activities, he did not deny the importance of external influences in achieving happiness. It was not enough for a person to exercise his or her "divine element" by thinking and contemplating. A person also needed to fulfill some of the desires of the body in order to achieve happiness. Aristotle explained,

> But being a man, one will also need external prosperity; for our nature is not self-sufficient for the purpose of contemplation, but our body also must be healthy and must have food and other attention.[7]

This need for some of the comforts of life was not confined to some lower class of people. Aristotle disagreed with Plato's notion that the highest class, the "guardians," or philosopher kings, should not have worldly goods. According to Aristotle, "a philosopher, as well as a just man or one possessing any other virtue, needs the necessities of life."[8]

Furthermore, Aristotle believed that the things that happened to a person during his or her lifetime helped to determine whether or not that person would have a happy life. Although happiness was "acting in accordance with virtue," the fateful occurrences of life were important. Aristotle declared that "a multitude of great events if they turn out well will make life happier . . . while if they turn out ill they crush and maim happiness."[9]

Aristotle concluded then that a person was happy if he or she was "active in accordance with complete virtue and is sufficiently equipped with external goods, not for some chance period but throughout a complete life."[10] Material things and physical well-being were not bad. They were important preconditions for a happy life.

The Indictment

When Alexander the Great died, long-suppressed feelings surfaced. The Athenians were suddenly free to vent their hatred of everything Macedonian. Throughout the city, statues that depicted Macedonians were pulled down. Orators appeared on the street corners urging a war of liberation from Macedonia. Aristotle, who had been identified in the popular mind with Alexander and Macedonia, was a likely target for angry mobs.

One of the foremost anti-Macedonians, Demophilus, charged Aristotle with impiety. The indictment cited a hymn that Aristotle had composed in honor of his friend and former patron, Hermias. Demophilus asserted that the song ascribed deity to Hermias. Because Hermias had once been a slave, it was considered obvious that he could not be divine.

On the basis of this formal indictment, Aristotle was summoned to appear before the Athenian assembly. There he would be expected to answer the charges brought against him.

The Decision

Aristotle realized that he would have to act quickly. He felt that the formal charges were fabricated. The real issue was his association with Macedonia.

Aristotle's political ideals were being tested by practical reality. Socrates had encountered a similar situation some seventy-five years before. He, too, had been indicted on fabricated charges. He had stayed and "fought" in his own way, finally choosing death over escape.

As Aristotle considered the situation, he thought about Socrates. Should he also stay and fight the charges? Or should he flee the city before some irrational mob seized him? If he left, what would become of his work, his school? How could he put his own philosophy into practice in this tense political situation? In this situation of injustice, how could he achieve happiness?

He did not have much time to decide.

NOTES

1. Plato, *The Republic*, trans. B. Jowett (New York: Random House, n.d.), 473 CD.
2. Aristotle, *Metaphysics*, 1072 b 19, cited in *Encyclopedia of Philosophy*, s.v. "Aristotle."
3. Aristotle, *The Nicomachean Ethics of Aristotle*, trans. with introduction by David Ross (London: Oxford University Press, 1925), 1181 b 12 (pp. 275–276).
4. Ibid., 1176 b 29 (p. 262).
5. Ibid., 1176 b 27 (p. 262).
6. Ibid., 1177 a 9 (p. 263).
7. Ibid., 1178 b 39 (p. 268).
8. Ibid., 1177 a 28 (p. 264).
9. Ibid., 1100 b 24 (p. 21).
10. Ibid., 1101 a 13 (p. 22).

BIBLIOGRAPHY

Primary Source

Aristotle. *The Basic Works of Aristotle*. Edited by Richard McKeon. New York: Random House, 1941.

Biography

Green, Majorie. *A Portrait of Aristotle.* Chicago: University of Chicago Press, 1963.

Interpretative Works

Adler, Mortimer. *Aristotle for Everyone: Difficult Thought Made Easy.* New York: Macmillan, 1978.
Anscombe, G. E. M., and Geach, Peter. *Three Philosophers.* Oxford, England: Oxford University Press, 1961.
Chroust, Anton-Hermon. *Aristotle.* Notre Dame: University of Notre Dame Press, 1973. Two vols.
Randall, J. H., Jr. *Aristotle.* New York: Columbia University Press, 1960.
Ross, W. D. *Aristotle.* New York: Meridian Books, 1959.

QUESTIONS FOR STUDY

1. Outline the elements that Plato and Aristotle shared in common as classical realists. Then contrast their views on metaphysics and epistemology.

2. How did Aristotle approach the problem of change differently than Plato? Why?

3. Discuss Aristotle's concept of cause and effect. Define and describe the function in Aristotle's philosophy of the following sets of principles:
    a. Actuality and potentiality
    b. Form and matter
    c. Four causes

4. Describe Aristotle's concept of God. What elements of similarity and difference does it have to your own views of deity?

5. Compare Plato's and Aristotle's views on how good government could be achieved. Discuss the relevance of their views in a modern state.

6. Define happiness according to Aristotle. Would this definition provide an adequate guide to living the good life for modern people? Why or why not?

A Contemporary Response

RALPH McINERNY

THE MORAL decision Aristotle faced in 323 B.C. as anti-Macedonian fever mounted in Athens is one that must have been influenced by the philosophical positions he had arrived at over the years. In the *Nicomachean Ethics,* he remarked that a good deal of experience is required in order to judge wisely in practical affairs. When we are young, we are apt to see things as black and white; whereas, as Aristotle said, "perhaps" is the adverb of age. He decided to leave lest, he said, Athens be given an opportunity to sin a second time against philosophy. The reference is to Socrates, and we must ask ourselves why Aristotle availed himself of the opportunity Socrates refused, namely, escape. What would be an Aristotelian justification of the decision to leave Athens—other than not wanting to be an occasion of sin to his hosts?

Aristotle would distinguish between two sorts of evil, the evil that befalls us and the evil we do. The first sort of evil is exemplified by misfortune or by an injustice that is done to us. Socrates was a victim of injustice. The great evil of condemnation to death and execution befell him but he was not for all that a worse man. Indeed, we are inclined to think him a better man. Aristotle chose to forego the honor of execution. His decision to flee will be judged good or bad and, if bad, Aristotle himself will be thought bad.

What are the criteria according to which an action can be judged good or bad? What is the human good? Aristotle, noting that we call a thing good if it performs its function well, calling a knife that cuts cleanly a good one, a car that runs economically a good one, said that that person would be called good who performed the specifically human function well—if human beings have a function, that is. Aristotle thought humans had a function, and it is important to get straight what he meant by this. What he meant was an action that is peculiar to humans and to nothing else, some action that sets the human agent off from all others.

This is not simply a matter of distinguishing between human beings and mice and elm trees. Rather, it is a matter of distinguishing from among the activities that are truly ascribed to humans those which are ascribed to them *as human beings*.

1. Jones is digesting his dinner.
2. Jones is plummeting down the elevator shaft.
3. Jones is whispering to Mrs. Jones.

Let us say that all these sentences are true. Each of them truly ascribes an activity to Jones. But only item 3 ascribes to Jones an activity that is peculiar to humans. Presumably all animals digest their food and any physical object could fall down a shaft, but only humans can whisper sweet nothings into the auricular cavities of their spouses. Thus, when we ask about the good of human beings, we are speaking of doing well such activities as that mentioned in item 3.

Specifically human activities are those we put our mind to; they are deliberate and purposive. That does not mean they are ordered to something beyond themselves. Jones might be perfectly content just to sit and hold Mrs. Jones's hand, something he does deliberately and intentionally and that he may do well or badly.

It is clear that when Aristotle spoke of the specifically human act, he did not mean some numerically one act that all humans perform, such as talking. The specifically human ranges over all kinds of actions: whispering to one's wife, pursuing the pleasant, avoiding the harmful, buying and selling, climbing mountains, making shoes, and so on. The list is all but infinite, and that is the rub. How can we possibly specify what doing so many different kinds of acts well would be? As Aristotle feared, we seem to have embraced a platitude; that is, "Do well what you do." Or, "Be good."

But Aristotle was not disheartened by this problem. He thought we could cluster these various kinds of acts into manageable categories, say something about what acting well would mean in this category or that, and go on to relate the kinds or categories of acts in a sort of hierarchy so that acting well in one category will take precedence over acting well in another.

That is a large order, but we can see the main outlines by noticing that Aristotle distinguished moral virtues from intellectual virtues. A virtue is an habitual disposition to act well. What is a moral virtue? Consider the following:

4. John trembles as the lion approaches.
5. John fights off the lion and saves the little old lady.

Item 4 is like items 1 and 2; that is, fearing is truly described to John but it is not a peculiarly human activity, because presumably lambs and perhaps lions are also fearful in the face of threats to their life. The difference between items 4 and 5 is like the difference between the following:

6. John's beard is growing.
7. John is growing a beard.

That is, items 5 and 7 express acts John deliberately or intentionally engages in.

A specifically human act does not just happen; it is brought about by the reasoned choice of the human agent.

This is why Aristotle used "rational activity" as descriptive of all specifically human action. But rational activity is either *participated* in, as when the growth of one's beard is fostered and intended the better to conceal a weak jaw, or *essential,* as when it is the activity of reasoning as such. Moral virtue, which brings our desires and appetites under the sway of reason, disposes for the acquisition of intellectual virtues, doing reasoning well; that is, arriving at truth. Finally, Aristotle spoke of doing well—or truly—the intellectual activity that is the contemplation of the divine and said it is in such contemplation that human happiness chiefly consists. Because he did not think any man could engage exclusively in contemplation, Aristotle did not *identify* happiness or the human good with contemplating well. That would be to identify happiness or the human good with a single virtue. The fact is that our good consists of a variety of virtuous activities, some of which are more necessary than others, some of which are more noble than others.

To return now to Aristotle's plight in Athens in 323 B.C. If he followed his own philosophy, he would ask himself what would be more in keeping with his nature as a rational agent: staying and facing execution, or fleeing and continuing his pursuit of truth. Aristotle did discuss the question of how much indignity can fittingly be borne by a human being. In discussing actions where our freedom is constrained, as for example if a tyrant forced us to sweep streets because he held our family hostage, Aristotle said that a point could be reached where what we are thus asked to do should not be done because it would be unbecoming to a human being. For example, if the tyrant demanded that we eat sand, we should refuse. Better death than dishonor, so to say. Of course, if a human being does sink below the level of acceptability, the circumstances might be such that his or her acts would elicit pity and pardon rather than condemnation.

One of the functions of Greek tragedy, for Aristotle, was to give us dramatic instances of human agents acting in situations where great misfortunes have befallen them. For example, there is the unwitting doing of a reprehensible deed, such as marrying one's mother. What should one do in the face of the tragedies that attend human life? What should one do in Athens facing indictment, condemnation, and death?

There is no single answer. In Aristotle's view, moral philosophy can put before us the moral ideal, the virtuous life; it can cite kinds of action that it would never be right for a human to do; but for the most part philosophy cannot give us an absolutely firm and unavoidable answer—certainly not an answer that will apply without pondering our circumstances. The reason is that philosophy must always proceed at the level of some generality, whereas Aristotle must perform a single act—he must leave or stay, in these circumstances.

Reflecting on the case of Socrates can produce some general considerations that by and large should guide those who find themselves in similar circumstances. But the results of such reflections, the rules or guidelines, must be applied. Is Aristotle's case identical with Socrates? One was an Athenian, the other was a Stagirite. That is a significant difference if staying is meant to serve as a lesson to one's fellow citizens. Finally it is the human agent, this one, who decides, and his action will be of the quality it is, not simply because of the moral philosophy or other general knowledge he has—one does not become good by philosophizing, Aristotle wrote—but because of the character he has, and one has a certain character because of one's past history of action. The saying attributed to Aristotle, that he chose not to give the Athenians an opportunity to sin twice against philosophy, may be regarded as rationalizing or it may be seen as the judgment that to provide others with an opportunity to act unjustly may, when one can avoid it, amount to an unfitting action on the part of the prospective victim.

Nowadays we are unlikely to find nobility in the spectacle of someone suffering misfortune or injustice. Perhaps our instinctive reaction is that Aristotle should stay, fight his enemies, and provide an example of philosophical courage. But then perhaps we think that the world is a perfectible place and that by way of effort and struggle evil and injustice can be driven from the world. Aristotle would not have been so optimistic. Surely history supports his view rather than that of the utopian idealist. He distinguished between timidity and foolhardiness; what he called courage or fortitude was a mean between these extremes. He did not think we could decide in advance or at the level of theory where that mean may lie. To find it, in our own case, in these circumstances, under the pressure of time and our limited knowledge, is the moral task.

We can describe Aristotle's plight in such a way that it would be incumbent on him to flee. But the human agent, when he or she acts, must assess *his* or *her* circumstances and do the right thing. And doing the right thing, for Aristotle, was less a matter of settling an abstract case than it was of assessing his circumstances in the light of his moral character, which entailed a stable love of the good. That is why, beside his interest in principles and guidelines of an abstract sort, Aristotle insisted that in moral matters, the good person is the measure. This is not relativism, any more than it was absolutism when Aristotle insisted that we can describe the moral ideal and say what is never compatible with it.

Did Aristotle act in a cowardly fashion? Was his a strategic withdrawal? Is it not a good thing to prevent others from committing an evil? How we construe the case will dictate our assessment. In the concrete historical deed, Aristotle would have been able to see what the right thing to do was and to do it only if his moral character was of the appropriate sort.

CHAPTER 3

The Case of Augustine

How Can We Make Sense of the Evil in the World?

As Augustine prepared to write the letter, he was struck by the strangeness of the situation. In his youth, he had converted his friend Honoratus to Manichaeism. Now, just a few years later in A.D. 391, Augustine was again trying to convert Honoratus: this time from Manichaeism to Christianity. Taking pen in hand, Augustine began to write:

> Thou knowest, Honoratus, that for this reason alone did we fall into the hands of these men, namely, that they professed to free us from all error and bring us to God by pure reason alone, without that terrible principle of authority. For what else induced me to . . . follow these men for almost nine years, except their assertion that we were terrified by superstition into a faith blindly imposed upon our reason, while they urged no one to believe until the truth was fully discussed and proved? Who would not be seduced by such promises: especially if he were a proud, contentious young man, thirsting for truth, such as they then found me?[1]

It was true. The Manichaeans had appealed to both his pride and his intellect. He had been proud that the leaders of a major religion had taken an interest in him: a middle-class boy from the African provinces. His intellect had found in Manichaean theology a solution to the troublesome problem of evil.

But Augustine had since abandoned his Manichaean beliefs. The attention of Faustus and the other Manichaean leaders no longer thrilled him. The clear answer to the problem of evil presented by the Manichaeans no longer seemed adequate. The certain reasonings no longer seemed so certain. Faith and the principle of authority were no longer abhorrent.

Sitting at his desk at the monastery in North Africa, Augustine thought about his own conversion. He remembered how he had reconciled his belief in the God of the Old Testament with the problem of evil. His notion of "disordered love" provided, for him, an adequate answer to the problem of evil. But

would his arguments be convincing to Honoratus? How could he persuade
Honoratus that faith and not reason alone led to God? How could he open his
friend to the illumination that alone came from God?

Early Life

Christianity had spread quickly throughout the Roman Empire. Despite
sporadic (and often brutal) attempts to eliminate the faith, Christians had
grown in numbers and power. By the early fourth century, Christianity had become the virtual state religion.

In the provinces of North Africa, towns had arisen, valleys and plains had
been planted with grain, and roads had been built. In one area of North Africa
an amphitheater nearly the size of the Colosseum in Rome had been built. At
the same time, Christianity had spread its influence. What had begun as a Jewish heresy soon became the dominant force in the religious life of North Africa.

But by the year 350 much of the economic growth of the provinces had
ceased. In North Africa, the Roman economy was crumbling. Wars with peo-
ples to the north and east of the empire had drained much of the economic
resources from the provinces. Corruption within the Roman government had led
to swindles that further crippled the outlying areas.

In 354 a relatively poor but respected man named Patricius and his wife
Monica had a son whom they named Aurelius Augustinus. Patricius was a
proud man from the North African town of Thagaste. He worked hard and sacrificed much to provide for Augustine's education. Patricius died when Augustine was still young. Augustine's mother, Monica, was a Christian.

As a young boy, Augustine was anxious to be accepted and to succeed in
life. Augustine enjoyed playing in the fields around Thagaste. His early days
were spent stalking birds, ripping the tails off lizards, and gazing longingly at
the mountains in the distance. In these early years, Augustine was especially
struck by the light that surrounded him. He portrayed the sunlight as the queen
of all colors, cascading over everything, and wrote a poem in praise of candle-
light.

In 371, at the age of seventeen, Augustine went to Carthage to pursue his
education. During his first two years in Carthage, Augustine discovered the
pleasures of the big city. He took a concubine as a sort of second-class wife. She
bore him a son, Adeodatus.

In 373, while reading Cicero's *The Hortensius*, Augustine was "converted"
to philosophy: the love of wisdom. Turning to the Bible in hopes of finding wisdom, Augustine was appalled at what he read. Being an educated young man,
he was put off by the uncultivated and unpolished language of the Latin Bible
of Africa. Furthermore, what Augustine found in the Bible seemed to have little
to do with the love of wisdom about which Cicero had written. The Bible
seemed to Augustine to be full of contradictions and inconsistencies. Finally, the
God of the Old Testament seemed to be a vengeful, spiteful god who did not

deserve respect or worship. How such a god who allowed evil could be considered loving completely escaped Augustine. Hence Augustine was initially drawn to a pagan position; a search for wisdom outside the bounds of any organized religion.

The Problem of Evil

The problem of evil in the world had troubled thoughtful people for centuries. They asked, "How could an all-loving, all-powerful God allow evil in the world?" The problem could be clearly seen by stating three propositions—one of which had to be either denied or revised. These three propositions were

1. God is good.
2. God is all-powerful.
3. There is evil in the world.

If there was evil in the world and God was good (in at least some sense of the word *good* that was understandable), then Item 2 must be false; that is, God wanted to wipe out evil, but he could not. If one maintained God's powerfulness, then either God desired that evil be in the world (and thus was not good) or else one was mistaken about the apparent evil in the world. It did not seem possible to hold all three of these propositions to be true without changing at least one of them.

As a pagan, the problem of evil ceased to be a real problem for Augustine. As a pagan, Augustine denied both that God was good (sometimes the gods acted in obviously evil ways) and that God was all-powerful (there might be many conflicting gods, or no God or gods at all). So, by denying the first and second propositions, Augustine was free from the problem of evil.

Manichaeism

While in Carthage, Augustine discovered the religion of Manichaeism. Believing that this religion would lead him to wisdom, he became a "Hearer," one of the faithful, among the Manichees. He even managed to win converts (such as his friend Honoratus) for his new religion.

The Manichees were followers of the prophet Mani, a Persian who called himself "the apostle of Jesus Christ." In the third century, Mani had founded a new religion based loosely on the teachings of Christ. The Manichees believed that they were the "true Christians" and that they alone possessed the truth. They rejected the Old Testament and the incarnation of Jesus holding Jesus to be a mere mortal who only seemed divine. They further rejected all authority, whether of the Bible or of the church, and accepted nothing that could not be proven by reason.

The Manichees believed that in people, as in the universe at large, two fundamental principles were struggling for dominance. One principle was evil, the other was good. Following an initiation service, the new inductees into the Manichaean religion would be "illumined, filled with light." In this "illumined" state, the inductee would realize the evil at war with the good in his or her own soul. The goal then became to separate the darkness (or evil) from the light. The method of doing this was through denying the flesh—that is, through celibacy, poverty, and vegetarianism. But not all Manichees went through such a rigorous program of self-denial. A small minority, called the Elect, lived the life of denial, while the majority of the faithful (like Augustine) were known as Hearers and lived a normal life.

The Manichees were relieved from having any sense of guilt. Because any evil they might do arose from their evil natures, their good natures remained untouched. For Augustine, this meant that his relationship with a concubine, his fights with his mother, all of the things that seemed to be from darkness rather than from light did not affect his soul. A principle of darkness was working within him that he could no more control than he could restrain the cosmic struggle of good and evil.

The Manichees answered the problem of evil by denying the proposition that God is all-powerful. God was powerful, but not powerful enough to do away with evil. Evil had an equal standing with goodness. There was no power that could do away with either one. God, therefore, was as incapable of dealing with evil as Augustine found himself to be.

Neoplatonism

Augustine returned to Thagaste in 375 to become a teacher. When his mother, Monica, found out that he had become a Manichaean, she expelled him from her house. Finding that his hometown lacked the thrill of the city, Augustine returned to Carthage the next year. There he remained for the next seven years, teaching and continuing his own studies.

During this time, Augustine became acquainted with Faustus, Manichaeism's foremost thinker. Although Faustus was clever, Augustine was profoundly disappointed by his lack of education and his inconsistent attacks on Christianity. The more Augustine read in the standard works of academic learning, the more he began to doubt the theories of his fellow Manichees. The Manichees prided themselves on their knowledge of the heavens and of the curious orbits of the planets, but Augustine found their calculations to be contradictory.

Like any young and ambitious scholar, Augustine longed to be closer to the center of learning. By 382 he had grown tired of Carthage and longed to go to Rome. His students in Carthage were undisciplined and unattentive, and he had heard that in Rome the students were better behaved. As Augustine prepared to go to Rome, his mother discovered his plans. She was angry that her son had abandoned Christianity, but now he was going to leave her as well. Augustine described his departure for Rome,

> I did not wish to go to Rome because of the richer fees and higher dignity which my friends promised me there. . . . My principal and almost sole motive was that I had been informed that the students there studied more quietly and were better kept under the control of stern discipline. . . . My mother, grieved deeply over my departure, . . . followed me down to the sea. She clasped me tight in her embrace, willing either to keep me back or to go with me, but I deceived her, pretending that I had a friend whom I could not leave until he had a favorable wind to set sail. . . . That night I slipped away secretly, and she remained to pray and weep.[2]

Arriving in Rome, Augustine was very disappointed. The aristocrats whom he wanted to get to know turned out to be pompous boors. After a year, Augustine left Rome for a teaching post in Milan.

While in Milan, Augustine encountered some of the writings of Plotinus and Porphyry. Plotinus was the founder of what later was called Neoplatonism. Porphyry was his disciple and popularizer. Following many of Plato's doctrines, the Neoplatonists had developed a quasi-religious doctrine of *logos,* or "word." This doctrine appeared to coincide with the doctrine of *logos* presented in the New Testament Gospel of John. In both accounts, the creative Word was understood to be immaterial, the transcendent cause of all things of flesh and blood.

The Neoplatonists had a convincing alternative to Manichaean dualism. Evil, they taught, was no substance at all, but simply a defection in substance. Evil had no being whatsoever apart from good. All things were good in so far as they existed. What constituted evil was imperfection in their existence, the corruption of their goodness. Starting from this premise, Augustine then inquired of his own experience "what wickedness was, and . . . found that it was no substance, but a perversion of the will, bent aside"[3] from God.

In terms of the three propositions that made up the problem of evil, Augustine's new position amounted to a denial of the third statement. The Neoplatonists denied that evil was a thing in the world. Evil did not exist. There was only a lack of the good.

Conversion to Christianity

As Augustine continued in his Neoplatonic studies, he came under the influence of a group of Christian Neoplatonists led by Bishop Ambrose. In 386, Augustine was in a garden thinking about his own life when he heard a child saying "pick it up, read it; pick it up, read it."[4] Augustine later recounted what happened:

> So I quickly returned to the bench . . . for there I had put down the apostle's book when I had left there. I snatched it up, opened it, and in silence read the paragraph on which my eyes first fell: "Not in rioting and drunkenness, not in chambering and wantonness, not in strife and envying, but put on the Lord Jesus Christ, and make no provision for the flesh to fulfill the lusts thereof." I wanted to read no further, nor did I need to. For instantly, as the sentence ended, there was infused in my heart something like the light of full certainty and all my gloom of doubt vanished away.[5]

Augustine's View of Faith and Reason

At the close of the fourth century, nearly all philosophers—Christian and non-Christian alike—believed that the goal of philosophy was wisdom and blessedness. No sharp distinction was made between philosophy and theology, and non-Christian philosophies were widely used by Christians. What distinguished Christians was their view that the ultimate Truth was to be found in Jesus Christ. Thus, although other philosophies (especially Neoplatonism) contained much truth for Augustine, they could never provide the heart of the Christian gospel—the life, death, and resurrection of Jesus. This was to be found only in the Scriptures and the tradition of the church. In order to find Truth, one appropriated the message of Scripture by faith and then sought to go from there to a full understanding. Augustine put it thus: "Believe in order that you may understand."

Augustine was far from being anti-intellectual in his emphasis on faith. Faith was the essential step to knowledge of God and salvation. But by itself faith could never satisfy the rational nature of humanity. Believing was a kind of thinking—"thinking with assent"—but only of an incomplete and elementary sort. It needed to be developed further, into real understanding. The object seen through faith was always distant and obscure and therefore not intellectually satisfying. It had to be refined and brought into sharper focus—that is, to be understood—by the exercise of the reason.

Two-Storied Universe

Fundamental to Augustine's thought was the duality of the universe. He asserted that there were two worlds: (1) an intelligible world where Truth itself dwelled and (2) this sensible world that people perceived by sight and touch. The sensible world was the "first" or "lower story" of the universe. This sensible world was the world of appearances. A person came to know this world of appearances by using his or her five senses. According to Augustine, this kind of knowledge, which he called *scientia,* was clearly inferior. Although one could have knowledge of appearances, that knowledge was always changeable and incomplete. Such knowledge could never lead one to decisions about how to live one's life. Still, such knowledge could be useful if kept within bounds.

In contrast to the sensible world was the intelligible world. This world was the "second" or "upper story" of the universe. This intelligible world was the world of eternal truths, or *rationes aeternae*. These *rationes aeternae* were eternal and unchanging. They were abstract concepts rather than particular instances. Concepts such as justice, beauty, and the truths of mathematics were all *rationes aeternae*. These *rationes aeternae* were located in the mind of God.

A person could have knowledge of the intelligible world by use of the reason. When the reason was directed toward understanding the *rationes aeternae,* toward attaining a knowledge of the Truth, then the reason was pursuing wisdom. This kind of knowledge Augustine called *sapientia*. However, for him reason never became the measure of all things, as it did for the Manichees. Because of the way one came to know the *rationes aeternae,* Truth always stood in judgment over the mind in spite of the use of reason in the process of gaining understanding.

In many ways, Augustine's idea of a two-storied universe was similar to Plato's theory of Forms. Augustine agreed with Plato that the Truth, which was the foundation of all else, was immaterial and eternal. Furthermore, Augustine also agreed that this Truth was perceived through the reason apart from the senses. Finally, Augustine agreed with Plato that in their present state persons were hindered from attaining a full knowledge of eternal Truth.

However, Augustine differed sharply from Plato on several key points. Augustine rejected the Platonic idea of a pre-existent soul that remembered the eternal truths from some past life. Augustine also believed that the sensible world or the world of appearances had a value. According to Augustine, God made the sensible world and was using it to bring about his eternal ends. Augustine further differed from his philosophical mentor, Plato, on why the reason was hindered in its quest for Truth. According to Plato, the reason once knew the eternal truths and simply forgot them when the person was born. Augustine, however, believed that sin had cut off God's direct illumination of the Truth so that people were in darkness.

Doctrine of Illumination

In order for a person to have knowledge of the intelligible world, the *rationes aeternae* had to be "illumined." Just as the physical eye needed light in order to see the things of the sensible world, so also the "eye of the mind" needed illumination in order to "see" the things of the intelligible world—the *rationes aeternae.* A person could no more "see" the things of the intelligible world (such as justice, beauty, the truths of mathematics, and so on) without some illumination than one could see trees, hills, and so on without the light of the sun. This illumination of the intelligible world came from God. It was divine illumination.

In one sense, this illumination was given in some measure to all people, because all people had the image of God in their souls. Even though this image was disfigured by sin, nevertheless it always remained. This image was the receiver of the divine illumination and was affected by this light even when the person who was in God's image did not have faith in God. Augustine explained,

> But [the mind] is reminded that it should turn to the Lord as to that light by which it was touched in some way, even when it was turned away from Him. For hence it is that even the godless think of eternity, and rightly condemn and rightly praise many things in the moral conduct of men.[6]

This divine illumination, available to all, explained for Augustine the common standards of justice and the common agreement on the truths of mathematics. Everyone was illumined on these matters.

But this general measure of illumination was not enough. Knowledge about God, which was the proper aim of all people, required participation by faith, a turning towards the light. Augustine explained that he had seen the *rationes aeternae* in his readings of the philosophers:

> I delighted in them, not knowing the real source of what it was in them that was true and certain. For I had my back towards the light, and my face towards the things on which the light falls, so that my face, which looked towards the illuminated things, was not itself illuminated.[7]

Augustine realized that he had been using his reason to understand some of the eternal truths in the divine light, but he had his back turned to the light and thus came to no satisfactory knowledge of God. True wisdom, true *sapientia,* the wisdom of knowing God, was only for those who actively participated in receiving God's illumination. Augustine said,

> Let [the mind] worship the God who was not made, but by whom it was made so that it is capable of Him and can be a partaker of Him; wherefore it is written: "Behold, the worship of God is wisdom;" and not by its own light, but by participation in that highest light, will it be wise, and where the eternal light is, there it will reign in blessedness. This wisdom is so called the wisdom of man, as to be also that of God. For it is then true wisdom, since if it is only human wisdom, it is vain.[8]

Thus knowing God through faith and divine illumination was not merely an intellectual matter, but was an act of the will. One had to "believe in order to understand."

Evil as Disordered Love

As a Christian, Augustine took the Neoplatonist answer to the problem of evil and modified it. He continued to agree with the Neoplatonists that evil was not a *thing,* but rather the absence of good. However, within his new Christian framework he found what he considered to be an adequate explanation of how evil (or rather, the lack of good) arose.

Everyone had the need to love. Because people were created incomplete, they needed some object of love to fulfill them. To love, for Augustine, was to focus one's attentions, emotions, and desires on an object of love. It was an act of the will. According to Augustine, there were four objects of love on which one could focus: things, other people, one's self, and God. Each of these were proper objects of love—provided that they were properly ordered. As long as one's love for things was secondary to the other three objects of love, it was proper. There was nothing wrong, for instance, with loving food when one was hungry. But if that love of food was stronger than love of another person who was also hungry and wanted to share some food, then it became evil. The highest love, the love that should be so strong as to make the others seem contemptible in comparison, was the love of God. People were made to love God. No finite thing or person was sufficient to fulfill the need to love God. So a properly ordered love was one where love of things, self, and others came after the love of God, which came first.

Evil, then, was simply disordered love. It was only through loving God first and foremost that people could achieve happiness. But people believed that they could achieve happiness through loving things, themselves, or other people. Although loving things, one's self, or other people were all proper objects of love, they had to be subordinated to the love of God. To expect happiness through loving things, oneself, or other people was to expect too much. These objects of love were simply not capable of providing happiness. A disordered love, a love where God was not the primary object of affection, simply could not bring happiness. A disordered love took the good of loving and turned it into evil because of the absence of a proper object.

The Letter

In 388, Augustine left Milan and, after a short visit in Rome, returned to North Africa. He visited Carthage and finally returned to his hometown of Thagaste. In 391 he was ordained as á priest and moved to the town of Hippo in North Africa to found a monastery.

While establishing the monastery, Augustine became concerned for his friend Honoratus. Just like Augustine, Honoratus had had trouble accepting the God of the Old Testament. He too had found such a God vengeful and cruel. He too had found a solution to the problem of evil in Manichaean dualism. But like Augustine, he also had some problems with Manichaean beliefs. The Manichees believed that all the references to the Old Testament in the New Testament were added by Christians who wanted to return to the old Jewish ways. Honoratus, being an independent thinker, found this position hard to accept.

Still, Honoratus was troubled by the problem of evil. If God was all-powerful and all-loving, how could God allow all the suffering that took place in the Old Testament or that was taking place in the fourth century? Furthermore, Honoratus asked, why should he begin with faith in the authority of scripture and the church?

Augustine knew of his friend's problems with the Christian faith. As he contemplated his own former involvement with the Manichees, he wondered what he could say that would be effective. How could he convince Honoratus that faith was not something that was to be avoided? How could he show that there was no contradiction in believing that the God of the Old Testament was not only all powerful, but also all loving? What could he say that would help Honoratus toward illumination by God?

NOTES

1. Augustine, *Letters,* Library of Christian Classics, vol. 7, trans. Albert C. Outler (Philadelphia: Westminster Press, 1955), p. 348.
2. Augustine, *Confessions,* trans. Albert C. Outler (Philadelphia: Westminster Press, 1955), pp. 103–104.

3. Ibid., p. 150.
4. Ibid., p. 176.
5. Ibid., p. 176.
6. Augustine, *The Trinity,* trans. Stephen McKenna, *The Fathers of the Church* (Washington, D.C.: Catholic University of America Press, 1963), vol. 45, p. 440.
7. Augustine, *Confessions,* p. 93.
8. Augustine, *The Trinity,* p. 432 (Scripture passage is from Job 28:28).

BIBLIOGRAPHY

Primary Sources

Augustine. *Augustine: Confessions and Enchiridion.* Translated and edited by Albert C. Outler. Philadelphia: Westminster Press, 1955.
Augustine. *The City of God.* New York: Doubleday, 1958.

Biography

D'Arcy, M. C., and others. *St. Augustine: His Age, Life, and Thought.* New York: World Publishing, 1957.

Interpretative Works

Battenhouse, Roy W. *A Companion to the Study of St. Augustine.* New York: Oxford University Press, 1955.
Bourke, Vernon J. *Augustine's Quest of Wisdom.* Milwaukee: Bruce, 1945.
Gilson, Etienne. *The Christian Philosophy of Saint Augustine.* Translated by L. E. M. Lynch. New York: Random House, 1960.
Guardini, Romano. *The Conversion of Augustine.* Translated by Elinor Briefs. Westminster, Md.: Newman Press, 1960.
Holmes, Arthur. "Christian Philosophy." *Encyclopaedia Britannica.* 15th ed.
Nash, Ronald H. *The Light of the Mind: St. Augustine's Theory of Knowledge.* Lexington, Ky.: University Press of Kentucky, 1969.
Van Der Meer, F. *Augustine the Bishop.* Translated by Brian Battershaw and G. R. Lamb. London: Sheed and Ward, 1961.

QUESTIONS FOR STUDY

1. Outline the logical propositions that compose the problem of evil as presented in the case. Indicate several methods by which people have tried to resolve this problem.

2. Describe the responses to the problem of evil by
    a. The Manichaeans
    b. The Neoplatonists
    c. Augustine

3. How was Manichaeism alike and different from the Christianity in which Augustine came to believe?

4. Explain Augustine's view of the relationship of faith to reason.

5. Contrast Augustine's concepts of *scientia* (science) and *sapientia* (wisdom). Explain the proper role of each in the process of acquiring knowledge.

6. Discuss Augustine's doctrines of general and divine illumination. Do these have any parallels in contemporary theory of knowledge?

7. What application to contemporary personal or social problems can you find in Augustine's notion of evil as disordered love?

A Contemporary Response

ARTHUR F. HOLMES

AUGUSTINE's treatment of the problem of evil has become a classic point of reference in philosophy of religion in three ways. First, he sees clearly the contrasting views of evil in dualism, pantheism, and Christian theism. The Manichees were, of course, dualists: they believed that two conflicting realities struggled for control, the evil one working through bodily things and the good one through our rational souls. Thereby they denied omnipotence to the good God, and so abandoned any sure hope that good could ever overcome or even limit evil. The Neoplatonists were pantheists, viewing all finite things as necessary emanations of divine being: because God was all-good, what humans called *evil* was then simply an unavoidable lack or privation of good. Consequently, evil was not an active force to be taken realistically.

Augustine, on the other hand, saw clearly the difference that Christian theism makes. The world of material things is neither an evil thing coeternal with divine being, as dualism proposed, nor a necessary outflowing of divine being, as pantheism supposed. It was rather created by God freely and *ex nihilo* (out of nothing). Evil therefore is neither eternal nor is it a built-in lack of finite things. Rather, evil perverts God's good creation. But because the creator-God remains transcendent, independent of creation, God is free to act, controlling evil and overcoming it with good. This plainly is impossible within either a dualist or a pantheist scheme, and Augustine could help Honoratus see the difference.

A second classic ingredient in Augustine's treatment of evil has become known as the "free will argument." As a perversion of the created order of things, evil can be traced to the free will of God's creatures. Rather than being a flaw in the very nature of reality or a byproduct of being finite, so that God is to blame, evil is instead a perversity for which we are rightly blamed.

Honoratus might have raised two objections. First, he individually, like any other individual, is not to blame for all the evils he must endure: the inhumanity of humans to one another exceeds by far what the victim him- or herself causes.

Second, many of the evils we face—such as earthquakes and disease—are beyond human causation; they are "natural" evils, not the "moral" evils Christians call sins. To the first objection, Augustine would reply that the sins of the
parents are visited on the children. That is, others' sinful choices and distorted
love affect all of us, for the corporate human condition is a result of human sinfulness generally—and that, in theological terms, is the result of Adam's disobedience and fall. To the second objection, Augustine might respond that natural
evils are due directly or indirectly to sin's perversion of nature (for instance
through the human greed and self-indulgence that rapes and contaminates the
environment). And if evils are not due to human sin, then they can be traced to
Satan's agency. This too is a "free will argument." Other Christian thinkers,
such as Irenaeus, have preferred what is called a "soul-making theodicy." A
theodicy attempts to justify the ways of God to humans, in this case by arguing
that God allows suffering as a catalyst for building faith and character in us.
Perhaps the soul-making function of much natural evil can be combined with a
free will argument in relation to moral evil. Augustine might even say that a
soul-making theodicy ascribes suffering to the free will of a good God and so
might well be subsumed in an enlarged free will argument. His point in any
case is that God is ultimately sovereign in permitting both the evil we do and the
evil we endure.

This is a largely theological response to Honoratus, for Augustine was one
of Christianity's first great theologians. He would point out that the whole of
Christian theology and Christian ethics may be seen as an extension of the free
will argument that retains all three propositions: God is all-good, God is all-
powerful, and evil exists in this world. But the argument also entails the Christian understanding of human beings as free and responsible agents made in
God's image and entails their resultant responsibility for sin. It leads to the conception of God acting freely through the advent of Christ and through the cruci-
fixion to overcome that sin. It involves the responsible role of the church in the
world and the belief that good will ultimately triumph through God's involvement with us in history. Augustine developed all of these themes in his various
writings and was the first to elaborate a Christian view of history in his famous
City of God. The point is that a full response to Honoratus would involve the
whole scope of Christian theology.

In all of this, the question of human freedom is crucial. In contemporary
terms, Augustine would distinguish between events and actions. An event is part
of a natural process: it has causes and consequences, and apart from additional
intervening causes its occurrence is inevitable and so are its consequences.
Events are part of a natural process, while actions are not. Events have causes,
but actions require personal agents. Causes have other antecedent causes, but
agents have intentions, reasons, and purposes of their own. Agents thus tran-
scend causal processes by acting in creative ways and producing consequences
that otherwise would not occur. Both events and actions have extended consequences, and the agent may not intend all of them. But one is responsible for
both one's action, because it was intended, and so for its consequences. The free
will argument agrees.

The Old Testament views human suffering in this way. Adam's sin has consequences that are traced to his action. Israel's unfaithfulness to God has consequences that are traced to Israel's misuse of freedom. The inhumanity of humans to each other is something for which humankind is accountable. Even Job's suffering is due to Satan's agency. And God's judgment on evildoers is an act of just punishment on free agents. Yet God acts to limit Job's torments. God acts to deliver Israel. Historical occurrences are treated either as "acts of God" or as human acts, or both.

The same kind of extended free will explanation can be applied today. For a tragically contemporary example, consider the evils of war. In its causes—unbridled aggressiveness, economic self-interest, international distrust, and deceit—it is evil. In its conduct and consequences—death and maiming, economic havoc, and excesses of violence—it is evil. Why does God allow it? Why does God not do something about it? Augustine's free will argument plainly applies, along with his reminder that God is still active in history. Christian ethics therefore includes both a pacifist tradition that bears witness by its nonviolence to another way of life, one of peace and love, and a "just war" tradition that limits the uses of force to what are necessary for defense against aggression and does so with a view to a just peace for all involved. Both traditions propose action to limit evil, or to overcome it with good, for the Christian hope remains one of universal peace with justice for all. Augustine in fact contributed significantly to the development of the just war theory and to other aspects of a Christian ethic addressed to the evils humans do. He developed an ethic of love, *agape*—sacrificial, redeeming love and its intentional actions—for his free will argument has as its logical extension an ethic that acts to limit evil and overcome it with good.

But Augustine's treatment of evil involves a third important feature that is readily apparent by now, because what he says about evil and about ethical action presupposes the truth of what the Christian faith teaches about human persons as sinners and God as redeeemer. Honoratus might well have asked why he should begin with the faith in scripture that all that requires.

One might well reply that any view of evil one adopts is part of a larger conceptual scheme: it involves presuppositions. This was plainly the case with both Manichaeism and Neoplatonism. The problem of evil involves more than the logical relationship between three bare statements: it involves the conceptual context those statements have in different philosophies. "God is good" means something very different in the context of Christianity than in the contexts of Manichaeism or Neoplatonism. Consequently they as well as Augustine have presuppositions or, if you like, a prior faith of some sort. Presuppositionless thinking is rare indeed. Contemporary thinkers often assert that there is no presuppositionless or value-free science, and philosophers of science assert that all scientific observations are "theoryladen." Rather than look for the "will o' the wisp" of presuppositionless assertions, then, we need to appraise the credibility of alternative theoretical or conceptual schemes in a more overall fashion.

Augustine's view of faith and reason contributes to this appraisal. "Faith is understanding's step," he claimed, "and understanding is faith's reward." Faith, then, is not blind but requires understanding. Two things are involved.

First, the credibility of a belief stems from its intelligibility, as if truth rides pig-gyback on meaning. "So, Honoratus," Augustine might say, "do you see how the whole scope of Christian theology and ethics addresses the problem of evil?" But, second, the justification of belief requires good and sufficient reasons: "So, Honoratus, your concern calls for honest thought."

Augustine would argue that the *rationes aeternae* provide a logical basis for arguing the existence of one God, altogether good, and that God's existence is attested by various historical evidences. I would rather cast the argument in con-temporary epistemological form. The "foundationalist" bases everything on premises that are beyond question and beyond any need for correction, and de-duces conclusions from these premises. The procedure is like that of geometry: you start with axioms and prove your theorems. But I question whether Augus-tine's *rationes aeternae* or any other premises are sufficient (or indubitable enough) to establish all the conclusive proofs he wants. Yet an alternative proce-dure is available. The "coherentist" regards beliefs as mutually supportive by their interrelatedness and by embracing all the pertinent empirical consider-ations. Thus we are justified in accepting the scientific theory that best explains the empirical phenomena it addresses and at the same time comports best with the body of scientific theories we already hold on similar grounds. Likewise with theoretical or philosophical beliefs. It is the coherence and explanatory range of a position that justifies its acceptance. And this, Honoratus, is why I think Christianity should be believed rather than dualism or pantheism. Augus-tine's handling of the problem of evil fares extremely well by comparison. He provides a plausible and satisfying explanation of the phenomena, and what he says fits well with the whole body of his beliefs.

CHAPTER 4

The Case of Anselm and Aquinas

Will Reason and Faith Work Together?

WHEN HE was last at the University of Paris in 1259, it had taken an edict from the Pope for him to gain admission to the faculty. Now, in 1269, as Thomas Aquinas considered his reappointment, he thought about the issues with which he would have to deal.

The debates that had so troubled the great university ten years before had grown more intense. The role of the mendicant orders in the church continued to be a controversial issue. The Augustinian-Platonic tradition of the church was still strong, and the church was resisting the intrusion of Aristotelian thought. The relationship of the sacred and the secular remained an unresolved problem as the conflict between the Pope and the Holy Roman Emperor intensified. The proper response of the church to the rest of the world was still very much in doubt.

With all of Christendom being shaken both from without and within, Thomas wondered what he had to offer. Had he managed to produce a better demonstration of God's existence than Anselm's ontological argument? Did his emphasis on the role of reason in leading to faith provide a needed link between the secular and the sacred? What was in store for Thomas as he returned to this hotbed of controversy?

Anselm

In 452, twenty-two years after Augustine's death, Rome fell. Following a period of conquest and chaos, a degree of order was ultimately realized through the emergence of feudalism. The church, which had managed to survive the social and political upheaval, gradually assumed responsibilities that previously had been relegated to the civil government. This involvement in government led in turn to a secularization of the church. Bishops became ministers of the state, church dignitaries became warriors.

In the tenth and eleventh centuries, many within the church were so involved in the secular world that a movement led to the emergence of the monastic life as a force within the church. Those who wanted to escape the temptations of the secular world and pursue holiness were naturally drawn to the monasteries. Among those who followed the monastic life was Anselm.

Born to well-to-do parents in the border region of northern Italy in 1033, Anselm was a devout, studious man. After quarreling with his father on his plans to forsake the worldly life of a landowner's son and join a monastery, Anselm left home in 1056. Following a period of travel, he arrived at the Norman Abbey at Bec, where he took his monastic vows in 1060. Within a few years, he became prior of the abbey, and finally, in 1078, he became the abbot. In 1093, Anselm became archbishop of Canterbury. He remained in Canterbury, fighting to free the church from the power of the English kings, until his death in 1109.

Relationship to Augustine

Following the tradition of Augustine, Anselm held that faith precedes and leads to understanding. Like Augustine, he believed that faith is the master of reason. As he wrote in the first chapter of the *Proslogion*,

> I do not try, Lord, to attain Your lofty heights, because my understanding is in no way equal to it. But I do desire to understand Your truth a little, that truth that my heart believes and loves. For I do not seek to understand so that I may believe; but I believe so that I may understand. For I believe this also, that "unless I believe, I shall not understand."[1]

In order better to understand his faith and present it more clearly to others, Anselm sought a proof of God's existence that "for its proof required no other save itself."[2] He wanted to find a proof that would not only show that God existed but would also clearly show God's attributes. The notion that "perfection implies existence" seemed to him to be the key to the proof he was seeking. In 1077, after much thought, Anselm laid out his proof of God's existence in the *Proslogion*.

The Ontological Argument

The argument, which was in the form of a prayer to God, began with a description of God as "something than which nothing greater can be thought."[3] (It was clear from the context that by "greater," Anselm meant "more perfect" rather than physically larger.) Using this description, Anselm pointed out that even the "fool [who] has said in his heart, 'There is no God' "[4] must have such an idea.

Anselm began the argument in the *Proslogion*, Chapter 2, by distinguishing between something existing only in the understanding (*in intellectu*) and something existing in reality (*in re*) as well. In this way, he was able to speak meaningfully of something that existed in the understanding before determining whether or not it also existed in reality.

If a being existed in reality as well as in the understanding, it must be greater (or more perfect) than one that existed only in the understanding. From this,
it followed that the "something than which nothing greater can be thought"
must exist in reality as well as in the understanding. If this being existed only in
the understanding, one would be left with the contradiction that it was possible
to conceive of a greater being—namely, the one that existed in reality as well as
in the understanding. Therefore, in order to avoid a contradiction, the greatest
conceivable being must exist in reality as well as in the understanding.

Put simply, this argument stated:

First premise:
  God is the greatest possible being.
Second premise:
  God exists in the understanding.
Third premise:
  A being that exists in reality as well as in the understanding is greater
  than one that exists in the understanding alone.
Conclusion:
  God exists in reality as well as in the understanding.

In the *Proslogion,* Chapter 3, Anselm continued the argument. Using the
same first two premises, he made a distinction between necessary existence and
contingent existence. The issue was no longer just God's existence but God's
uniquely necessary existence. God was defined in such a way that it was impossible to conceive of God not existing. The core of this notion of necessary being
was self-existence, or *aseity.* Anselm later expanded on this by claiming there
could never be a time when God came to exist or a time when God might cease
to exist, because God was not limited by time. Therefore God's nonexistence
was simply impossible.

If the most perfect conceivable being was one that had contingent existence—that is, one whose existence was not necessary—then one could conceive
of a more perfect being. A being that had necessary existence and could not be
conceived *not* to exist. If the most perfect conceivable being was one that had
contingent existence—that is, one whose existence was not necessary—then one
could conceive of a more perfect being. A being that had necessary existence and
could not be conceived *not* to exist would be greater. Once again, in order to
avoid a contradiction, the necessary existence of the most perfect conceivable being must be affirmed. In summary form,

First premise:
  God is the greatest possible being.
Second premise:
  God exists in the understanding.
Third premise:
  A being that has necessary existence is greater than one that has contin-
  gent existence.
Conclusion:
  God has necessary existence.

Thirteenth-Century Europe

The thirteenth century brought more struggles to Europe. Having survived the collapse of the Roman Empire, the church was now being threatened by the Islamic world. As the church became more aware of the world beyond its borders, it came to see how small and limited the Christian world really was.

The predominant philosophy in the West was still the Platonism of Augustine. This philosophy put great emphasis on the world of "ideas" or "Forms." The sensible world was held to be simply a reflection of those eternal unchanging "Forms" that were in the mind of God. In order to understand the things of the sensible world, one must first know the Forms. Because these were in the mind of God and could only be known through God's illumination, faith in God was held to precede understanding.

Although the dominant philosophy of the West remained the Platonism of Augustine, the Islamic world developed a distinctly different way of thinking. Whereas the Christian Church had based its thought on the works of Plato, the Moslems had built on the ideas of Plato's pupil, Aristotle. Aristotle had taught that the sensible world was real. In order to know reality, one must study the world around oneself, not just "contemplate" some eternal "Form."

In addition to these external pressures, there were problems within the church as well. Despite the monastic revivals, the church had become even more secularized. As the church gained more political power, it came into conflict with the secular government and, in particular, the emperor. Both the pope and the emperor involved themselves in political intrigues and military conquests.

The Franciscan and Dominican orders sought to reverse this trend toward secularization. Known as the "mendicant orders," these groups led a life of service and lived by begging as they traveled.

They were considered spiritually extreme by many in the church. The Franciscans tended to be theologically conservative, holding to the Platonism of the past. The Dominicans were innovators who used Aristotle's philosophy freely in developing their theology. The Dominicans, in particular, put a strong emphasis on education. They established schools and had members appointed to faculty seats in all the major universities. As the Dominicans took over more and more of the teaching positions, the conservative, traditional priests began to fight back. Nowhere was this conflict more visible than at the University of Paris.

Thomas Aquinas

Born of noble parents in 1225 near Naples, Thomas Aquinas was raised amidst controversy within the church. At the age of five, Thomas went to the conservative Abbey of Monte Cassino where he stayed until forced to flee because of the struggles between the pope and the emperor. Arriving back in Naples at age fourteen, Thomas attended the Imperial University for three years. During this time, he discovered the thought of Aristotle and the life-style of the

Dominicans. At age seventeen, Thomas decided to become a Dominican novice, a decision greeted with horror by his conservative noble family. At the instigation of his mother, his brothers kidnapped him and held him captive in the family castle. After a year of reasoning, shouting, intimidating him, and tempting him with women, Thomas's family finally released him and allowed him to follow the Dominicans. Thomas went to the Dominican school in Paris where he studied under Albert the Great, an early exponent of Aristotle. Following Albert to Cologne where he was transferred in 1248, Thomas continued his studies and was ordained in the Dominican Order. In 1252, Thomas returned to Paris for graduate studies at the University.

As Thomas concluded his studies at the University of Paris, it seemed natural that he would take up a faculty chair and teach. But the antimendicant movement was strong enough to prevent this from happening immediately. In fact, it took a letter from the pope himself before Thomas was accepted onto the faculty.

In addition to the controversy over the mendicant orders, Thomas became involved in the question of what to do with Aristotle. Although officially banned as heretical, Aristotle's philosophy had been taught at the university for years. With its emphasis on the sensible world, the world of sin, combined with its history of being used by the Moslems, this philosophy was held to be dangerous by many in the Christian world. While not accepting Aristotle's thought uncritically, as some at the university were doing, Thomas nevertheless felt that this rediscovered philosophy could provide a solid philosophical basis for much of Christian thought as well as a possible evangelistic link to the Moslem world.

Thomas's Critique of the Ontological Argument

In many ways, Thomas Aquinas believed that it was possible to approach God from the standpoint of God's creation rather than from the standpoint of God's transcendent nature. For this reason, Aquinas was not impressed with the ontological argument. There were two fundamental problems Aquinas found with Anselm's proof.

In the first place, Thomas did not accept Anselm's notion that real things exist in the understanding. Even if the conception of God used in the argument was clearly understood, it would not prove that God really existed. It would only prove that God must be thought of as existing. Thomas said:

> Granted that everyone understands that by this name *God* is signified something than which nothing greater can be thought, nevertheless, it does not therefore follow that he understands that what the name signifies exists actually, but only that it exists mentally. Nor can it be argued that it actually exists, unless it be admitted that there actually exists something than which nothing greater can be thought; and this precisely is not admitted by those who hold that God does not exist.[5]

But for Thomas, the conception of God used in the ontological argument was *not* clearly understood. Clearly to understand any conception of God, one must know God's nature or essence. God's existence was self-evident only if one knew the essence of God. But who could know God's essence? Thomas said,

> Therefore I say that this proposition, *God exists,* of itself is self-evident, for the predicate is the same as the subject, because God is His own existence. ... Now because we do not know the essence of God, the proposition is not self-evident to us, but needs to be demonstrated by things that are more known to us, though less known in their nature—namely, by his effects.[6]

Natural and Special Revelation

Following Aristotle, Thomas held that one could discover God by examining God's effects in the sensible world. Thomas believed that the unaided human reason could know the things of this world. The reason could know the forms embedded in matter. In addition, the reason could know certain things about God. Without any divine illumination, apart from the Bible and the tradition of the church, the reason could know that God existed, that God was one, and that God was perfect. This was not to say that the reason could comprehend God, but that the reason could know a few basic things about God. These truths, which all people could know apart from faith or illumination, were known through natural revelation. God was revealed through nature so that simply by using the reason to examine nature, one could discover truths about God. By observing the world, one could discover certain truths about the creator in the creation. Thomas declared, "The existence of God and other like truths about God, which can be known by natural reason, are not articles of faith, but are preambles to the articles; for faith presupposes natural knowledge."[7]

This was not to say that a person must have intense reasoning powers in order to know that God existed. One could take God's existence on faith. But it *was* possible for this truth to be known by the reason alone apart from faith.

There were, however, certain truths about God that the unaided reason could never discover. These truths, such as God's triune (three-part) nature and the creation of the world out of nothing (*ex nihilo*), were revealed by God through the Bible and the tradition of the church. These truths were known by faith through special revelation. Reason was not capable of knowing these truths because it was too weak—not because it was too sinful. The will, but not the reason, was affected by sin. So reason and faith were not in conflict. Natural revelation (which the reason discovered) and special revelation (which faith discovered) manifested the same truth.

The Five Ways

Believing that reason was sufficient to show God's existence, Thomas set out five ways by which this could be proved. Drawing from many sources, he hoped to appeal to the Moslem world. He felt that he could not use either a preconceived conception of God or the testimony of the scriptures in the arguments. Therefore, it was necessary "to go back to natural reason, to which all are obligated to assent."[8] Using the Aristotelian method of beginning with objects in the sensible world, he argued inductively to God's existence. In all five of the arguments, he began with an observation of the sensible world. Finding some feature of this world to be unexplainable in terms of the sensible world itself, he argued that there must be a God who was responsible for the given feature.

In the first argument, Thomas argued from the fact of motion to the necessity of a first mover. By motion, he meant not movement from one place to another but rather "the reduction of something from potentiality to actuality."[9] He stated,

> Whatever is moved must be moved by another. If that by which it is moved be itself moved, then this also must needs be moved by another, and that by another again. But this cannot go on to infinity. . . . Therefore it is necessary to arrive at a first mover, moved by no other; and this everyone understands to be God.[10]

Thomas used the Aristotelian notion of efficient cause in his second argument. Pointing out that "in the world of sensible things we find there is an order of efficient causes,"[11] he went on to state,

> There is no case known . . . in which a thing is found to be the efficient cause of itself; for so it would be prior to itself, which is impossible. Now in efficient causes it is not possible to go on to infinity, because in all efficient causes following in order, the first is the cause of the intermediate cause, and the intermediate is the cause of the ultimate cause. . . . Now to take away the cause is to take away the effect. Therefore if there be no first cause among efficient causes, there will be no ultimate, nor any immediate, cause.[12]

For this reason, "it is necessary to admit a first efficient cause, to which everyone gives the name of God."[13]

The third way turned on the notions of possibility and necessity. Because all things in the sensible world were created and decayed, it was possible for these things to be or to not be. But if all things had the possibility of not existing, "then at one time was nothing in existence."[14] This being the case, Thomas asserted,

> It would have been impossible for anything to have begun to exist; and thus even now nothing would be in existence, which is absurd. Therefore, not all beings are merely possible, but there must exist something the existence of which is necessary. But every necessary thing either has its necessity caused by another, or not. Now it is impossible to go on to infinity in necessary things which have their necessity caused by another, as has been already proved in regard to efficient causes. Therefore we cannot but admit the existence of some being having of itself its own necessity, and . . . this all men speak of as God.[15]

The fourth way that Thomas sought to prove God's existence was by the "gradation to be found in things."[16] Because there were beings that were greater and lesser, better and worse, there must be, Thomas felt,

> Something which is truest, something best, something noblest, and, consequently, something which is most being. . . . Therefore there must also be something which is

to all beings the cause of their being, goodness, and every other perfection; and this we call God.[17]

Lastly, by examining the world, Thomas held that one could see that all natural things sought their final ends. Potentiality always sought to actualize itself. But, because objects had no knowledge, how was it that they could move toward their ends

> Unless [they] be directed by some being endowed with knowledge and intelligence; as the arrow is directed by the archer? Therefore some intelligent being exists by whom all natural things are directed to their end; and this being we call God.[18]   ,

The Return to Paris

In 1259, Thomas left the University of Paris and took on a succession of tasks within the church. He was called to the papal court on several occasions over the next ten years. In 1260, he was named the preacher-general of the Dominicans. While in this office, he traveled extensively in Europe until he was made the regent master of the Dominican House of Studies at Rome in 1265. Two years later he began teaching at the University of Bologna. At this time, Thomas began writing his *Summa Theologica*. Beginning with Aristotle's philosophy, Thomas synthesized Aristotle with the traditional thinking of the church and produced a massive systematic theology.

In early 1269, Thomas was reappointed to the faculty of the University of Paris. The controversy over the Dominicans and Aristotle continued to rage. As Thomas prepared to begin teaching again, he wondered what would happen. Did his Aristotelian ideas have anything to offer the changing church? More specifically, could this emphasis on natural, unillumined reason provide a bridge between the sacred and the secular, the Christian and the Moslem? Did his five ways really prove the existence of God? Was he still operating within the tradition of the church? As he reflected on these questions, he realized how great was the task that still lay ahead of him.

NOTES

1. Anselm, *Proslogion*, chap. 1, in M. J. Charlesworth, *St. Anselm's* Proslogion (Oxford, England: Clarendon Press, 1965), p. 115.
2. Ibid., preface, p. 103.
3. Ibid., chap. 2, p. 117.
4. Ibid.
5. Thomas Aquinas, *Summa Theologica*, from *Basic Writings of St. Thomas Aquinas*, ed. Anton C. Pegis (New York: Random House, 1945), as quoted in *Classical and Contemporary Readings in the Philosophy of Religion*, 2nd ed., ed. John Hick (Englewood Cliffs, N.J.: Prentice Hall, 1970), p. 40.
6. Ibid., p. 39.
7. Ibid., p. 41.

8. Thomas Aquinas, *Summa Contra Gentiles*, from *Basic Writings*, as quoted in Josef Pieper, *Guide to Thomas Aquinas*, trans. Richard and Clara Winston (New York: Pantheon Books, 1962), p. 100.
9. *Summa Theologica*, p. 42.
10. Ibid.
11. Ibid.
12. Ibid.
13. Ibid.
14. Ibid., p. 43.
15. Ibid.
16. Ibid.
17. Ibid.
18. Ibid.

BIBLIOGRAPHY

Primary Sources

Anselm. *St. Anselm, Basic Writings*. Translated by S. N. Deane. 2nd ed. LaSalle, Ill.: Open Court, 1974.
Aquinas, Thomas. *Basic Writings of St. Thomas Aquinas*. Edited by Anton C. Pegis. New York: Random House, 1955.

Biographies

Southern, R. W. *Saint Anselm and His Biographer*. Cambridge, England: Cambridge University Press, 1963.
Grabmann, M. *Thomas Aquinas: His Personality and Thought*. New York: Longmans, Green, 1928.

Interpretative Works

Anscombe, G. E. M., and Geach, Peter. *Three Philosophers*. Oxford, England: Oxford University Press, 1961.
Charlesworth, M. J. *St. Anselm's* Proslogion. Oxford, England: Clarendon Press, 1965.
Chesterton, G. K. *St. Thomas Aquinas*. New York: Doubleday, 1936.
Copleston, Frederick. *Aquinas*. Baltimore: Penguin, 1955.
Gilson, Etienne. *The Christian Philosophy of St. Thomas*. New York: Random House, 1956.
Hopkins, Jasper. *A Companion to the Study of St. Anselm*. Minneapolis: University of Minnesota Press, 1972.

QUESTIONS FOR STUDY

1. Debate the following proposition: The example of medieval Europe offers a model of ordered society toward which we should strive to return.

2. Outline two forms of Anselm's ontological argument.
   a. Explore the question "Is existence a predicate (or attribute)?"
   b. What was Thomas Aquinas' critique of Anselm's argument?

3. Describe the relationship between natural revelation and special revelation in the theology of Thomas Aquinas. How is this similar to or different than concepts of revelation in religious traditions with which you are familiar?

4. Briefly define the Aristotelian principle that informs each of Aquinas's five ways to know God.
    a. Prime mover
    b. First cause
    c. Necessary being
    d. Absolute value
    e. Divine designer

5. How were Anselm and Aquinas alike and how were they different in their understanding of the relationship between faith and reason? Relate each of their positions to its philosophical roots in Plato and Aristotle.

A Contemporary Response

MARILYN McCORD ADAMS

CAN WE know or prove the articles of the Nicene Creed to be true without believing them first? Aquinas thought unaided natural reason could demonstrate the truth of some articles (about the existence and nature of God) and not others (about the Trinity and Incarnation). Anselm, on the other hand, ends the opening prayer of the *Proslogion* with the declaration that he does not try to understand so that he may come to believe but believes so that he may understand, and that unless he believes he will not understand. Is Anselm giving a negative answer to our original question?

To find out, we must ask what Anselm takes these Biblical and Augustinian formulas—"I believe so that I may understand" and "unless I believe, I shall not understand"—to mean. Various interpretations might occur to us. First, surely Anselm is not proposing the general epistemological thesis that *unless I believe (assent to) what is expressed by a sentence, I cannot understand the meaning of that sentence.* I can understand the meaning of the sentence "The moon is made of green cheese," all the while believing the moon to be made of cheddar. If anything, the reverse claim appears closer to the truth: *unless I understand the meaning of a sentence, I am not—except in special circumstances— in a position to use it to express any of my beliefs.*

Second, is Anselm saying that *unless I believe (assent to) a proposition, I will not be able to prove it or to come to know that it is true?* Once again, as a general thesis, this is too implausible to attribute to Anselm. To set out to prove a proposition, I may have to entertain it as a hypothesis, but I do not have to give it my full assent. Did Anselm think this principle held good for the special case of theological truths? We know that Aquinas did not. For he maintained that a reader of the *Summa Contra Gentiles* or the *Summa Theologica* might start as an atheist and come to know that God exists after reading the five ways and various other articles. In fact, the *Summa Contra Gentiles* was intended as a handbook of arguments for missionaries to use in convincing their prospective converts. I believe that Anselm did not really differ from Aquinas on this point. In his earlier book, the *Monologium,* Anselm set out to prove, by reason and arguments without any appeals to authority, that God exists, has a certain nature, is triune, made everything, and is worthy of worship. So startling was his procedure in eleventh-century Europe that Lanfranc, his superior and eventual predecessor as archbishop of Canterbury, urged him not to publish it after all. The expressed purpose of Anselm's later book *Why Did God Become Man?* was to demonstrate the necessity of the incarnation to infidels by necessary reasons. Apparently, Anselm thought that one could come to know the existence and triune nature of God and the necessity of the incarnation by following the arguments of these two treatises, even if one began to read assenting to neither. If so, Anselm was even more optimistic about the scope of natural revelation than Aquinas was!

Third, I suggest that Anselm did restrict the preceding formulas to matters having to do with the existence and nature of God, primarily to God as God is in essence. But he construed belief as faith in God, not as assent to propositions about God, while understanding was ideally exemplified in the awareness of and attitude toward God had by those who saw God face to face. Anselm tells us in the preface that his original title for the *Proslogion* was *"Faith* Seeking Understanding." He opens Chapter 2 by calling on "the Lord, who gives understanding to *faith."* The prayer in Chapter 1 characterized the attitude of faith in terms of love and desire for God. And he laments there the fact that he has never seen God face to face and deplores the fall and sin that have exiled him from the vision of God to blindness. When he cries for understanding, he wants to see, appreciate, and take delight in the riches of the divine nature. On this reading, Anselm's declaration at the end of his opening prayer reflects a fundamental truth of biblical religion: *unless one has faith, not merely to assent to propositions about God, but to love God in a deep and persistent way, one will never be able to see and enjoy God as God is in essence.*

What is the relevance of Anselm's claim, on this interpretation, to the task of natural theology, focused as it is on showing that it is reasonable (or at least not unreasonable) to assent to the truth of various religious doctrines? An analogy may help here. Consider a musicologist who has spent his entire working life studying Mozart's music. He has analyzed and remembers the structure of every piece; he knows which themes recur where and exactly how each is varied; he has a complete knowledge of the order in which Mozart wrote his various works and can trace the development of his style away from Haydn and toward Beethoven. He has written many authoritative books on the music and has concluded that Mozart is the most creative composer who ever lived. Such professional accomplishment is compatible with any one of a number of attitudes toward Mozart's music. It might be that he hates or is indifferent to it. Perhaps he got into the field by a number of professional accidents and has been driven by ambition to become a leading expert in the subject anyway. If it were not for his professional responsibilities, he would positively prefer or at least not mind never hearing Mozart's music again. Such attitudes would doubtless have made his work more difficult and error more likely, but their effects could have been counterbalanced by unusual talent for musical analysis coupled with grim determination to succeed and/or fear of professional embarrassment. His analyses of the music might be impeccable, such antipathy or indifference notwithstanding. Alternatively, it may be that he loves Mozart's music. He may report that nothing he has written captures its riches and that each listening brings the awareness of something new. It is not that he finds some detail that he had omitted from his analysis and will rush to include it in the appendix of the next edition. What he grasps new with each hearing is not even the kind of thing that could be adequately communicated on paper. In the last case, the musicologist has a deeper appreciation of the beauty of Mozart's music. And this is not merely a matter of how he *feels* about it. There is a cognitive difference: loving the music, he *hears* more, and the more is there to be heard. The same is true of his readers. Students who never listened to Mozart or who hated or were bored by his music might still work through the book and get a perfect score on the examination. But only someone who went on to listen with love could *appreciate* what the book was about.

Likewise, faith is not necessary for reading and understanding a textbook of natural theology such as Anselm's *Monologium* or Aquinas's *Summa Theologica*. A violent hope that God does not exist, or boredom with the whole subject, might make the task more difficult. Yet other motives could overcome these obstacles, and a reader who hates or is indifferent to God might still follow the proofs and give some degree of assent to their conclusions—we might even be willing to say that he or she believed them. If such assent does not presuppose faith, it does not suffice for it either. According to Anselm, the natural condition of fallen humanity is hardness of heart; one's natural response to the claim "God exists and is worthy of worship"—whether presented in revelation or as the conclusion of sound arguments—is the rebellion or indifference with which our supposed reader began. The alternative response of faith is possible only by divine grace.

Is faith a necessary condition for inventing the proofs and writing the theology textbook in the first place? Love of Mozart was not necessary for writing expert works of musicology. Anselm would find a difference between the two cases. He has insisted that only those who love God will see God. A faithless theologian would be better compared to a deaf musicologist, because he would not be able to go beyond his own analyses to appreciate what his textbook was all about. The work would not be impossible, because the musicologist would have the scores and the theologian the world of space and time as data for their analytical skills. But each would be operating under a considerable handicap.

By the time Anselm wrote the *Proslogion,* he had already written a book of natural theology, the *Monologium,* which he thought proved that a supreme nature exists through whom everything else exists and to whom everything else owes worship and obedience. Having received the gift of faith, Anselm has committed himself to love and serve God as much as he can. In Chapter 1 of the *Proslogion,* he begs God to cure his blindness. Let us return to the argument of

Proslogion, Chapter 2, and consider how it is related to this prayer.

As reconstructed in the preceding case, the argument goes as follows:

> *First Premise:*
> God is the greatest possible being.
> *Second Premise:*
> God exists in the understanding.
> *Third Premise:*
> A being that exists in reality as well as the understanding is greater than one that exists in the understanding alone.
> *Conclusion:*
> God exists in reality as well as in the understanding.

To be convinced by this argument, one must be in a position to ascertain the truth of the second premise. In Chapter 2, Anselm finds this an easy task. Even the fool who says in his heart "There is no God" understands the expression "something than which nothing greater can be thought" when he hears it. Hence, on such occasions, something than which nothing greater can be thought is the object of his thought and accordingly exists in his understanding. This result combines with the first premise to yield the second. Such a justification of the second premise moves too fast, however, as Anselm himself admits by Chapter 4. A person who hears the words "something than which nothing greater can be thought" may have any of a variety of things in mind: (1) He may think only of the spoken words themselves. (2) Or he may think of the meanings of those words taken one by one and have some composite of concepts as the object of his thought. (3) Or he may misunderstand the words and have some other combination of concepts in mind. (4) Or he may actually think of the thing itself. It is one thing to think of the spoken words, another to think of some general description that God does or does not in fact fit, and still another to think of God as God. According to Anselm in the *Proslogion,* Chapter 4, only a thought of the last sort will ground the second premise. On the other hand, anyone who does think of God as God will immediately run through the reasoning of the *Proslogion,* Chapter 2, and consent to God's real existence. Anselm concludes that the fool who continues to say in his heart "There is no God" must have a thought of a different kind.

It is precisely at this point that Aquinas' remarks in *Summa Theologica* (I, q.2, a.1) become relevant. Aquinas agrees that if we could think of God as God or the divine essence we would immediately assent to the proposition "God exists," because we would see that the predicate is identical with the subject. Following the Artistotelian tradition, however, Aquinas thinks that the human mind is so built that all of its knowledge comes from sense experience and the only natures that can be the immediate objects of human understanding are the natures of material things. We have no immediate experience of anything immaterial, and we conceive of immaterial things only analogically. By abstraction and negation, we can form a composite concept that corresponds to phrases such as "something than which nothing greater can be thought" or "a being that has all perfections *per se*"—that is, we can have thoughts of the sorts presented in

Items 2 and 3. But such a composite of abstractions and negations was not the being whose real existence was at issue. Nor could Anselm's style of reasoning show that what we *do* have in mind when we hear such expressions exists in reality. Aquinas would deny the possibility of such a conjunction of abstractions and negations existing by themselves in reality.

Would Anselm have disagreed with Aquinas about our *natural* capacity to have God as God or the divine nature as the object of our thought? I speculate that the answer is no. After explaining in the *Proslogion,* in Chapter 4, how one must have the thing itself as the object of one's thought to carry the discourse of Chapter 2 through to a successful conclusion, and how the fool's understanding will not really do after all, Anselm thanks God for the illumination that enabled him to understand. Can it be that what divine illumination consists in here is God's supernaturally enabling Anselm's mind to have God's own nature as its object of thought and thereby see clearly how God exists in reality (Chapter 2) and necessarily (Chapter 3) and how God is supreme knowledge, power, goodness, life, eternity, and so on (Chapters 6–8, 18–22)? Would this not constitute a significant positive response to Anselm's opening prayer to see God face to face?

On this interpretation, Anselm would not see the *Proslogion* as a replacement for the *Monologium.* As noted, he thinks that the latter proves—from initial data provided by the world of space and time and by arguments that even an infidel could follow by his or her natural faculties—that there is a supreme nature that exists through itself and through which everything else exists; that this nature is supreme wisdom, power, goodness, life, eternity, and simplicity; that this nature is triune; and that it is worthy of all worship. One who is thus convinced and who loves God will want to see all these things more clearly and directly than is possible through God's effects. (After all, the *Monologium* is seventy-nine chapters long!) Such direct knowledge is not naturally possible for human beings in this life. Nevertheless, God rewards faith seeking understanding with illumination and makes the divine nature itself the object of thought. Those and only those who receive such a divine gift will be able to see the cogency of the reasoning Anselm goes through in the *Proslogion,* Chapter 2.

Can this interpretation of Anselm's project in the *Proslogion* really be correct? It may be arued that it cannot. After all, Anselm acknowledges in the opening prayer that God dwells in *inaccessible* light (Chapter 1). If he could think of God as God and not merely the words "something than which nothing greater can be thought" or some general description under which God falls, would Anselm not thereby have access to the inaccessible? Again, in Chapter 13, after further meditation on God's knowledge, power, goodness, life, and eternity, he complains that he was seeking God and yet seems to have no *experience* of God yet. In Chapter 15, he confesses that God is not only a being than which nothing greater can be conceived, but also a being greater than we can can conceive. In Chapter 16, he returns to the theme of God's dwelling in inaccessible light, and in the closing prayer of Chapter 26 he implies that the desire behind his opening petition has not been fully satisfied.

These considerations are not conclusive, however. It is a commonplace of sense perception that I can see something without being aware of all or even its essential properties. For example, the object I see moving across the horizon may in fact be a horse, while I can tell only that it is a moving brown body. According to Augustine's theory of divine illumination, the same goes for the objects of the mind's eye. When Euclid first demonstrated that the interior angles of a triangle equal 180 degrees, the reality he saw was God or the divine word itself. But he did not recognize it as such and would have denied that he had thereby *experienced* God. Perhaps Anselm's remarks about divine inaccessibility should be taken to mean not that God is not the object of thought for faith seeking understanding, but that even divinely enabled human faculties have a limited view of God in this life. Thus, in Chapter 14, after puzzling about how he can have seen the light and truth of the more direct demonstrations of God's existence and nature without seeming to have any experience of God, Anselm suggests that it is God that he has seen, but he saw God in a certain degree and not just as God is. Not even the blessed will be able to comprehend God fully, but they will see clearly enough to experience God and their joy in God will be full (Chapter 16).

I believe that Anselm and Aquinas agree that we can know certain articles of the Nicene Creed to be true without assenting to them first. To find out if they were right about this, we should have to determine whether there are any sound arguments for these doctrines whose premises could be known to be true without inferring them from their conclusions. Anselm and Aquinas themselves used many assumptions from Platonic and Aristotelian philosophy, some of which were called into question during the Middle Ages and many of which would be at least as controversial today as the existence of God itself. Do you agree with Aquinas that there are no uncaused motions (the first way)? Are we in a position to know, as he claims in the first three ways, that an infinite series of causes, each of which is caused by and causes another member of the series, is impossible? Is it true, as Anselm assumes at the beginning of the *Monologium* and Aquinas proposes in the fourth way, that whenever some things have a property, F-ness, in varying degrees, there is something that is F in the supreme degree? Is Aquinas right to take for granted in the fifth way, that the only adequate explanation of the regular life cycle in plants or the regular behavior of inanimate objects lies in their having been designed that way by someone who is intelligent and made them that way on purpose? If we are not in a position to know any of these premises, or if we find them at least as questionable as the conclusion inferred from them, we can neither come to know nor be persuaded of the existence of God by these arguments. But if these premises are unacceptable, can they be replaced with others? Are there other, completely different strategies for proving the existence and nature of God? What do you think?

Part Two

THE MODERN MATRIX

The Renaissance

The Renaissance and Reformation were movements of reaction and renewal. The Renaissance of the fourteenth and fifteenth centuries was, as its name indicates, a time of rediscovery and rebirth. People rediscovered the cultural heritage of ancient Greece and Rome. And, in doing so, people felt themselves to be reborn. People became interested in themselves. Human, rather than heavenly, concerns became the normal order of the day. People turned from metaphysical and theological speculations to study more practical, this-worldly matters. These studies became known as the "humanities." The ideal person was one of all-around competence, a "humanist." The norm was no longer scholarly work pursued in monastic isolation, but an active public life in which learning was applied.

The Renaissance fostered a critical use of ancient sources rather than a slavish reliance on authorities. This era was the first to identify itself as a distinct epoch. Its scholars termed the previous, medieval period "the Dark Ages." Renaissance scholars felt that, for the first time in a long time, light was breaking forth from the past. Lawyers, for example, reexamined the codes of ancient Roman law. They were no longer interested in reiterating the rules. Now they examined the context and sought to understand the intent of the ancient lawgivers so that their insights could be applied in appropriate ways in a new period.

Progress, in the Renaissance, was made by way of return to the classical past. Aristotle was studied for new ideas in physics, and Galen was consulted for fresh insights in medicine. Not until the Renaissance was nearly over did new ideas about the universe and humanity arise from fresh investigations done in the present. Copernicus' work on the solar system was published in 1543, and Vesalius' description of human anatomy was known in the same year.

The Reformation

The Reformation of the sixteenth century was also a movement that attempted to recover the past in order to renew church and society in the present.

Erasmus, Luther, and Calvin reacted against what they considered to be the decadent authority of medieval scholasticism and went back to earlier sources. Their model of the church was what they viewed as the pristine period of the first few centuries of the Christian era. Theologically, they went behind Thomas Aquinas to Augustine. And philosophically, they rejected the reigning Aristotelian scholasticism and adopted an earlier Neoplatonic style.

Most important of all to church reformers was their return to the Bible as the basic source document of their faith. They accepted its authority with personal trust. But they studied the text critically with the tools of Renaissance scholarship. Erasmus, while remaining a loyal Roman Catholic, provided Protestantism its most basic tool with his critical edition of the Greek New Testament. The Latin Vulgate, approved by the medieval church, was no longer normative. Luther took the next step by translating the Bible into German so that every burgher could read it. Calvin applied his Renaissance training in understanding the law to the interpretation of the Bible. He examined the historical and cultural context and sought meaning in an empathy with the intentions of the original authors.

The Bible now had new and powerful influence. The printing press had been invented. In 1454 Gutenberg produced the first printed Bible. In 1450 less than 100,000 handwritten manuscripts had been in existence. Just fifty years later there were 9 million printed books. The invention of printing thoroughly and rapidly revolutionized human life. Printed books gave people new ideas and a new independence from authorities. The printed word stirred criticism of the church and society.

Preparation for the Modern Era

The modern era really began in the seventeenth century. It was the matrix, the womb, in which the concepts that condition our contemporary thought were nurtured and finally brought to birth. In philosophy, "modern" denotes the seventeenth and eighteenth centuries, which set the scene for the "contemporary" period of the nineteenth and twentieth centuries. The modern period introduced in a rudimentary way the problems with which we still must deal.

Two discoveries near the end of the Renaissance and Reformation decisively formed the seventeenth and eighteenth centuries. The first was the development of modern mathematics, usually attributed to Christopher Clavius (1537–1612). Clavius, a Jesuit priest, was known as the "modern Euclid." He asserted the superiority of mathematical demonstrations over dialectical disputations. Mathematics, for him, was the most fundamental science. It alone gave certainty. This discovery spurred the philosophical development known as "rationalism" in the seventeenth century. Rationalism was Platonism taken to one of its extremes. The emphasis was on innate ideas and the ability to deduce all other knowledge from them.

The second discovery was the introduction of methods of observation, especially by instruments, fostered by Galileo Galilei (1564–1642). Galileo invented a telescope. Through it he saw, with his own eyes, that the earth rotated around the sun and that there were mountains on the moon. Both of those observations contradicted long and firmly held assumptions grounded in the statements of ancient authorities. The issue was method. Galileo did not consult authorities; he looked! This was a decisive break with the past. Now knowledge came from experiments in the present, which opened up new possibilities for the future. This new approach opened the philosophical possibility of eighteenth-century empiricism. Empiricism developed one side of Aristotle. Its stress was on sense data as the primary source of information from which all other knowledge could validly be induced.

Rationalism in the Seventeenth Century

Rationalism in the seventeenth century was developed by three great thinkers of three differing nationalities: Descartes (French), Spinoza (Dutch), and Leibniz (German). The latter two built on and expanded the approach that we find developed in the case of René Descartes.

Descartes (1596–1650) was a scientist who made significant contributions to physics, optics, and physiology. He is considered the founder of modern analytical geometry. For Descartes, mathematics was the one language that could express scientific ideas with perfect clarity.

His most important contribution was his method. He decided to doubt everything he had ever been taught until he came to some clear and evident idea, a first principle, that could not be doubted. He finally concluded that he could not doubt that he was doubting. If he was doubting, then he was thinking. And if he was thinking, then he existed as a thinking being. *Cogito ergo sum,* "I think, therefore I am," was Descartes' clear and evident first principle. Human nature was basically mind, to which a body was attached. Rationality was the key to reality.

By his mathematical method, Descartes believed that he could come to certain knowledge of everything. He began with an idea within himself that seemed obvious to his reason. Then by rational deduction he went on to demonstrate the existence of everything, including God and the world.

Baruch Spinoza (1632–1677) was a Dutch Jew who made his living grinding lenses. Descartes had left behind a significant problem, on which Spinoza worked. Mind and body seemed like two separate and incompatible substances. How did they function together? Spinoza accepted Descartes' mathematical model for synthesizing all knowledge into one system. He further tightened its systematic consistency by positing not two substances, thought and extension, but one divine substance, which he called alternately *God* or *nature.* Spinoza was thus considered an atheist or "that God-intoxicated man" depending on which dimension of his system was emphasized.

Gottfried Wilhelm Leibniz (1646–1716) was the son of a university professor at Leipzig, where he was also educated. In addition to being a jurist, he was a mathematician, scientist, historian, diplomat, theologian, and philosopher. He studied the other philosophers of his day and interacted with them. He traveled widely and met leading thinkers of his day, including Huygens, Newton, Boyle, and Spinoza.

For an active person like Leibniz, philosophy had to be done in "odd moments," in the form of letters, memoranda, and articles. But Leibniz' dream was the same as that of Descartes and Spinoza. He hoped for a systematic organization of all conceivable knowledge. His own effort was to reform all science through the use of two instruments of his devising. First, he sought to perfect a universal scientific language that would reduce all thoughts to mathematical symbols. Second, he succeeded in developing one of the first forms of calculus. (There was later a dispute with Isaac Newton over who had first formulated what they had each apparently come to independently.) With this reasoning tool, Leibniz hoped to bring all thought under the reign of symbolic logic.

Empiricism in the Eighteenth Century

Philosophical theories are seldom rejected because they have been proved wrong. Rather, they are abandoned because they have failed to solve all the problems and people hope that a new approach will be more successful. Deduction from seemingly obvious first principles had occupied the best minds on the European continent for over a century. The mathematical side of the new science had been in focus. But not all the problems had been solved.

In Great Britain as the eighteenth century approached, a new philosophical movement was growing that emphasized the other side of the new science. The observational and experimental was in focus. The interest of philosophers in the eighteenth century shifted to an empirical and inductive approach to knowledge. The new effort among philosophers in the eighteenth century was to develop all knowledge by induction from sense experience alone. A philosophy was sought that would be in harmony with the developing science.

In science, the greatest name was Isaac Newton. He appeared as the culmination of a century of preliminary efforts to produce an experimental science. Newton was born in 1642, the year that Galileo died. He elaborated the essentials of calculus, apparently quite independently of Leibniz. He discovered that white light is the presence of all colors. And, most important of all, he grasped the principle of gravity.

Some claim that the age of "Enlightenment" began with the publication of Newton's *Mathematical Principles of Natural Philosophy* in 1687. Just as Renaissance persons felt that they had been reborn, people in the Enlightenment believed that they had grown to maturity. Humankind was now able to solve all of its problems through the use of human intelligence. A "scientific method" had been articulated by Newton. In a letter to the secretary of the Royal Society of London for the Improvement of Natural Knowledge in 1672, Newton wrote,

> The best and safest method of philosophizing seems to be, first, to inquire diligently into the properties of things and to establish those properties by experiments, and to proceed later to hypotheses for the explanation of things themselves. For hypotheses

ought to be applied only in the explanation of the properties of things, and not made use of in determining them.[1]

The method of observation, experimentation, and generalization seemed to provide a new method that gave certain knowledge. The poet Alexander Pope expressed Newton's impact on his age:

> Nature and Nature's Laws lay hid in Night
> God said, "Let Newton be!" and all was Light.[2]

For over one hundred years in Great Britain, philosophers attempted to work out the metaphysical and epistemological implications of Newtonian science. They proposed to found all knowledge on what could be derived by induction from sense experience alone.

Eighteenth-century empiricism was developed by three great thinkers in the British Isles: Locke (English), Berkeley (Irish), and Hume (Scottish). We will delve into the details of their thought in the case of David Hume.

John Locke (1632–1704) took an approach almost exactly opposite to that of Descartes. According to Locke, at birth our minds are *tabula rasa,* blank tablets. All our ideas originate in sense experience coming to us from outside our minds. A fundamental question was "What causes sensations?" Locke's answer was to posit the existence of "matter." Matter was that stuff external to us that had power to cause the sensations received by our sight, hearing, taste, touch, and smell.

In Ireland, an Anglican bishop, George Berkeley (1685–1753), was disturbed by Locke's conclusions. Berkeley reasoned that if people believed that the source of all our ideas was inert, unthinking matter, they would become materialists and atheists. Berkeley did not reject Locke's method. Berkeley insisted that he too was a strict empiricist. But, Berkeley argued, on the basis of our experience we know that no ideas exist except in minds. Indeed, nothing exists, in human experience, unless it exists as perceived by some mind. The only mind capable of causing all the richness and diversity that we experience with our senses, for Berkeley, was the mind of God. Berkeley thus had an alternate empirical solution to Locke's question, "What causes our sensations?" Berkeley's answer was "God." Only God was a sufficient source and cause of all sensations and ideas everywhere.

A Scot, David Hume (1711–1776), inherited these arguments from Locke and Berkeley. Hume agreed with Locke that there were no innate ideas. All the ideas in our minds come originally from sense experiences. When Hume approached the question to which Locke and Berkeley gave different answers, "What causes our sensations?" Hume was honest enough to say, "We don't know!" On the basis of sense experience alone, all we know with certainty is that we have sensations. After one hundred years of empiricism, the result was skepticism. Many traditional philosophical notions had no empirical basis. According to Hume, from sense experience alone, one could not know with certainty that cause and effect were necessarily connected or, that there was an external world, a self, or God. All of these ideas could be accounted for psychologically. By custom or habit, we associate ideas with experiences when there is no demonstrable connection. We may retain our beliefs for practical purposes if we wish, said Hume. But as a philosopher he had to say that empirically we know almost nothing!

Kant's Synthesis

Two opposite philosophical methods had dominated the best minds of the continent and Great Britain for a century each. Philosophers on the continent had followed rationalism during the seventeenth century. They had developed the ideal of a few innate principles from which they had attempted to deduce all knowledge. They had not been decisively proved wrong. But neither had they solved all problems. Philosophers in Great Britain had tried to be rigorously empirical during the eighteenth century. They had sought comprehensive knowledge by induction from sense experience alone. The result, finally, was David Hume's skepticism.

The person who attempted to bring order out of the chaos resulting from these two competing and inconclusive efforts was Immanuel Kant (1724–1804). He never traveled more than thirty miles from the sleepy university town of Königsberg, Germany, where he was born. He seemed like a stereotypical ivory-tower academician, a bachelor who lived by a rigid routine, interested only in books. But ultimately his thought revolutionized philosophy, and we still wrestle with problems in the context that Kant created.

Kant was raised by his parents in a pietistic Christian home. At Königsberg University, he was trained in the rationalism of Christian Wolff, who transmitted the tradition of Descartes and Leibniz. After becoming a lecturer in philosophy at the same university, Kant was redirected by his reading. He declared that studying David Hume's radical empiricism awakened him from his "dogmatic slumbers." Another new element came when he read Rousseau. Kant became so absorbed in this new approach that for the first time in his adult life he missed his regular four o'clock afternoon walk. In Rousseau, Kant was introduced to the influence of feelings and conscience. Here were elements not derived either from logical arguments or sensory evidence.

Kant raised the fundamental question "How is knowledge possible?" He set out to perform a "transcendental critique" of human knowing. The term *transcendental,* in Kant's sense, referred to that which did not fall within experience, but that which made experience possible. His transcendental critique sought for the *a priori* (prior to experience) conditions in the mind itself that made knowledge possible.

Kant presented a new synthesis of the conflicting methods that had been handed down to him. According to Kant, both empiricism and rationalism were partly right, but each was more limited in its scope than its proponents believed, and both had to work together. Empiricism was right in that the material of our knowledge came from the senses. If we had no sense data, we would have no knowledge. But rationalism was right in that the form of knowledge was supplied by the mind. We would have no knowledge except that certain categories in our minds gave meaningful shape to the data that the senses provided.

The knowledge humans had was limited to the "phenomenal world." It was knowledge of how things (phenomena) appeared to people. People had no knowledge of things as they are in themselves. They did not know essences, but only appearances. This meant that metaphysics in the traditional sense was impossible. Humankind could not know reality as it is but could only have a "scientific" knowledge of the way in which things appeared to human senses and minds. Epistemology had become the overriding philosophical concern. "How do we know?" had replaced "What do we know?" as the principal question of philosophy. This was a "Copernican revolution" in philosophy, Kant contended. No longer did philosophers ask themselves how knowledge could conform to the nature of objects outside themselves. "Now," said Kant, "we make nature." Nature was understood as a system of objects manifesting an order on which predictions could be based. Kant contended that the human mind provided that order. Objects therefore conformed to human understanding. Yet knowledge was objective, because, according to Kant, all people's minds were structured so as to order the same sense data into identical patterns.

There was also a "noumenal world" for Kant, a world outside of human sense experience. Included in that world were things-in-themselves, essences, values, moral absolutes. Kant wanted objective knowledge in the moral realm as much as in the scientific. Indeed, for Kant, the realm of human values was more important than the realm of nature. But Kant was convinced that one could not have knowledge of values from either the reason or from sense experience. The answer to knowledge of the noumenal world, for Kant, lay inside the individual. Morality was a postulate of the "practical reason." All people had within them, Kant believed, a sense of duty, a conscience, feelings of oughtness that rightly guided them. On the basis of this "inner sense," people could have practical certainty, what Kant called a "rational faith" that they were free and immortal and that God existed. Why? Otherwise people's inner sense of oughtness would not conform to reality outside of them. Kant could not bear that thought.

For himself, Kant had reconciled the opposing, formerly mutually exclusive, approaches to knowledge of the preceding two centuries. The mechanistic view of modern science rightly applied to the world of appearances. Empirical evidence and mathematical reasoning enabled people to understand and, to some extent, control the world as they perceived it. At the same time, Kant was able to hold to a belief in human freedom and moral responsibility that exempted humankind from being just another cog in the cause-and-effect chain of science. Human beings were citizens of two worlds, the noumenal as well as the phenomenal.

Kant's synthesis did not last long in its original form. Soon after him, other philosophers emphasized one side of his thought to the exclusion of the other. Either scientific facts or human values became paramount, but rarely were they held in balance. The problems with which Kant wrestled are still our problems. We work with those problems in a context that Kant helped to develop. The epistemological problem is still uppermost in contemporary philosophy. In our section on the contemporary context, we will deal with the diverse schools of thought that have evolved since Kant.

The work of Descartes, Hume, and Kant truly laid the foundations of the contemporary era. As we understand them, we will better comprehend the intellectual factors that have shaped our lives.

NOTES

1. Cited in Peter Gay, *Age of Enlightenment*, Great Ages of Man (New York: Time-Life, 1966), p. 19.
2. Ibid., p. 18.

CHAPTER 5

The Case of Descartes

Dare We Risk Being Honest in a Culture That Resists New Ideas?

RESPONDING to the shocking news that Galileo had been condemned by the Catholic Church, René Descartes wrote,

> I cannot imagine that an Italian, and especially one well thought of by the Pope from what I have heard, could have been labeled a criminal for nothing other than wanting to establish the movement of the earth. I know that this had been censured formerly by a few cardinals, but I thought that since that time one was allowed to teach it publicly even in Rome. I confess that if this is false, then all the principles of my philosophy are false also.[1]

In the year 1633, it seemed incredible that such a thing could happen. Galileo's *Dialogue on the Two Chief Systems*, which sought to prove that the earth revolved around the sun, was hardly irreligious. Still, the Pope had declared that it was in error, and Galileo was being punished. As Descartes considered the forthcoming publication of his *Le Monde* ("The World"), he wondered what he should do. Living in Protestant Holland, he was beyond the reach of the Catholic Church. But Descartes wanted his ideas accepted in Paris and Rome as well as in Holland. Should he proceed with the publication of his work, knowing that it would probably be condemned by the church? Or should he wait until a more judicious occasion? What insights could his newly discovered method bring to this issue?

Renaissance and Reformation

In 1340, Francis Petrarch was named poet laureate of Rome. Petrarch's poetry had a certain quality that set it apart from previous writings. Whereas earlier poets, such as Dante, had rarely focused their attention on themselves, Petrarch was constantly trying to express his own passions and sufferings. Petrarch was also very interested in the writings of ancient Rome. These ancient writings, which had been preserved in medieval monasteries, seemed to him to have a richness and depth that was lacking in the literary works of the previous centuries. This emphasis on the self, combined with an appreciation of ancient culture, made Petrarch "the first writer of the Renaissance."[2]

The Renaissance, or "rediscovery," which began with Petrarch in Italy, slowly spread to other countries. When Constantinople fell to the Turks in 1453, trade routes to the East were cut off. This, in turn, led many countries to seek new routes to the East. The explorers who sought these new routes inadvertently discovered whole new continents. These discoveries forced a rethinking of scientific theories that had been accepted for centuries. People became more interested in the world around them and less interested in the life to come.

In astronomy especially, many established ideas were being challenged. Using a model of the universe devised by the Egyptian astronomer Ptolemy, most medieval thinkers had believed that the earth was at the center of the universe. Moving outward from the earth, one encountered first the sun, then the moon, then the planets, and finally the fixed stars. All of these, including the fixed "orb" of the stars, rotated around the earth.

According to medieval theologians, when humankind fell in the Garden of Eden the entire landscape of earth "fell." Weeds, briars, mosquitos, and other banes of humanity suddenly appeared. Instead of the perfect flat landscape of the garden, there were mountains and valleys. Mountains became the symbols of sin. People looked forward to the day when "Every valley shall be exalted and every mountain and hill made low" (Is. 40:4).

But this "fall" of earth did not extend to the heavens. The moon, the sun, the planets, and especially the fixed stars were untouched by the effects of sin. They all continued to move in the same perfect rotation as when God first created them.

In the early 1500s, the Polish astronomer Nicolaus Copernicus (1473–1543) presented the first major challenge to this model of the universe. Using mathematical principles and a desire for simplicity, Copernicus claimed that the earth, the planets, and the fixed stars rotated around the sun. The moon was the only heavenly body that rotated around the earth. This new idea generated interest and excitement on the part of the church and the thinkers of the day. In fact, Copernicus' ideas were widely accepted—at first.

In 1517, the Protestant Reformation began in Germany. Reformers such as Martin Luther and John Calvin sought to replace the authority of the hierarchy in Rome with the authority of the Bible in their hands. Luther and Calvin used Renaissance scholarship to translate and interpret the biblical texts. They used these ancient sources as the basis for a wide-ranging critique of church and culture.

The Roman Catholic Church, in response to the Reformation, began a Counter-Reformation. At the Council of Trent, many of the excesses of the church were corrected. Ideas that had previously been freely discussed were now banned and their authors punished. A group called the Society of Jesus (Jesuits) was formed to help spread the orthodox Catholic position and defend it against heresy. These Jesuits soon dominated the major Catholic centers of learning.

Despite these attempts to stem Protestant advances, by the end of the sixteenth century a significant portion of the Western world was no longer under the control of the Catholic Church of Rome. The declining power of the Roman Catholic Church, the new emphasis on the self and the natural world, the new ideas about the structures of the universe, and the rediscovery of ancient art and culture forced a radical change in Western thinking. One such new way of thinking was formulated by René Descartes.

Early Life

René Descartes was born in Touraine, France, on March 31, 1596. His paternal grandfather was a doctor and his father a member of the nobility. His family was independently wealthy, and young René never had to work. In 1606, at age ten, Descartes began a nine-year course of study at the Royal Jesuit College of La Fleche. During his first six years at the college, Descartes studied the humanities and theology. The next three years were spent studying philosophy. Philosophy, which was not distinguished from the special sciences at that time, included morals, logic, mathematics, physics, and metaphysics.

Descartes was a good student and did well at the College. But as his studies ended Descartes came to a very negative conclusion about his education. As he later wrote,

> From my childhood I have been familiar with letters; and as I was given to believe that by their means a clear and assured knowledge can be acquired of all that is useful in life, I was extremely eager for instruction in them. As soon, however, as I had completed the course of study, at the close of which it is customary to be admitted into the order of the learned, I entirely changed my opinion. For I found myself entangled in so many doubts and errors that, as it seemed to me, the endeavor to instruct myself had served only to disclose to me more and more of my ignorance. [I was led] to conclude that there was no body of knowledge in the world of such worth as I had previously been led to expect.[3]

There was, however, one subject that Descartes found to be of value: mathematics. In the rigors of mathematics, Descartes found the certainty that was so lacking in all of the other disciplines. Whereas the humanities and the sciences of the time were based on conflicting, unprovable presuppositions, mathematics was based on the certainty of deductive reasoning. In fact, it seemed odd to Descartes that a foundation "so firm and solid should have nothing loftier erected upon [it]."[4]

Descartes' interest in mathematics grew after he left the college. Following some study at Poitiers, he joined the army of Maurice of Nassau in 1618 and served as a gentleman volunteer. Having been left a sizable inheritance by his father, Descartes was free to pursue his own interests. While serving as a volunteer, he carried on intense mental struggles over the place of mathematical reasoning in science. Descartes became more and more convinced that the whole approach to understanding of the world was incorrect. In 1619, following a period of especially intense reasoning, he had a series of dreams that convinced him that the "spirit of truth" had been inspiring him and that his mathematical studies had divine approval. Traveling, soldiering, and writing, Descartes spent the next ten years developing and testing his new principles. In 1629, he moved to Holland, where there was a greater degree of intellectual freedom than anywhere else on the continent, and began to prepare his writings for publication.

The Rules

Throughout his studies, Descartes found uncertainty and contradiction. Each thinker he encountered seemed to have a different approach to the quest for truth that conflicted with other thinkers. Many learned men of the past had relied on the authority of the church or sacred writings to guide them. But this dependence on authority also led to contradictory results. As Descartes continued his studies, he became "obsessed by the eager desire to learn to distinguish the true from the false, that [he] might see clearly what [his] actions ought to be, and so as to have assurance as to the path to be followed in this life."[5] It seemed to Descartes that mathematics was the only discipline that supplied the kind of certainty he was seeking. Therefore, he decided to use the principles of mathematics to construct a system of knowledge. He began by establishing twenty-one *Rules for the Direction of the Mind*. The most important of these rules were

> *Rule 3.* In treating of objects proposed for investigation what we have to examine is not what others have opined, nor what we ourselves may conjecture, but what we can clearly and evidently intuit, or can deduce with certainty: knowledge is not obtainable in any other way. . . .
>
> By *intuition* I understand, not the fluctuating testimony of the sense, nor the misleading judgment of a wrongly combining imagination, but the apprehension which the mind, pure and attentive, gives us so easily and so distinctively that we are thereby freed from all doubt as to what it is that we are apprehending. . . .
>
> By way of *deduction* . . . we understand all that is necessarily concluded from other certainly known data. . . .
>
> *Rule 4.* In the search for the truth of things method is indispensable.
>
> *Rule 5.* Method consists entirely in the orderly handling of the things upon which the mind's attention has to be concentrated, if any truth bearing on them is to be discovered. We shall comply with it exactly, if we resolve involved and obscure data step by step into those which are simpler, and then starting from the intuition of those which are simplest, endeavor to ascend to the knowledge of all the others, doing so by corresponding steps.[6]

To find certain truth, then, one must begin with what could be "clearly and evidently intuited." Such "clear and evident" intuitions could not be derived from sense-perception. The senses provided only blurred information. Certain knowledge had to come from someplace else. But if "clear and evident" intuitions did not come from the senses, then where did they come from? Following Plato's theory of Forms, Descartes claimed that they were innate. One could never derive, for example, the concept of a perfect triangle from sense experience. Any attempt to draw a triangle would necessarily fall short of the mark. No matter how carefully drawn, the triangle would always have imperfections. But the "clear and evident" intuition or idea of a "plane figure formed by three lines intersecting by twos in three points" could be known apart from sense experience. It could be known with certainty.

Plato held that sense experience served to remind people of the eternal truths they already knew. Aquinas, following Aristotle, held that sense experience provided the basis for one's knowledge of universals. But for Descartes sense experience played no role whatsoever in the search for truth.

Once one had established "clear and evident" intuitions, Descartes claimed, then one could move deductively to build on them. Just as mathematics began with basic postulates and then used these to form theorems, Descartes began with basic intuitions and then used them to discover other certain knowledge.

Descartes began with himself, with his own ideas, in his search for truth. He put aside the authority of past thinkers, the church, sacred writings, and even his own sense experience and sought to discover ultimate truth by using only his reason.

Methodological Doubt

The key issue for Descartes was to find the "clear and evident" intuition (or intuitions) that would lead him to truth. It seemed to Descartes that the best way to find such intuitions was the process of methodological doubt. This process involved examining every idea that he had been taught or had come to believe to see whether there was a chance it might be incorrect. If there was a chance of being mistaken, however remote, the idea was to be set aside or "doubted." In this manner, Descartes hoped to find one (or more) things that could not be doubted. As he explained it,

> In respect . . . of the opinions which I have hitherto been entertaining, I thought that I could not do better than decide on emptying my mind of them one and all, with a view to the replacing of them by others more tenable, or, it may be, to the re-admitting of them, on their being shown to be in conformity with reason.[7]

Descartes began his methodological doubt by doubting everything he had been taught. Holding that they could possibly be mistaken, he doubted every theory of science that was held in his time. After all, Galileo was attempting to prove that the earth rotated around the sun, not the sun around the earth, as was commonly supposed. If the commonly held opinion was wrong in this instance, could one trust it in other cases? He doubted all of the theology and metaphysics that he had learned from the Jesuits. Next he doubted ideas that seemed more certain: his own bodily existence and the truths of mathematics. Descartes came to the conclusion that even in these matters he might possibly be mistaken. There was always the possibility that he might be insane or even that some evil god was deceiving him. As Descartes explained this process of methodological doubt,

It may be said, although the senses sometimes deceive us regarding minute objects ... There are yet many other things which ... are too evident to be doubted; as for instance, that I am in this place, seated by the fire, attired in a dressing-gown, having this paper in my hands, and other similar seeming certainties. Can I deny that these hands and this body are mine, save perhaps by comparing myself to those who are insane.... None the less I must bear in mind that I am a man, and am therefore in the habit of sleeping, and that what the insane represent to themselves in their waking moments I represent to myself, with other things even less probable in my dreams. How often, indeed, have I dreamt of myself being in this place, ... lying undressed in bed! ... On more careful study ... I see that there are no certain marks distinguishing waking from sleep....

Let us, then, suppose ourselves to be asleep, and that all these particulars—namely, that we open our eyes, move the head, extend the hands—are false and illusory; and let us reflect that our hands perhaps, and the whole body, are not what we see them as being.... This, perhaps, is why we not unreasonably conclude that physics, astronomy, medicine, and all other disciplines treating of composite things are of doubtful character, and that arithmetic, geometry, etc. ... have a content that is certain and indubitable. For whether I am awake or dreaming, 2 and 3 are 5.... Yet even these truths can be questioned.... How ... do I know that [God] has not arranged that there be no Earth, no heavens, no extended thing, no shape, no magnitude, no location, while at the same time securing that all these things appear to me to exist precisely as they now do? Others, as I sometimes think, deceive themselves in the things which they believe they know best. How do I know that I am not myself deceived everytime I add 2 and 3? ... But perhaps God has not been willing that I should be thus deceived, for He is said to be supremely good....

[But] I shall now suppose, not that a true God, who as such must be supremely good and the fountain of truth, but that some malignant genius exceedingly powerful and cunning has devoted all his powers in the deceiving of me....

What is there, then, which can be esteemed true? Perhaps only this, that nothing whatsoever is certain.[8]

Cogito Ergo Sum

While in the process of this universal, all-encompassing doubt, Descartes came across one thing that he simply could not doubt: that he doubted. Even if there was a "malignant genius" who was misleading him at every point, there still had to be a "him" to mislead. There had to be a person who was doubting. This led Descartes to affirm the one proposition that could not be doubted, "*Cogito ergo sum*—I think, therefore I am." Descartes reflected,

> But I immediately became aware that while I was thus disposed to think that all was false, it was absolutely necessary that I who thus thought should be somewhat; and noting that this truth *I think, therefore I am*, was so steadfast and so assured that the suppositions of the skeptics, to whatever extreme they might all be carried, could not avail to shake it, I concluded that I might without scruple accept it as being the first principle of the philosophy I was seeking.[9]

Having established that there was at least an "I" that was doubting, Descartes went on to examine the nature of this "I." It seemed clear to Descartes that this "I" was, by nature, a thinking thing. He wrote,

What then is it that I am? A thinking thing. What is a thinking thing? It is a thing that doubts, understands, affirms, denies, wills, abstains from willing, that also can be aware of images and sensations.[10]

Proof of God's Existence

Included among the ideas that this "thinking thing" had was the idea of God. Where did such an idea come from? Certainly the idea of God did not come from within the "thinking thing" itself, because the self was finite and could not conceive of something infinite. In fact, the awareness that this "thinking thing" was finite only came through comparison with something infinite. The idea of God, then, had to come from a source outside the "thinking thing." Furthermore, this idea of God had to come from a source adequate to produce such an idea. The only adequate source was God. Descartes explained,

> I resolved to inquire whence I had learned to think of something more perfect than I myself was; and I saw clearly that it must proceed from some nature that was indeed more perfect. . . . Thus [I am] committed to the conclusion that [the idea of something more perfect] has been placed in me by a nature which is veritably more perfect than I am, and which has indeed within itself all the perfections of which I have any idea, that is to say, in a single word, that is God.[11]

Having proved that there was a perfect God, Descartes argued that "it is impossible that He should ever deceive me, since in all fraud and deception there is some element of imperfection."[12] Therefore, he concluded that his God-given judgment, if used properly, could never lead him astray. Even his senses could be trusted—*if* they were subject to his reason. By using his reason alone, Descartes was able to come to truth.

Body and Mind

The affirmation "I think, therefore I am" was absolutely certain because it applied only to the conscious self. The "I" that Descartes found at the conclusion of his methodological doubt was not "that assemblage of limbs we call the human body."[13] What then was the relation of this conscious self or mind to the body?

According to Descartes, the body was a part of the material world. As a part of the material world, two important things about the body became clear. Like all other objects, the body was subject to the laws of motion. Each bodily motion was determined by some antecedent movement. So the body, taken by itself, was simply a complex machine. Like all other objects in the material world, the body's essential characteristic was extension. Using a piece of wax as an example, Descartes explained what he meant by extension. One could easily describe the taste, color, shape, and size of the wax. But when the wax melts "What remains of the taste exhales, the odor evaporates, the color changes, the shape is destroyed, its size increases,"[14] and so on. Yet through all of these changes, the piece of wax remained a piece of wax before and after heating—and common to all material things, including the body—was the "character of being spacially extended. It is the capacity to assume, under certain and different conditions, this or that determinate size and this or that determinate shape."[15]

The mind, on the other hand, had nothing whatsoever to do with the material world. Whereas the body was determined by the laws of motion, the mind was totally free. The essential characteristic of the mind was thought. The mind was the "self" Descartes found at the end of his process of doubt.

From this distinction between body and mind, Descartes concluded that the world of experience was dual. On the other hand, there were the material objects, which were distinguished by extension: the world of bodies. On the other hand, there were the human selves, which are distinguished by thought: the world of minds.

The problem that remained for Descartes was to explain the interaction of the body and the mind. If they belonged to such totally different worlds, how could one affect the other? How could the body, for example, cause the mind to become disoriented when tired? Conversely, how could the mind direct the body to write down ideas?

Descartes attempted to answer this question by referring to the pineal gland. This small gland, attached to the brain, provided the bridge between "thinking substance" (mind) and "corporeal substance" (body). When the body was stimulated by some material object acting on the senses, one of two things happened. Either the body responded on its own, or else through the pineal gland the body caused changes in the mind. For example, if one's hand became hot from being too near a flame, the body would independently respond to the heat stimulus by causing the hand to move away. If another person held one's hand over a flame, the body would act on the pineal gland, causing a change of mind. The mind would then understand that the other person was up to something evil and might attempt to do that person harm.

Conversely, the mind could act on the body through the pineal gland. If, for example, the mind should desire intellectual stimulation, it might direct the body to move to the library. Descartes contended, "Solely because it desires something, [the mind] causes the little gland to which it is closely united to move in the way requisite to produce the effect which relates to this desire."[16]

Galileo's Condemnation

In 1604 a new star appeared in the constellation of Cassiopeia. The appearance of this new star was devastating to the intellectual life of Europe. Ptolemy and even Copernicus had held that the stars were fixed. The stars were the furthest things away from the fallen earth and the closest things to God. It was inconceivable that these perfect creations of God could ever change.

Around this time, an Italian by the name of Galileo began experimenting with lenses. In 1609, Galileo built a telescope that could enlarge by thirty diameters. Pointing this telescope at the heavens, Galileo made several startling discoveries. He discovered that the Milky Way was actually an incredible number of stars. He discovered that the planet Jupiter had at least four moons—much like the moons of earth. And, most important, he discovered that the earth's moon had mountains.

Galileo's discoveries and his conclusions, which supported a position similar to that of Copernicus, were unacceptable to the Roman Catholic Church. Whereas Copernicus had written in a period of relative freedom of ideas, Galileo was writing in a period of fear and distrust following the Reformation. Whereas Copernicus had based his theories on mathematical principles and a desire for simplicity, Galileo based his theories on observations. Whereas Copernicus' theories had left medieval theology essentially undisturbed, Galileo's discoveries threatened to undermine it. That mountains, the symbols of sin, could be found in the perfection of the heavens was unthinkable! In 1616 Galileo was "strongly counseled" by the Pope not to publish any findings that he might make. However, in 1632 Galileo finally published his theories in the *Dialogue on the Two Chief Systems*. In 1633, Galileo's work was declared heretical by the Roman Catholic Church. Galileo was called before the Inquisition and forced to renounce his ideas. He spent the rest of his life under house arrest at his small estate near Florence.

When Descartes heard the news, he was dumbfounded. He had thought that Galileo's work was gaining general acceptance everywhere. The severity of the sentence especially frightened him and forced him to rethink his plan to publish his work. Although his method was different from that of Galileo, he came to many of the same conclusions. In his application of mathematics to astronomy, he, too, held that the earth revolved around the sun. But even apart from this specific area, his whole work was radically new and would probably breed controversy. He had begun with the self, the thinking "I." God had been introduced into his philosophy only to assist in the search for truth. God had been found to be a useful aid in humankind's quest for knowledge. Surely, such a philosophy would be condemned by the Roman Catholic Church.

As Descartes considered publication, he was uncertain as to his course of action. He could proceed with publication, knowing that his work would probably be censured. But that would mean his ideas would not reach the centers of learning in the church-controlled universities. He could postpone publication and hope for a softening of the church's hard-line position. But was such a change forthcoming? By waiting, he would rob himself of the opportunity to interact with other thinkers about his ideas. In confusion, Descartes pondered his alternatives.

NOTES

1. René Descartes, *Oeuvres*, ed. Cherks Adam and Paul Tannery (Paris: Cerf, 1897–1913, Fin novembre 1633), 13 vols., pp. 241–242, trans. Jack Rochford Vrooman in *René Descartes: A Biography* (New York: Putnam's, 1970), p. 84.

2. See Maynard Mack and others, *World Masterpieces* (New York: Norton, 1965), vol. 1, pp. 1141–1143.
3. René Descartes, *Discourse on Method,* from *Descartes' Philosophical Writings,* trans. Norman Kemp Smith (New York: Random House, 1958), p. 95.
4. Ibid., p. 97.
5. Ibid., p. 99.
6. René Descartes, *Rules for the Guidance of Our Native Powers,* from *Descartes' Philosophical Writings,* pp. 8–21.
7. Descartes, *Discourse,* p. 103.
8. René Descartes, *Meditations on First Philosophy,* from *Descartes' Philosophical Writings,* pp. 177–182.
9. Descartes, *Discourse,* pp. 118–119.
10. Descartes, *Meditations,* p. 186.
11. Descartes, *Discourse,* p. 120.
12. Descartes, *Meditations,* p. 212.
13. Ibid., p. 185.
14. Ibid., p. 188.
15. S. V. Keeling, *Descartes,* rev. ed. (London: Oxford University Press, 1968), p. 113.
16. René Descartes, *Philosophical Works of Descartes,* trans. E. S. Haldane and G. R. T. Ross (Cambridge: University Press, 1931–1934), pp. 347–350.

BIBLIOGRAPHY

Primary Source

Descartes, René. *Descartes Philosophical Writings.* Selected and translated by Norman Kemp Smith. New York: Random House, 1958.

Biography

Haldane, E. S. *Descartes: His Life and Times.* New York: Dutton, 1905.

Interpretative Works

Campbell, Keith. *Body and Mind.* New York: Doubleday, 1970.
Gibson, A. B. *The Philosophy of Descartes.* London: Russell and Russell, 1932.
Keeling, S. V. *Descartes.* Rev. ed. London: Oxford University Press, 1968.
Kenny, Anthony. *Descartes: A Study of His Philosophy.* New York: Random House, 1968.
Smith, Norman Kemp. *New Studies in the Philosophy of Descartes.* London: Russell and Russell, 1952.

QUESTIONS FOR STUDY

1. Outline the factors introduced during the periods we call Renaissance and Reformation that contributed to the shaping of a "modern" mentality.

2. Describe Descartes' process of methodological doubt. Indicate several implications of the conclusion to which he came at the end of his doubting process.

3. Explain how Descartes arrived at each of the following certainties, and show how each of these three certainties relate to each other:
   a. *Certainty 1.* I think, therefore I am.
   b. *Certainty 2.* God exists.
   c. *Certainty 3.* Within the bounds of reason, the senses can be trusted.

4. Sketch Descartes' argument for the existence of God. How was it like and how was it different from the ontological argument of Anselm?

5. What were the characteristics of body and mind for Descartes? How were they related to each other?

6. In what ways are body-mind dualisms with us today? Give examples.

A Contemporary Response

ROBERT C. LEVIS

What to Do?

Should he publish? This was an important question for Descartes as he arrived at the completion of his work.

At the outset, he had made a pact with himself—namely, to lead a sort of double life. When in public, he would "obey the laws and customs." But in the privacy of his study he would question everything. As he tells us,

> It is not sufficient, before commencing to rebuild the house which we inhabit, to pull it down and provide materials and an architect . . . unless we have also provided ourselves with some other house where we can be comfortably lodged during the time of rebuilding.[1]

But now the sanctity of his study had served its purpose. His initial mission was accomplished. It was a time of decision—a decision that could involve his own condemnation and possibly his death—a situation that would truly leave him without a house in which to live! What should he do?

As he "pondered his alternatives," he was no doubt reminded of his reasons for setting out on this intellectual venture in the first place. He remembered how he had been torn between the truth as presented by the church and as reflected in the science of his day—and how, in vain, he had looked around in search of philosophers who were attempting the needed reconciliation.

Also, as he reflected, he might well have realized that underlying his whole approach was a fundamental trust in his ability to reason—plus a capacity for being radically honest with himself in a very personal way. These were the factors responsible for his success. The next logical step consistent with the spirit of his venture was to risk sharing his views with others—with his contemporaries—asking only that they reciprocate in kind. And so he decided to publish.

Now it is up to us to react. And here I like to think that his greatest concern would be that we each, in our own way, simply follow his example—that we too have the courage to question him and, in turn, begin anew. As Edman Husserl puts it at the beginning of his book, *Cartesian Meditations,* "anyone who seriously intends to become a philosopher must 'once in his life' withdraw into himself and attempt, within himself, to overthrow and build anew all the sciences that, up to then, he has been accepting."[2]

Let me begin with *Cogito ergo sum.*

Overthrowing the Thinking Man

Descartes takes me on an impressive journey as he proceeds to doubt the world, God, and, finally, the self. Most of all, the resistance I encounter in myself when I try to doubt my own efforts to doubt is very obvious. My very act of doubting presupposes a doubter—a thinker—me. There is no way of getting around it. But when Descartes posits this thinker as essentially a thinking thing I am confused. Just what does he mean here?

I can come up with some plausible explanations. For example, he can be seen as beginning with Galileo's view that the mathematically formulable primary qualities are the real aspect of material bodies. This leads to the positing of extension as a fundamental substance. Then, with extension accepted as given, there arises the problem of those aspects of human experience, such as feeling and willing, that seem to fall outside the categories of extension—thus the need for another kind of substance. And so he posits the idea of thinking things.

But does such an explanation really bring me any closer to an understanding of what Descartes himself meant by a thinking thing, and, even more important, have I come any closer to an understanding of my own self? He presents me with a vision of who I am, but is it a vision that somehow corresponds with what I find myself to be?

Actually, what happens in my encounter with Descartes is that he raises the fundamental question "Who am I?" But, finding his answer rather obscure, I tend to reject it. As a result, I am thrown back on myself in quest of a more adequate answer. The question "Who am I?" has now become a problem. It is very much like the situation in which a girlfriend asks, "Do you love me?" and I reply, "Well, now that you ask!" The question "What is love?" like the question "Who am I?" has suddenly become real.

"I Can" as an Alternative to "I Think"

The adequacy of Descartes' view of the self has been under constant criticism by those that have followed him. For instance, Michel Henry, a contemporary French philosopher, rejects the notion of a static substance closed in on itself. For him, "the ego is a power. The *cogito* does not signify an 'I think,' but an 'I can.' "[3] My essential self is not reducible to some thinking thing or even to some molecular process as the materialists would have it. Both of these are abstractions—ways of talking about the self. My essential self is rather what I am aware of when I sense myself as one who is able—an "I can"—a unity of body and will.

I want to explore this alternative, but before doing so I would like to indicate that what follows has been greatly influenced by an argument that arose in one of my philosophy classes when discussing the Descartes case. The "Buddhists" insisted on rejecting the notion of any permanent self, while the "Christians" supported the view of an unchanging soul.

As I examine myself as an "I can," I can look in two directions: back toward the "I" and outward from the "can." And then, finally, I can look at my looking in these two directions. These three ways of looking at the "I can" point to three basic relationships that I want to propose—the I-I relation, the I-other relation, and the I-object relation. Let me take each of them in turn.

Looking Back Toward the "I": The I-I Relation

In each moment—each now—I am aware that I am what I am. I am something for myself. This is the level of the self that the Zen Buddhists call experiencing what we are—be it breathing, desiring, thinking or any other activity.[4] Michel Henry calls it self-feeling or *ipseity* ("selfness," in Greek). The key for him is the subjective body—the body as it is immediately present for itself at any moment. For example, when I take a breath there is a oneness between my bodily "pulling in" and my bodily being alive. As he puts it,

> My body is the movement which proves itself in functioning, that is to say which vouches for itself by itself within itself, it is my action in so far as I live in an immediate experience which defies all commentary and, even more strongly, all contestation.[5]

One of the important characteristics of this self-feeling or this being there for myself is that it is an ever-present given as long as I am alive and well. Also it is a given over which I have no control. The I is not free to be what it finds itself to be. It is simply what it discovers itself to be. This comes out when we reflect on the question "Why am I me—the particular me that I find myself to be?" In moments of happiness, we can rejoice and have a deep appreciation in being what we are. Likewise, in moments of despair we can regret our existence—even, for some, to the point of suicide. But we cannot be other than what we are. It is as inconceivable that I be other than what I find myself to be as it is to doubt that I am a doubter when in the act of doubting.

Another characteristic of this self-feeling—this I-I relation—is that it involves a continuity. Even though I may grow as the circumstances of my life change, I am still aware of being the same I. Should my wife ask, "Why did you marry me?" I somehow feel responsible. The I that decided to marry her and the I that is being questioned are one and the same. My memory is witness to the fact that it was I and not somebody else that proposed and said "I do." I can rejoice or feel guilty about having said this, but to remember it is to realize that it was in fact I that said it—and meant it—the same I that is now being questioned. Such continuity is the very basis of all human commitment.

Looking Outward from the "Can": The I-Other Relation

I have said that my essential self is what I am aware of when I sense myself as one who is able—as an "I can." But this raises the question—able to do what? After all, the "I can" that I find myself to be never operates in a vacuum—out in limbo someplace. Rather, it is always in process—always up to something—always on the way.

So to answer the question "Able to do what?" I am directed to all that I am involved in along the way. And it is here that I note that, within limits, I am able to do—or not to do—such things as breathe, touch, love, see, hear, and decide. But the important thing here is that I can only do all of these things within limits because it is this that points to the fact that I am dependent on that which is other than myself. For example, I can play with the air as I breathe, but being in a world with air to breathe is something that I discover. It is other than me, as is evidenced by the fact that it can be taken away. Also, I am capable of love—of what Martin Buber calls the I-Thou relation. But, again, in the absence of other persons the I-Thou happening need not happen. Others, like the air, can be taken from me—and I die.

Such reflections make me realize that, just as I am not free to be other than me, so also there is a sense in which I have no choice in the unique circumstances—the other—that I encounter along the way. I am only free to relate to the other that I find given. I am never free to instantaneously make it other than what it is.

Looking at Our Looking at "I Can": The I-Object Relation

As far as I am concerned much of what I have tried to point to in both the I-I and the I-other relationships could well apply to all living things—and especially my dogs! The main difference is that they are not capable of being aware of themselves in the objective fashion that we are. And it is to this aspect the "I can"—the ability to think—that I now want to turn.

According to the philosopher Ernst Cassirer, a major difficulty in understanding human thought is that it has already passed through a long period of development before it is able to turn in on itself and attempt to determine its own nature. It is for this reason that he looks with special interest at the accounts of such people as Helen Keller, the famous blind deaf-mute. He tells us that, although the usual methods of psychological observation are not much help, in the case of Keller "nature itself has, so to speak, made an experiment capable of throwing unexpected light upon the point in question."[6] Let us look briefly at her teacher's account of the day she learned to use words as names for kinds of things, as universals.

This morning, while she was washing, she wanted to know the name for "water."
When she wants to know the name of anything, she points to it and pats my hand. I
spelled "w-a-t-e-r" and thought no more about it until after breakfast. . . . [Later on]
we went out to the pump house, and I made Helen hold her mug under the spout
while I pumped. As cold water gushed forth, filling the mug, I spelled "w-a-t-e-r" in
Helen's free hand. The word coming so close upon the sensation of cold water rushing over her hand seemed to startle her. She dropped her mug and stood as one trans-
fixed. A new light came into her face. She spelled "w-a-t-e-r" several times. Then
she dropped to the ground and asked for its name. . . . Everything must have a name
now. Wherever we go, she asks eagerly for the names of things she has not learned at
home.[7]

In reconstructing what must have preceded this eventful discovery that everything has a name, it seems plausible to discern at least three stages. First, as
a result of repeated experiences, Helen must have become familiar with the special sensation of water with the unique pattern *w-a-t-e-r* being made in the
palm of her hand. Second, through imitating her teacher she gradually learned
to associate with each individual thing like water a specific name like *w-a-t-e-r*.
Then, finally, the third stage began with the major breakthrough indicated in
the preceding quote when she recognized that water and *w-a-t-e-r always* went
together, that they were paired. And as she became aware of one such "paired"
relationship she was in a position to look for others, such as earth and *e-a-r-t-h*.
Also, she could begin using the symbol *w-a-t-e-r* to point to water even though
she might not actually be experiencing it. She could begin using symbols to communicate the objects of her concern. It is this last step that, according to Cassirer, is the crucial one for human beings. As he tells us,

Helen Keller had previously learned to combine a certain thing or event with a certain sign of the manual alphabet. A fixed association had been established between
these things and certain tactile impressions. But a series of such associations, even if
they are repeated and amplified, still does not imply an understanding of what human speech is and means. In order to arrive at such an understanding the child had
to make a new and much more significant discovery. It had to understand that *everything has a name*—that the symbolic function is not restricted to particular cases but
is a principle of *universal* applicability which encompasses the whole field of human
thought.[8]

Can anything more be said about this? What is involved in this crucial step
of understanding "that everything has a name?" As I try to identify with Helen
just prior to her discovery, I feel that there must have been a "reaching out" on
her part. It is almost as if her teacher and the things in her world were inviting
her to relate to them in some special way, that laying there among all of her familiar surroundings was something that she needed to see, and that it was somehow *up to her* to find it. Those around her could only wait. But what did she
need to do? As I see it, a fundamental need at this point was to learn to *play
with possibility*. She needed to perfect her capacity for envisaging the future. By
withdrawing imaginatively from the present and remembering the past, she
needed to learn to anticipate in a new way what was to come. Then, out of the

remembered correlation between water and *w-a-t-e-r* could come the vision of a similar correlation in the future, followed by the realization that it might hold for *all possible* future encounters-always.

Concluding Comments

Whereas in Descartes we have a radical split between the self as "I think" and the world as extension, this analysis of the self as "I can" makes us whole again. In fact the questions "Who am I?" and "What is the nature of the world?" become inseparable—they are basically the same question.

Likewise, in place of a radical dualism we have interdependence. "Looking at" the I-I and the I-other relations presupposes the power to reflect—the I-object relation. *And* the I-object relation presupposes that I am something for myself in a world of the other—the I-I and the I-other relations.

Concerning the nature of the soul and its possible permanence, the important thing is to make a distinction between what we are witness to in the primitive feeling of being something for ourselves *and* our efforts to reflect on this essential given and understand it. Here as in all other areas, except perhaps math and logic, our understanding will always entail an approximation. I can know with absolute certainty that there is continuity between the "I" that began this discussion and the "I" that is now about to terminate, but to say that this "I" will continue beyond the grave is something that I, for the moment, can *neither* affirm *nor* deny with any complete assurance.

NOTES

1. René Descartes, *Discourse on Method,* from *Descartes' Philosophical Writings,* selected and trans. Norman Kemp Smith (New York: Random House, 1958), p. 20.
2. Edmund Husserl, *Cartesian Meditations,* trans. Dorion Cairns (The Hague: Nijhoff, 1960), p. 2.
3. Michel Henry, *Philosophie et Phenomenologie du Corps* (Paris: Presses Universitaires de France, 1965), p. 71. English translation by Robert Levis.
4. Jacob Needleman, *The New Religions,* quoted in Roger Eastman, *Coming of Age in Philosophy* (San Francisco: Canfield Press, 1973), p. 371.
5. Michel Henry, "Le Concept d'Ame a-t-il un Sens?" *Revue Philosophique de Louvain,* February 1966, 64:27. English translation by Robert Levis.
6. Ernst Cassirer, *An Essay on Man* (New Haven, Conn.: Yale University Press, 1944), p. 33.
7. Ibid., p. 34.
8. Ibid., p. 34.

CHAPTER 6

The Case of Hume

Is There a Place for Miracles in the Secular World?

WITH ALL the religious controversy going on in England at the time, David
Hume wanted to be sure that his *Treatise of Human Nature* was not misunder-
stood. The Deists and the orthodox Christians were attacking one another in almost every book that appeared in the 1730s, and Hume wanted to do more than
simply defend one side. In fact, he felt that his *Treatise* would show both sides of
the controversy to be wrong.

But Hume's desire to avoid religious controversy ran counter to his desire to
include in the *Treatise* a chapter on miracles. Entitled "Reasonings Concerning
Miracles," this chapter pointed out the problems associated with miracles.
Using the principles established at the beginning of the *Treatise*, Hume argued
that one could never provide even a probable argument for the occurrence of
miracles.

As Hume completed the *Treatise* and began to look for a publisher, he had
second thoughts about including this chapter. Would his views on miracles force
him into the middle of the Deist–Christian controversy? Would he appear to be
simply another Deist, or would people be able to see that he was attacking the
Deists as well as the traditional Christians? If he did not include the chapter,
would the *Treatise* be damaged? Would the work still incite the debate and discussion Hume was expecting? Would people be able to realize the staggering
implications of Hume's reworking of Locke's philosophy without examples such
as "Reasonings Concerning Miracles"? As Hume considered these questions,
he realized he had a difficult decision to make.

John Locke

René Descartes (1596–1650) was the first of the "continental rationalists."
These thinkers, who dominated the philosophy of the continent of Europe until
the end of the 1700s, held that truth was derived from reason. All knowledge

was deducible from certain "clear and evident" ideas. Reason was independent of sense experience. In fact, reason was prior to and superior to sense experience. Among the philosophers who held to this view of knowledge were Benedict Spinoza (1632–1677) and Gottfried Wilhelm Leibniz (1646–1716).

Philosophy developed quite differently in the British Isles. The British Empiricists, as they were called, believed that there was no such thing as an innate idea. A person was not born with certain truths already implanted in the mind. Rather, knowledge came from observation, from sense experience. Even the idea of God was not innate—it was a conclusion drawn from observations.

John Locke (1632–1704) was the first philosopher clearly to lay out a form of empiricism. According to Locke, the mind was at birth a *tabula rasa*, a blank tablet. All ideas that were imprinted on this blank tablet came from experience. Experience could be either external, coming from sensations produced by objects outside the person, or internal, coming from reflection on external experience. In either case, all knowledge had to originate in sense experience.

Sense experience, and reflection on sense experience, gave rise to simple ideas. These simple ideas could be any one of four kinds. There were those simple ideas received through one sense only, such as ideas of taste, color, and smell. Next, there were the simple ideas that were obtained by a combination of two or more senses, such as the ideas of space, extension, and motions. Thirdly, there were the simple ideas that were obtained by reflection alone. These ideas included such things as remembering, judging, and knowing. Finally, there were those simple ideas that arose from both sense and reflection. Such ideas included the ideas of pleasure, existence, and unity. These simple ideas were combined by the mind to form an infinite number of complex ideas. The idea of God, for example, was a combination of the simple ideas of existence, unity, knowledge, and so on. This meant, for Locke, that no matter how complex an idea might be it could in principle be reduced to simple ideas that came from sense experience. Therefore, all knowledge was derived from the senses.

Locke also made a distinction between simple and complex ideas and external objects. Ideas, whether simple or complex, were caused by "things outside" the person. These "things outside" the person had certain powers that included the power to cause changes in other objects and the power to produce sensations. So all ideas came from sensations, and all sensations came from external objects.

Locke used this concept of the power of external objects to prove God's existence. His "first-cause argument" was similar to the first of Aquinas' "five ways." The world is known by ideas that are caused by sensations. These sensations are caused by external objects. It follows, said Locke, that something must have caused these external objects. This "something" that caused external objects must, in turn, have had a cause, and so on. Locke posited that there could not be an endless series of causes and effects, so he concluded that there had to be a first cause. Because external objects ultimately gave rise to the orderly perceptions and ideas by which the universe was known, these objects must have been created in an orderly manner. Because thinking was the end product of the power of objects, thinking must have caused the objects in the first place. Therefore there had to be a supreme thinking source that corresponded to (and ultimately gave rise to) the complex idea of a divine being.

The identification of God as the first cause of the universe led Locke to affirm a religion of Deism. According to the Deists, God created the world to operate in a certain way. God both caused the world to begin and established the laws of nature to govern it. Having laid down the laws of nature, God would not violate them. Hence, God did not work miracles, answer prayer, or in any other way interfere with the operation of natural laws. Humankind's job was to discover these natural laws and live in accordance with them.

David Hume

David Hume was born in Edinburgh, Scotland, in 1711. His father, Joseph, was a lawyer who died before young David was two years old. As Hume later recalled his childhood, his father's death left him "with an elder Brother and Sister under the care of our Mother, who, though young and handsome, devoted herself entirely to the rearing and educating of her children."[1] David's mother, Katherine, was a deeply religious person who raised her children to be God-fearing members of the Scottish Church. Young David also took his religion seriously. While still a young boy, he made lists of his vices so that he might properly seek forgiveness from God.

Even though he grew up under the strict rules of the Scottish Presbyterian Church, David had a pleasant childhood. The family estate, called Ninewells, sat on a bluff overlooking the Whiteadder River in southern Scotland. As a boy, Hume lived part of the year in this charming country estate and part of the year in a small flat in Edinburgh. When he was twelve years old, Hume went to the University of Edinburgh. Like his father before him, he did not study for a degree. As Hume described his university life, "I passed through the ordinary Courses of Education with Success . . . and was seized early with a passion for Literature."[2] While a student, Hume encountered the writings of John Locke. As a result of his readings in Locke and other philosophers, Hume abandoned his religious beliefs.

The Hume family was certainly not poor, but neither was it rich. When Joseph died, he did not leave David enough money to live a leisurely life of studying and writing. As a result, David's family encouraged him to learn some profession. Because his father had been a lawyer, it was decided that he should be a lawyer too. Hume later explained,

> My studious Disposition, my Sobriety, and my Industry gave my Family a Notion that the Law was a proper profession for me: But I found an unsurmountable Aversion to everything but the pursuits of Philosophy and general Learning; and while they fancyed I was pouring over Voet and Vinnius, Cicero and Virgil were the Authors which I was secretly devouring.[3]

In 1729, Hume made what he considered to be some startingly new discoveries in philosophy. He found what he held to be "A new Science of Thought, which transported [me] beyond measure and made [me], with an ardour natural to a young man, throw up every other pleasure or business to apply entirely to it."[4] He announced to his family that he was going to give up his pretense to law and become a philosopher. For the next several years, Hume worked on developing his new ideas. The pace at which he worked on his studies soon made him quite ill. He moved to France, where the weather was less severe and his limited money would go further.

In 1735, Hume retired to the town of La Fleche. The college in this small town where Descartes had gone to school was one of the centers of continental rationalism. Living quietly in a small cottage, Hume continued his studies and his writing. In 1738, Hume finished the *Treatise of Human Nature*.

The Treatise: Impressions and Ideas

A monumental work, the *Treatise* contained sections dealing with logic, morals, criticism, and politics. Logic, which Hume held to be an explanation of "the principles and operations of our reasoning faculty and the nature of our ideas," took up the whole of Book 1.

Hume agreed with Locke that there is no such thing as an innate idea. He also agreed that all knowledge must come through sense experience. But as he worked out the implications of his empirical (or "sense-experience based") theory of knowledge, he came to some very different conclusions from those of Locke.

Hume began his exposition in the *Treatise* by dividing the perceptions of the human mind into impressions and ideas.

> All the perceptions of the human mind resolve themselves into two distinct kinds, which I shall call impressions and ideas. The difference betwixt these consists in the degrees of force and liveliness, with which they strike upon the mind, and make their way into our thought or consciousness. Those perceptions which enter with most force and violence, we may name *impressions;* and under this name I comprehend all our sensations, passions, and emotions, as they make their first appearance in the soul. By *ideas* I mean the faint images of these in thinking and reasoning; such as, for instance, are all the perceptions excited by the present discourse, excepting only those which arise from the sight and touch, and excepting the immediate pleasure or uneasiness it may occasion.[5]

In distinguishing between impressions and ideas, Hume used an empirical distinction: impressions strike the mind with more "force and liveliness" than ideas. He made no assumptions about where these impressions came from or why they had more "force" than ideas. To deal with such questions would have been to move beyond the world of sense experience. Next, Hume divided impressions and ideas into simple and complex.

> Simple perceptions, or impressions and ideas, are such as admit of no distinction nor separation. The complex are the contrary to these, and may be distinguished into parts. Though a particular colour, taste, and smell, are qualities all united together

in this apple, it is easy to perceive they are not the same, but are at least distinguish-
able from each other.[6]

At this point, Hume did make one nonempirical assumption. Just as Locke had
assumed that all complex ideas could be reduced to distinct simple ideas, Hume
assumed that every simple impression was a distinct, single unit. He further assumed that every simple idea was a memory copy of a simple impression.

Besides the distinction between simple and complex, impressions could be
further divided into impressions of sensation and impressions of reflection. Impressions of sensation were the original impressions, the cause of which was unknown. Impressions of reflection were derived from ideas. Hume outlined the
process:

> An impression first strikes upon the senses, and makes us perceive heat or cold, thirst
> or hunger, pleasure or pain, of some kind or other. Of this impression there is a copy
> taken by the mind, which remains after the impression ceases; and this we call an
> idea. This idea of pleasure or pain, when it returns upon the soul, produces the new
> impressions of desire and aversion, hope and fear, which may properly be called im-
> pressions of reflection, because derived from it.[7]

Because every simple idea was a distinct unit, it should follow that any one
idea might precede or follow any other one idea. But this was clearly not the
case. Ideas in the mind followed one another in an orderly progression. Hume
concluded that there must be "some universal principles" that connected ideas.
He wrote in the *Treatise,*

> Were ideas entirely loose and unconnected, chance alone would join them; and it is
> impossible the same ideas should fall regularly into complex ones (as they commonly
> do) without some bond of union among them, some associating quality, by which one
> idea naturally introduces another.[8]

Treatise: Cause and Effect

There were, according to Hume, three principles by which the mind moved
from one idea to another: resemblance, contiguity in space and time, and cause
and effect. These three principles were not ideas because they did not come from
impressions. Rather, they reflected the habitual way the mind worked. Hume
explained the principles of resemblance and contiguity in space and time in the
following way:

> It is plain, that in the course of our thinking . . . our imagination runs easily from
> one idea to any other that *resembles* it, and that this quality alone is to the fancy a
> sufficient bond and association. It is likewise evident, that as the senses, in changing
> their objects, are necessitated to change them regularly, and take them as they lie
> *contiguous* to each other, the imagination must by long custom acquire the same
> method of thinking.[9]

By means of the principle of resemblance, the mind connected ideas that appeared similar to one another. By means of the principle of contiguity in time

and place, the mind connected ideas that appeared to arise from sensory objects that followed one another. Hume gave an example:

> That these principles serve to connect ideas will not, I believe, be much doubted. A picture naturally leads our thoughts to the original [resemblance]: the mention of one apartment in a building naturally introduces an enquiry or discourse concerning the others [contiguity in space and time]: and if we think of a wound, we can scarcely forbear reflecting on the pain which follows it [cause and effect].[10]

The principle of cause and effect was of special interest to Hume. Locke had held that external objects had the power to cause changes in their objects and to give rise to sensations. In fact, all philosophers before Hume, whether rationalists or empiricists, Platonic or Aristotelian, had held that every effect must necessarily have a cause. For every event that occurred, the thinking went, something must have caused it.

Hume denied that there was such a necessary connection between cause and effect. According to Hume, people simply experienced one impression followed by another. After a period of time, people concluded that the second impression was caused by the first. But no one could ever give a reason for believing that any occurrence should follow another. No one could ever have an impression of one thing *causing* another. Hume declared,

> When we look about us towards external objects, and consider the operation of causes, we are never able, in a single instance, to discover any power or necessary connexion; any quality, which binds the effect to the cause, and renders the one an infallible consequence of the other. We only find, that the one does actually, in fact, follow the other ... we never can observe any tie between them. They seem *conjoined*, but never *connected*. And as we can have no idea of any thing which never appeared to our outward sense [impressions of sensation] or inward sentiment [impressions of reflection], the necessary conclusion *seems* to be that we have no idea of connexion or power at all, and that these words are absolutely without any meaning, when employed either in philosophical reasonings or common life.[11]

For example, when a person repeatedly observed the movement of one billiard ball followed by the movement of another, he or she inferred that there was a necessary causal connection. The movement of the first ball seemed to be *causing* the second ball to move. In truth, there was nothing necessary about the second ball's movement. The reason people assumed that there was a necessary connection was that they were accustomed to seeing one ball's movement follow the other's. For Hume, the cause-and-effect relation was simply a matter of habit.

Treatise: Empirical Criterion of Meaning

According to Hume, all complex ideas were combinations of simple ideas and all simple ideas were copies of simple impressions. Because all ideas ultimately came from impressions, any given idea had meaning only if there was an impression (or combination of impressions) that it was copying. For example, the idea *house* arose from a combination of impressions of certain colors, shapes, and sizes.

This criterion of meaning led Hume to question ideas that had been accepted by philosophers for centuries. The idea of *substance,* that which was left when all the sensory properties of a thing were removed, had been an important idea in the philosophy of Aristotle and others. But Hume found it to be a meaningless idea. As he put it,

> I would fain ask ... philosophers ... whether the idea of *substance* be derived from the impressions of sensation or reflection? If it be conveyed to us by our senses, I ask, which of them, and after what manner? If it be perceived by the eyes, it must be a colour; if by the ears, a sound; if by the palate, a taste; and so of the other senses. But I believe none will assert, that substance is either a colour, a sound, or a taste. The idea of substance must, therefore, be derived from an impression of reflection, if it really exists. But the impressions of reflection resolve themselves into our passions and emotions; none of which can possibly represent a substance. We have therefore no idea of substance, distinct from that of a collection of particular qualities, nor have we any other meaning when we either talk or reason concerning it.[12]

Locke had assumed that all sensations ultimately arose from external objects. These external objects in an external world were beyond sense experience. They gave rise to sense experience but could not themselves be experienced. According to Hume, the idea of an external world was meaningless. There were no impressions that could give rise to such an idea. The senses could "give us no notion of continued existence (that is, of an external world), because they do not operate beyond the extent, in which they really operate."[13] The senses, which provided all knowledge, could never get outside of themselves to experience their own relationship to some supposed external world. Hume concluded that there was no need to assume an external world of objects. Whether or not impressions were impressions *of* something was a question that could not be answered.

Finally, Hume held that the idea of *self* was also meaningless. Descartes had founded his philosophy on the "clear and evident" intuition "I think, therefore I am." But for Hume, there was no such thing as an "I": no self. He asserted,

> When I enter most intimately into what I call *myself,* I always stumble on some particular perception or other, of heat or cold, light or shade, love or hatred, pain or pleasure. I never can catch *myself* at any time without a perception, and never can observe anything but the perception.[14]

Hume concluded, therefore, that the self or "I" was nothing but "a bundle or collection of different perceptions, which succeed each other with an inconceivable rapidity, and are in a perpetual flux and movement."[15]

Miracles

Given that all knowledge began with impressions or the relations of ideas, Hume held that metaphysical systems that talked about God, the nature of what was real, and so on, had no meaning. Because it was not possible to have a simple impression of things that transcended human experience, it was not possible to talk meaningfully about such things. More specifically, because there was no necessary relation between cause and effect, all proofs for God's existence that depended on God's being the necessary cause of some feature in the world were meaningless. Thus the five ways of Thomas Aquinas and the first-cause argument of Locke were worthless. Further, any proofs for God's existence that sought to build necessary connections between the idea of God and the idea of existence were equally doomed to failure. Because the idea of existence was not something separate from the idea of an object, it was ridiculous to conclude that the idea of God (which was meaningless itself) had the unique characteristic of entailing the idea of existence. Thus the ontological proof of Anselm and Descartes' proof of God's existence on the basis of the idea of God were also doomed to failure.

Applying his philosophy to miracles, Hume pointed out that a miracle was, by definition, a violation of a law of nature. But the laws of nature that were known were founded on repeated observation. They were based on extensive and carefully recorded experience. For that reason, known laws of nature had the highest degree of probability. Therefore, Hume concluded that one should believe the testimony for a miracle, a violation of a law of nature, only if it would require more of a miracle for the testimony to be false than for there to have been an actual miracle. For example, someone might claim that they had seen an entire mountain moved. This person's testimony should be believed, according to Hume, only if the possibility of this person's lying or being mistaken was less than the possibility of a mountain moving. It was hard to imagine someone whose testimony would be that sure. It was, of course, possible that this could happen. The laws of nature were sometimes in need of revision. Perhaps this person had seen an earthquake of a force not previously observed. But it was usually more likely that such testimony to a miracle was either false or at least confused.

Hume took this argument a step further by claiming that there was not really even a probable argument for miracles. In the first place, most miracles were reported among ignorant and barbarous nations. In the second place, the testimony for miracles in the past had been less than unimpeachable. In fact, the history of supposed miracles seemed so tainted to Hume that he concluded it was always more probable that a miracle had been made up than that one had actually occurred. Finally, all religions claimed miracles. But not all religions could be true, because they had conflicting truth claims. Therefore, many of these claimed miracles had to be deceptions. Hume concluded that given any miracle claim, there was always a very good chance that it was false. In no way could such suspect miracles be taken as proof of any religion.

Publication

It was obvious that the orthodox Christians would not appreciate this commentary on miracles. But the Deists were also opposed by Hume. Holding that there was a God who, as the first cause, established universal and immutable laws, the Deists engaged in metaphysical speculation that was meaningless for Hume. The whole notion of a first cause was absurd.

Still, as he considered the upcoming publication of the *Treatise,* Hume was wary. His attack on miracles was directed much more obviously at traditional Christians than at Deists. Did he want to bring on the wrath of the Christian community with a frontal attack? If he did not include the section on miracles, would the book be taken more seriously as a philosophical work? Would his readers be able to grasp the implications of his philosophy and his reaction to Locke without the specific example of "Reasonings Concerning Miracles"?

NOTES

1. David Hume, quoted in Ernest Mossner, *The Life of David Hume* (Oxford, England: Clarendon Press, 1954), p. 26.
2. Ibid., p. 40.
3. Ibid., p. 52.
4. David Hume, *A Treatise of Human Nature,* ed. with an introduction by D. G. C. Macnabb (Cleveland: World, 1962), p. 7.
5. Ibid., p. 45.
6. Ibid., p. 46.
7. Ibid., p. 51.
8. Ibid., p. 54.
9. Ibid., pp. 54–55.
10. David Hume, *An Enquiry Concerning the Human Understanding,* ed. L. A. Selby-Bigge (Oxford, England: Clarendon Press, 1902), p. 24.
11. Ibid., pp. 63–74.
12. Treatise, p. 59.
13. Ibid., p. 242.
14. Ibid., p. 301.
15. Ibid., p. 302.

BIBLIOGRAPHY

Primary Source

Hume, David. *A Treatise of Human Nature.* Edited with an introduction by D. G. C. Macnabb. Cleveland: World Publishing, 1962.

Biography

Mossner, Ernest. *The Life of David Hume.* Oxford, England: Clarendon Press, 1954.

Interpretative Works

Hendel, Charles W. *Studies in the Philosophy of David Hume.* New York: Liberal Arts Press, 1963.
Laird, John. *Hume's Philosophy of Human Nature.* London: Methuen, 1932.

Smith, Norman Kemp. *The Philosophy of David Hume.* New York: St. Martin's Press, 1941.
Zabech, F. *Hume: Precursor of Modern Empiricism.* New York: Humanities Press, 1960.

QUESTIONS FOR STUDY

1. Examine and outline the differing premises about how knowledge was acquired and held by the seventeenth-century continental rationalists and the eighteenth-century British empiricists.

2. Describe Locke's proof for the existence of God. Compare and contrast it with one of Thomas Aquinas' five ways of knowing God.

3. Define the terms *impressions* and *ideas* in Hume's philosophy. What were their various sources and how were they related to each other?

4. Discuss Hume's treatment of the concept of cause and effect. Explain his treatment, using the illustration of billiard balls striking each other.

5. What was Hume's attitude toward miracles? Give an example of a miracle reported by someone in your lifetime. Examine it, using Hume's criteria of validity. Reflect on Hume's criteria in light of his discussion of cause and effect.

A Contemporary Response

GEORGE I. MAVRODES

DAVID HUME may have been wary, as the case suggests, of including a discussion of miracles in his writings on general philosophy. He was very much interested in applying his philosophical talents to questions of religion, as he shows in his *Dialogues Concerning Natural Religion*. But he may have wished to avoid having his more general philosophical works embroiled in controversies over religion.

At any rate, Hume finally did include a chapter on miracles in his later *Enquiry Concerning Human Understanding*. Maybe he thought that, in the end, it would be strange if a philosopher who professed to be a radical empiricist were to say nothing at all about possible empirical evidence of God's existence or actions. It was one thing for Hume to reject rationalistic arguments for God's existence, such as those of Anselm and Descartes. He might also reject Locke's rather speculative "first-cause" line of argument. But there were some Christians who claimed that God had become involved in some day-to-day affairs in the world-within the historical past, or even in Hume's own lifetime. They maintained that God was not a sort of absentee landlord of the world, whose existence must be proved by convoluted lines of reasoning. Instead, they said, God's hand was pretty clearly evident in certain special events that were "empirical." That is, these events were open to sense perception, so they could be experienced by ordinary human beings in ordinary ways. And the records of such events would be transmitted by ordinary historical methods; that is, by oral or written testimony. These special events were miracles, such as the miracles of Jesus and especially his resurrection. There was therefore, according to some of these Christians, a substantial body of empirical evidence supporting the truth of Christianity. Must not a philosopher of empiricism pay some attention to it? Hume finally did.

Even as Hume wrote his chapter, however, he may still have been a little uneasy. He was unusually cautious. The official conclusion of his argument was, "Therefore we may establish it as a maxim, that no human testimony can have such force as to prove a miracle, and make it a just foundation for any such system of religion."[1] And he immediately emphasized the limited scope of this conclusion by adding,

> I beg the limitations here made may be remarked, when I say, that a miracle can never be proved, so as to be the foundation of a system of religion. For I own, that otherwise, there may possibly be miracles, or violations of the usual course of nature, of such a kind as to admit of proof from human testimony.[2]

Notice how little Hume claimed here to show about miracles. He did not say that miracles could not happen, or that they did not happen. He didn't say that people could not know about miracles, or that miracles could not be the foundation of a religion. He claimed only that *testimony* could not be sufficient to establish a miracle and make it a foundation of a religion. And that was really a very restricted conclusion.

We cannot go into all of the restrictions here, but we should take special notice of one. There could not be any sincere testimonial evidence for a miracle, even if it was mistaken, unless there were someone who believed that he or she had a different kind of evidence. A sincere testimony would be given only by a person who believed that he or she had *seen* one of these striking events. But being an eyewitness of an event was not the same as hearing someone's testimony about it. In fact, there could not even be a *lying* testimony unless there were someone who *claimed* to be an eyewitness. It looked, therefore, as though testimonial evidence depended, in the end, on another kind of evidence—the evidence of someone's own senses. And this fact could hardly have escaped Hume.

In his whole argument about miracles, however, Hume had nothing at all to say to a person who saw, or thought that he or she saw, a miracle. He did not say whether such a person could know that a miracle had occurred, whether a miracle could be the foundation of his or her religious faith, and so on. And that is very curious.

You might guess that Hume thought that all of the claimed miracles were in the distant past, so that his readers would have nothing but testimonies to go on. Maybe that is part of the explanation, but something that Hume said casts a great deal of doubt on it. I will come back to that later.

Why can't testimony establish a miracle? Hume made a special point of saying that there is hardly anything that is more useful to human life and thought than the evidence of testimony. Hume himself was a writer of history ("David Hume, the historian," he is called in the card catalogue of the British Museum Library), and he relied almost entirely on testimony in his historical work. Why should testimony fail when it came to miracles?

Hume's main argument on this point takes up most of the chapter. The gist of it is captured in this passage:

> When anyone tells me, that he saw a dead man restored to life, I immediately consider with myself, whether it be more probable, that this person should either deceive or

be deceived, or that the fact, which he relates, should really have happened. I weigh the one miracle against the other; and according to the superiority, which I discover, I pronounce my decision, and always reject the greater miracle. If the falsehood of his testimony would be more miraculous, than the event which he relates; then, and not till then, can he pretend to command my belief or opinion.[3]

This is an argument based on probabilities. Hume thought that we ought always to believe, if we believe at all, whatever was more probable on our evidence. (Maybe that is something like advising someone always to bet, if he or she bets at all, on whatever horse is most likely to win, based on past records, and so forth. In fact, that is a rather poor strategy for someone who wants to make money at the racetrack. But that is another story.) And, as the case says, Hume thought that it was always more probable that a testifier was lying or mistaken than that such a bizarre event as a miracle really happened. So we should always believe one of those explanations of the testimony rather than believing that the testimony is true.

But why should we think that the probabilities always come out that way? On this point Hume, true to his empiricist theory, wanted to(rely on experience. It is a "commonplace," he said, that people lie or are mistaken. So presumably the probability of any particular testimony's being false was not terribly low. On the other hand, Hume said, there must be a very large body of experience in support of any known law of nature. A miracle was defined as a violation of a law of nature. It must, therefore, be very, very unlikely. And consequently the probability of the testimony's being false must always be much greater than the probability that the miracle happened.

To many people, this argument may seem initially plausible. But it may be, as C. S. Peirce suggested, "based upon a misunderstanding of the doctrine of probabilities."[4] That there is something phony about it is suggested by the following sort of observation. We may sometime read in the newspaper an account of a bridge tournament. And the story may describe the play of one of the more interesting hands, beginning by telling us what cards each player was dealt. But in fact the probability that any player will actually be dealt any specified set of thirteen cards is very, very low. No matter what thirteen cards are mentioned, there is only one chance in many, many millions that exactly that hand will come up on any particular deal. When four bridge players around a table pick up their cards they are looking at a distribution that is so unlikely that it may well never have been dealt before in the whole history of bridge playing.

What we have in the newspaper, however, is just some reporter's testimony that these hands were dealt. If we applied Hume's procedure, it would turn out to be absurd to believe the news story. We would say that it is much more probable that a reporter be mistaken or lying than that such a fantastically improbable set of cards should actually be dealt.

Furthermore, there isn't anything special about the card game. Almost any event we read about in the paper, or in a history book, or that we hear about from our friends—that exactly that event should happen is very, very improbable. So Hume's procedure, if we followed it consistently, would allow us to believe practially nothing on the basis of testimony. And that seems to be very odd. Neither we nor Hume seem willing to go anywhere like that far with it.

Well, what has gone wrong? Here we should notice a very important fact about philosophical procedure. Hume has proposed a sophisticated theory about how we should evaluate testimony. But how can we evaluate Hume's theory itself? We have seen that Hume's procedure seems to bar us from accepting a miracle on the basis of testimony. But it turns out that there is nothing special about miracles in this regard. His procedure would also prevent our accepting the testimonial account of any ordinary event—a card game, for example. But we already know—do we not?—that such a result is absurd. Consequently we can judge that there is something wrong with Hume's theory.

Notice that we can know that there is *something* wrong with the theory even if we do not know exactly *what* is wrong. There is nothing special about that sort of situation. Many people know that they are sick even if they do not know what illness they have. I can know that my car will not start even if I do not know just what keeps it from starting. We need not be embarrassed in saying, sometimes, that we know a philosophical view to be wrong even if we have not figured out just what is wrong with it.

Can we say anything more about Hume's procedure? Maybe. Just what does our experience tell us, after all, about the probability of miracles? I have experienced a small sample of the enormous set of events that make up the history of the world. Suppose that my experience is "uniform," as Hume says. That is, no event in my sample is a miracle. Does that show that it is very unlikely that there are any miracles in the world? Not at all. My sample is far too small to support any such probability judgment. Even if I add the experiences of my friends the sample remains too small. I could expand the sample greatly by including the experience of people generally, but the only way I can know what their experience has been is by way of their testimony. And, unfortunately for Hume's procedure, the history of the world includes many testimonies about the occurrence of miracles. It would be totally arbitrary to exclude such testimonies when we are trying to set up a basis for evaluating testimonies.

It looks, therefore, as though I do not have a basis in experience for thinking that it is unlikely that there have been any miracles.

But surely there is *something* improbable about miracles? Yes. If my experience has included no miracles then it seems reasonable to suppose that miracles are not commonplace, that most events are not miracles, and so on. So it is improbable that the next event I see, or any arbitrarily selected event, will be a miracle. And that seems right. So my experience seems to suggest that some claims about miracles, but not all of them, are improbable. It is important to keep that distinction in mind.

Now, what about testimony? I have much experience of lies and mistakes, of course, so something about them is not terribly improbable. But what about the actual bridge story in the newspaper? What is the probability that, if the reporter were lying or mistaken, he would have told exactly this story which is actually here? That probability is fantastically small, only one in many millions. For, if the reporter were lying, this particular distribution of cards is only one of many millions that he could have chosen. And that will generally be the case. For any reasonably detailed piece of testimony, it will be fantastically improbable that exactly that testimony would be given as a mistake or a lie. There will always be a vast number of other ways in which the mistake or lie could have come out.

I suspect that this fact explains why we often believe the newspaper story about the bridge game, and why it is reasonable to do so. It is, of course, very unlikely that anyone would get exactly those cards. But it is also very unlikely that a lying or mistaken reporter would report exactly that hand. These improbabilities are of the same order of magnitude, and so we make our judgment—to believe or not—largely on other grounds.

In the case of miracles, Hume invites us to compare the probability of a generality (people lie or are mistaken) with that of a specific event (such and such a miracle occurred). Those probabilities are indeed much different from one another. But that is irrelevant. We need to compare the probability of claims of the same specificity. But our experience, as we have seen, gives us no reason to think that the probability of the generality, "there are some miracles in the history of the world," is low. So, if we compare generality with generality, there is no reason to suppose that miracles must always come out on the short end.

Suppose, on the other hand, we focus on some very specific miracle claim. In such a case, it will indeed be antecedently improbable—improbable, that is, before we collect any evidence about it—that just such an event actually occurred. But it will often also be antecedently improbable—with roughly the same improbability—that just that story would be told as a mistake or a lie. And so here again this comparison of probabilities will not serve to settle the question for us. We will have to bring in something else.

My own judgment, therefore, is that there is something correct in Hume's procedure, but that he goes wrong in inviting us to compare the wrong probabilities. When we get that straightened out, we have no reason to suppose that the comparison must always be unfavorable to the miracle. Sometimes it may be, but sometimes it will be the other way around.

Several times I have mentioned bringing in other factors when trying to decide about a miracle story. Of course we do that, and rightly so. There are many such factors, too many even to start on here, and some of them are extremely subtle and hard to describe. Hume recognized that there were such factors, and in a secondary argument he claimed that miracle stories always failed in these respects also. He said, for example (but of course you should read his own statement of it), that such stories always originated in "barbarous and ignorant nations,"[5] that they are never attested to "by a sufficient number of men, of such unquestioned good-sense, education, and learning,"[6] that such events never happen in our own times, and so on.

Well, those things, if true, would seem to be relevant. Just what force they should have would be, perhaps, a matter of subtle judgment, but they certainly seem like relevant sorts of consideration. But there is a very curious question

about just how seriously Hume took them, and indeed, of what really lies behind his own rejection of miracles. Hume says that all miracle stories fail to satisfy these requirements. But in this very same chapter he goes on to report some
miracle accounts from France, accounts originating in his own lifetime. These
miracles, he says, were "proved upon the spot, before judges of unquestioned integrity."[7] They were "attested by witnesses of credit and distinction."[8] They
originated in "a learned age"[9] (his own, naturally!) and in a cultured and eminent nation. Learned and resourceful investigators completely failed to refute
them. And so on.

Well, that would seem to be a pretty strong case, wouldn't it? Maybe one
would expect an empiricist to accept it, or at least to allow it as a live possibility.
But no. Hume flatly rejected these alleged miracles. Why? I will leave you to
read his reason for yourself, and to reflect about what that reason may tell us
about the way in which Hume is actually proceeding.

NOTES

1. David Hume, *An Enquiry Concerning the Human Understanding*, ed. L. A. Seby-Bigge (Oxford, England: Clarendon Press, 1902), p. 127.
2. Ibid.
3. Ibid., p. 116.
4. Charles Sanders Peirce, *Collected Papers of Charles Sanders Peirce*, ed. Charles Hartshorne and
   Paul Weiss (Cambridge, Mass.: Harvard University Press, 1935), 6.512.
5. *Enquiry*, p. 119.
6. Ibid., p. 116.
7. Ibid., p. 124.
8. Ibid.
9. Ibid.

CHAPTER 7

The Case of Kant

Can We Think About Reality Beyond Our Own Experience?

IMMANUEL KANT felt that he was near the end of what had been a quiet life. He read the edict once more before making his reply. For over seventy years, he had lived in Königsberg, Prussia, developing his philosophy under the approving eye of Frederick the Great. Now, in 1794, eight years after Frederick's religiously orthodox nephew had succeeded to the throne, the aging Kant was being censored for his religious beliefs. Did his philosophy provide a new and adequate basis for thinking and talking about God? How could he defend his innovative theory of knowledge without attacking the religious powers? What kind of response could he make that would bring out his philosophy without further offending the authorities? Slowly he began to pen his painful reply.

Kant's Early Life

Kant was born in 1724 of poor parents in the university town of Königsberg. His parents belonged to the pietist movement, which stressed both the personal aspects of religion and high moral standards. It was through his mother's favorite preacher that the young Immanuel was able to begin his studies. This man was both a professor at the university and the director of a local high school, to which Kant was admitted at the age of eight. There he received a pietistic education with solid training in the classics. Kant studied there until at the age of sixteen he was admitted to the university.

At the university, Kant entered the department of philosophy. He was influenced greatly by a professor, Martin Knutzen, who introduced Kant to mathematics and Newtonian physics. Under the influence of Knutzen, Kant developed a great interest in the philosophy of Christian Wolff, an extreme rationalist who followed Descartes and Leibniz.

Kant heard lectures for some years at the university. Following this, he spent a few years tutoring in the Königsberg area.

In 1755, Kant returned to the university as an instructor. He continued in this position for fifteen years becoming very popular not only with students, but also with men of high rank. During his early years as a lecturer, Kant's interest was primarily in the external world. Along with his lectures on logic, metaphysics, and mathematics, he dealt especially with physics. He initiated the first lectures on physical geography at the university. In 1755, he published a work called *Universal History of Nature and Theory of the Heavens,* in which he attempted to explain the structure of the universe exclusively on the basis of Newtonian physics. In this system, there was absolutely no need for the intervention of God. Kant felt that true religion had no interest in limiting mechanical explanations of the universe.

During the 1860s, Kant's interests began to shift toward the inner world of human beings and their moral nature, as was the general movement of the time. He began to move away from the mathematical orientation of such thinkers as Descartes and became acquainted with the writings of Hume. Hume's writings presented a challenge to the whole rationalist approach. This challenge forced Kant to rethink much of his philosophy. He later declared that Hume's writings had awakened him from his dogmatic slumbers. The writings of Rousseau also had a profound influence on Kant. While Hume provided a challenge to Kant, Rousseau gave him a new direction. From this French thinker, Kant developed a new valuation of knowledge: the primacy of the moral over the intellectual. Moral reflection came to replace metaphysical speculation as primary in Kant's thinking.

In 1770, Kant received the professorship in logic and metaphysics at Königsberg he had so long desired. One major factor in his appointment was the high esteem in which many prominent officials held him. Another important consideration was that many of the current professors were being replaced because they would not cooperate with the government. In his inaugural address, entitled *Dissertation on the Form and Principles of Sensible and Intelligible Worlds,* Kant revealed his intention to reconstruct philosophy. This intention was fulfilled in 1781 with the publication of his *Critique of Pure Reason.*

Kant's *Critique of Pure Reason*

In the *Critique of Pure Reason,* Kant elaborated his basic theory of knowledge. He presented the mind as active in knowing, as asking specific questions of accumulated data and demanding specific answers. The mind was not merely a blank tablet on which data was deposited. Knowledge involved both the mind of the knower and the object known. Using this model, Kant argued that the mind had fixed laws according to which it organized data just as science had theories according to which it organized its data.

Kant concurred with the British empiricists, Locke and Hume, that sensation was the source of these data. However, Hume had taken the argument to the extreme by holding that it was unnecessary to assume sensation to be anything but a state of mind, a tingle in the brain. This led Hume to deny the necessity of a world external to the mind. Kant rejected this conclusion, holding that it was absurd to think there could be an appearance without there being something that appeared. Kant held that there was a world outside experience that was made up of "things-in-themselves." These "things-in-themselves" were the "noumenal" world and gave rise to the things that were in the world of experience, called the "phenomenal world." For example, the color, texture, and shape of a chair could be experienced, but the "essence" of a chair could not. The experienced characteristics of the chair belonged to the phenomenal world, while the essence (or "being") belonged to the noumenal world. Still, although there was a noumenal world, it was beyond the world of experience and so could not be known by the reason. People were limited by their reason to the phenomenal world—that is, to experience.

With the rationalists (Descartes, Spinoza, Leibniz), Kant agreed that concepts were formed by the mind. Sensations, taken by themselves, could not lead to concepts. The mind had to play an active role in developing concepts. But, whereas the rationalists had held that knowledge could be found apart from sensations, Kant held that knowledge resulted from a combination of mind and sensation. Sensations, apart from the concept-forming mind, were meaningless and chaotic. The mind, apart from data-providing sensations, was ignorant and blind. Using Aristotle's terminology, the "matter" of knowledge came from the senses, as the empiricists claimed. The "form" of knowledge came from the understanding—which was similar to the positions of the rationalists.

Kant felt that he had performed a Copernican revolution in philosophy. Copernicus had rejected the notion that heavenly bodies revolved around earthly observers of them, and instead "made the spectator to revolve and the stars to remain at rest."[1] Kant's revolution reversed the relationship between human knowledge and its objects. Kant declared,

> Hitherto it has been assumed that all our knowledge must conform to objects. . . . We must therefore make trial whether we may not have more success in tasks of metaphysics, if we suppose that objects conform to our knowledge.[2]

Certain factors, structures, or elements within the human mind imposed ordered relationships on the world of sense experience, according to Kant. Nature was, by definition, a system of objects manifesting an order on which predictions could be based. For Kant, then, there was the possibility of the human understanding "prescribing laws to nature, and even of making nature possible."[3] The factors within the mind that imposed meaningful order on the world external to the human knower, for Kant, were three: the forms of intuition, the categories of the understanding, and the ideas of reason.

The Forms of Intuition

In all knowledge that one could have about the phenomenal world, there were three factors that had to be considered. In the first place, everything that occurred in the phenomenal world occurred in space and time. All people apprehended (or experienced) whatever occurred to them as being ordered in space and time. All people thought and spoke in these categories: "This house is to the left of that tree;" "Karl went to the store after Fritz came home."

All people experienced what they considered to be objects outside themselves. Kant said, "By means of outer sense, a property of our mind, we represent to ourselves objects as outside us, and all without exception in space."[4] This space was not some real thing. It "does not represent any property of things in themselves."[5] Neither was space an empirical concept derived from experience. Instead, it was the precondition for experiencing anything as outer. In short, it was simply a form of intuition: one of the ways the mind worked.

Similarly, all people experienced what they considered to be the succession of one idea following another or one event following another. All experience, whether of external objects or of inner states seemed to take place in time. Kant stated,

> Time is the formal *a priori* (or necessary) condition of all appearances whatsoever. Space, as the pure form of all *outer* intuition, is so far limited; it serves as the *a priori* condition only of outer appearances. But since all representations, whether they have for their objects outer things or not, belong, in themselves, as determinations of the mind, to our inner state.[6]

Like space, time was neither some real thing nor some empirical concept derived from experience. It was simply another form of intuition. Space and time were the preconditions for a person ever experiencing anything.

The Categories of the Understanding

A second factor in gaining knowledge was the unifying activity of the mind. Everything that was perceived by the mind was organized according to certain categories into concepts. Through the senses, the mind received intuitions that were spontaneously acted upon by the categories. This yielded understanding of the intuitions as concepts. Kant claimed that by carefully analyzing the basic level of knowledge he discovered that there were twelve categories. Two of these categories were those of substance and cause.

Kant believed that one never had an experience of substance or cause. Rather, those were structures of the mind that brought together sensations. Kant did not believe that the categories were God-given nor innate ideas. In the case of substance, for example, he replaced the innate idea of something enduring beyond sense experience with an empirical relation: endurance through time. A substance was a collection of sensations that were experienced as permanent and unified.

Hume had denied that there could ever be a necessary cause-and-effect relationship between two things. People talked about such a relationship because they observed one thing following another often enough to expect a connection. When people saw one billiard ball's movement followed by another ball's movement often enough, they assumed that there was a necessary causal relation.

Kant agreed that the cause-and-effect relation did not arise from experience. Agreeing with Hume that no one ever had a sensation of a cause-and-effect relation, he concluded that the relation was supplied by the understanding.

According to Kant, there were two ways in which one sensation (or impression, using Hume's terminology) followed another. In the first case, there were those times when Sensation B followed Sensation A because the mind's attention had been turned from A to B. In this case, the mind could have done otherwise. Using Kant's example, this was similar to a person looking at a house from top to bottom. He or she received a series of sensations that followed one another, but were not causally related. The person could just as easily have looked from bottom to top or from side to side. On the other hand, there were times when the order of sensations was fixed and independent of any given mind. Using the example of the house, one had to begin at the bottom in building a house. In this kind of case, there was a necessary connection between one sensation and another. This connection was supplied by the category of cause.

The Ideas of Reason

The third group of factors within the mind that imposed meaningful order on the world external to the human knower Kant called the *ideas of reason.* Kant held that these were the three unifying, guiding ideals of complete knowledge. These three were (1) "The absolute unity of the thinking subject" (the soul or the mind), (2) "The absolute unity of the series of conditions of appearance" (the world), and (3) "The absolute unity of the condition of all objects of thought in general" (God).[7]

For Kant, as for Hume, none of these three ideas were really part of experience. No one ever had an experience of his or her own soul, the world (that is, the noumenal world), or God. Hence, no one could ever have knowledge of these things. But these ideas were important as guides to knowledge. These ideas did not give information—only the senses gave information. But they directed the investigation of objects. Knowledge was always of appearances, the phenomenal world—not of things-in-themselves. But without the ideas of a soul, a world, and a God, there would be no way to organize knowledge. These three ideas were useful tools rather than actual things existing beyond the world of experience.

So all one could know for sure was his or her own mental states. Although there had to be something beyond these mental states, one could never know what it was. Hence, knowledge about the soul, the world, and God was impossible. Neither from sense experience nor from reason could one gain knowledge of what really is. The ideas of reason were important as a regulative force. They gave direction to the search for knowledge and limited the reason itself to the phenomenal or empirical world. Kant asserted,

> It is thus evident that reason has here no other purpose than to prescribe its own formal rule for the extension of its empirical employment, and not any extension *beyond all limits of empirical employment.*[8]

For Kant, these great ideals (self, world, and God) gave meaningful unity to human experience and stimulated the pursuit of knowledge. Metaphysics, the search for knowledge of reality as a whole, could never be a science but remained a disposition of the human mind. The ideas of reason did not describe realities in the phenomenal world but pointed beyond themselves to possibilities in the noumenal world where science could not reach. Reason thus gave certain knowledge—but only of appearances in the phenomenal world of sensation. To gain knowledge of realities in the noumenal world of ideas and things-in-themselves, Kant sought another avenue—not the pure reason, but the practical reason.

Kant's *Critique of Practical Reason*

Kant wrote a second extensive critique called the *Critique of Practical Reason*. It was designed to ensure objectivity in the area of moral judgments and moral behavior despite the limited and relative character of science. Kant contended that moral action was demanded by the very nature of rational human beings. Morality, for Kant, was a categorical imperative. An act was good only if one behaved according to a built-in moral law rather than because such an act would benefit the doer. Kant stated the command of this inner moral law in two formulations:

> Act only on that maxim whereby thou canst at the same time will that it should become a universal law. [And,] so act as to treat humanity, whether in thine own person, or in that of any other, in every case as an end withal, never as means only.[9]

Because, according to Kant, this moral law was present within all rational beings he felt justified in drawing certain conclusions about human beings and reality in the noumenal world. First of all, humans were free. Kant reasoned that if people felt obligated to obey the moral law within them then they had to be able to do so. Thus, people had free will. Human beings were citizens of two worlds, in Kant's view. As a part of the phenomenal (appearance) world, a human was subject to causal laws. But as a member of the noumenal (thing-in-itself) world a human enjoyed freedom. In the phenomenal world persons were objects. In the noumenal world, humans were subjects, imposing laws on themselves.

Kant drew a second conclusion from his awareness of the moral law within people. Humans were immortal. The moral law demanded perfection. So perfection had to be within human power. Yet people were not perfect in this world. Thus humans had to live on beyond this life in order to have further opportunity to advance toward the goal of perfection.

Finally, Kant postulated that God must exist. Humans desired that obedience to the inner moral law be accompanied by happiness. But happiness belonged to the (phenomenal) realm of what was while duty operated only in the (noumenal) realm of what ought to be. Kant held that it was a rational faith to believe that God existed who brought the two realms together and united obedience to the moral law with happiness.

Kant's Moral Religion

Kant had remained a pious person throughout his life. For him, this piety was not inconsistent with his attack on the traditional empirical or rational arguments for the existence of God. Kant pointed to flaws in the evidence or logic of each of the arguments for God's existence. But he ultimately rejected empirical or rational proofs for God because they were applicable only to objects in the phenomenal world of time and space. God by definition was not an object in time and space. Arguments therefore could neither prove nor disprove God's existence. God transcended the phenomenal realm to which empirical and rational demonstrations applied.

Kant felt that he had not threatened religion. He had only placed it on a more firm foundation, that of morality.

> Morality thus leads ineluctably to religion, through which it extends itself to the idea of a powerful moral lawgiver, outside of mankind, for Whose will that is the final end of creation which at the same time can and ought to be man's final end.[10]

Far from being an enemy of religion, as some apparently thought him, Kant felt that he had done the cause of religion a service. He had shown that one could not make vital affirmations such as the reality of God, freedom, and immortality on the basis of scientific (pure) reason. Only in the realm of duty, that of the practical reason, could these values be found. Kant expressed his intellectual and religious choice unambiguously: "I have therefore found it necessary to deny *knowledge,* in order to make room for faith."[11]

The Edict

Kant had feared that the edict would come. Publication of *Religion Within the Limits of Reason Alone* had been opposed by the authorities, but it contained the results of his life's work. Did it offer a different but viable way of thinking and speaking about God? How could he deny the logical conclusions of his own theory of knowledge? Was it possible still to hold to the orthodox theology of his day without denying his theories? What effect would all of this have on his quiet way of life? It was time to make a response.

NOTES

1. Immanuel Kant, *Critique of Pure Reason,* trans. Norman Kemp Smith (New York: St. Martin's Press, 1929), p. 22.
2. Ibid.
3. Ibid., p. 170.
4. Ibid., p. 67.
5. Ibid., p. 71.
6. Ibid., p. 77.

7. Ibid., p. 323.
8. Ibid., p. 560.
9. Immanuel Kant, *Fundamental Principles of the Metaphysic of Morals,* trans. T. K. Abbott (New York: Longmans, Green, 1909), cited in Robert F. Davidson, ed., *The Search for Meaning in Life: Readings in Philosophy* (New York: Holt, Rinehart and Winston, 1962), pp. 309, 311.
10. Immanuel Kant, *Religion Within the Limits of Reason Alone,* trans. Theodore M. Greene and Hoyt H. Hudson (New York: Harper & Row, 1960), pp. 5–6.
11. Kant, *Critique of Pure Reason,* p. 29.

BIBLIOGRAPHY

Primary Sources

Kant, Immanuel. *Critique of Pure Reason.* Translated by Norman Kemp Smith. New York: St. Martin's Press, 1929.
Kant, Immanuel. *Religion Within the Limits of Reason Alone.* Translated by Theodore M. Green and Hoyt H. Hudson. New York: Harper & Row, 1960.

Biography

Paulson, Friedrich. *Immanuel Kant: His Life and Doctrine.* Translated by J. E. Creighton and Albert LeFerre. New York: Ungar, 1963.

Interpretative Works

Ewing, A. C. *A Short Commentary on Kant's Critique of Pure Reason.* London: Methuen, 1950.
Hendel, Charles W., ed. *The Philosophy of Kant and Our Modern World.* New York: Liberal Arts Press, 1957.
Koerner, S. *Kant.* Baltimore: Penguin Books, 1955.
Smith, Norman Kemp. *A Commentary to Kant's Critique of Pure Reason.* London: Macmillan, 1930.

QUESTIONS FOR STUDY

1. Discuss the influences on Kant from the seventeenth-century rationalists and the eighteenth-century empiricists. How did he respond to these influences?

2. Illustrate and explain the factors present in the mind, according to Kant, that give meaningful shape to our sense data.
   a. The forms of intuition
   b. The categories of the understanding
   c. The ideas of reason

3. Argue, from Kant's perspective, against Anselm's ontological proof and Aquinas' cosmological proof for the existence of God. On what rational grounds did Kant find belief in God justified?

4. Define Kant's "categorical imperative." What are its implications for morality?

5. Describe the phenomenal and the noumenal worlds as Kant did. How was the human person related to each?

6. Debate the following proposition: "In our society today, Kant would be considered a conservative."

A Contemporary Response

ALVIN PLANTINGA

CAN WE really think and talk about God? Or is God so completely beyond our grasp, so far above us, that our concepts and ways of thinking simply do not apply? This is one important question we must ask in thinking about Kant and his contribution to philosophy. Kant's work has had an enormous impact on present-day thinking about God; probably no other single person (with the possible exception of God) has been as influential. I am sorry to say, however, that much of this influence has been harmful rather than helpful. Let me explain why.

Kant's most influential work was the *Critique of Pure Reason*. The details of this book are extremely hard to figure out, but the central idea goes as follows. Our categories and concepts—our ways of thinking about the world—apply only within the realm of experience. More specifically, they apply only to the phenomenal world, the world of appearance. This is the world we all live in—the world of tables and chairs, plants and animals, mountains and oceans, planets and stars.

And according to Kant, this world is, in an important sense, of our own making. The world of everyday experience—the phenomenal world—is one we ourselves have constructed out of the raw material of sensation. The activity of the *noumena,* or *things-in-themselves,* as Kant calls them, produce in us smells, feels, sights, and sounds—in a word, sense data. The mind then works on these data and somehow forms them into the objects of everyday experience. The mind combines and unifies the sense data coming from the outside; it imposes a kind of structure and organization on these raw sensations and sights and sounds, and in so doing it creates our phenomenal world of everyday objects.

Now how, exactly, does the mind manage to do a thing like that? Again, the details are thoroughly obscure. For our purposes, however, that does not matter; what is important to see is that the result of this formative and structuring activity is the world in which we live. So in an important sense we ourselves create that world.

Now obviously there are some enormous problems with Kant's thinking here. What he says, if we take him seriously and at face value, is that we ourselves create the world we live in. Houses and trees, planets and stars—the objects of everyday experience generally—these are created by our activity. But if so, they depend for their existence on us. If there had been no human beings, there would have been no mountains, or oceans, or forests—indeed, there would have been no earth, or sun, or stars. *Before* there were human beings, furthermore, there were no such things. And this is not easy to believe. According to contemporary science, the sun, moon, and stars, for example, all existed for enormously long periods before there were any human beings. If Kant is right, however, then there were not any such things as the sun, moon, and stars before human beings appeared on the scene—in fact there was no *scene* before human beings showed up. Furthermore, if some cataclysmic disaster should befall the human race, so that all human beings should go out of existence, then, in Kant's view, the sun and stars—indeed, the entire physical universe—would also disappear. And these things seem quite preposterous.

For present purposes, however, this Kantian scheme has an even more unhappy consequence. According to Kant, our concepts are something like rules the mind uses to "unify the manifold" as he put it. They are rules according to which sense data are combined and unified. But of course if that is so, then our concepts do not apply to what lies beyond experience—to the world of noumena, or things-in-themselves. Kant clearly thinks there *are* noumena or things-in-themselves, but he also says that our concepts do not apply to them. And if our concepts do not apply to them, then we cannot think about them, because thinking about something is a matter of applying concepts to that thing. But if we cannot think about a thing, obviously we cannot hold any beliefs about it. If our concepts do not apply to things-in-themselves, we cannot believe, for example, that there is *just one* thing-in-itself; for that would be to apply the concept *just-one* or *uniqueness* to the realm of things in themselves. On the other hand, we also cannot believe that there is more than one thing-in-itself—for that is to suppose that our concept *more-than-one* or *plurality* applies to the realm of things-in-themselves. You may think that makes the whole idea of things-in-themselves pretty unlikely; nonetheless this seems to be what Kant said.

For present purposes, however, it is extremely important to see the following point. If there are any noumena, or things-in-themselves, at all, then, clearly enough, God is among them. God, surely, is as ultimately real as anything could possibly be; if this distinction between noumena and phenomena (between things-in-themselves and things as they appear to us) is a real distinction, then God would surely fall on the noumenal side of the distinction. But then, if Kant is right, none of our concepts applies to God. And, if none of our concepts applies to God, we cannot so much as think or talk about God. We cannot form beliefs about God, because any belief we held about God would apply a concept to this one to whom our concepts do not apply. We could not, for example, believe that God is wise, or almighty, or the creator of the heavens and the earth, because to believe these things is to apply the concepts *wisdom, being almighty,* and *being the creator of the heavens and the earth* to God. In fact, if our concepts do not apply to God, then God wouldn't *be* wise, or almighty, or perfectly good, because if a being is wise, say, then our concept *wisdom* applies to it. If, therefore, our concepts do not apply to God, then our concepts of being loving, almighty, wise, creator, and redeemer do not apply to him, in which case he is not loving, almighty, wise, a creator, or a redeemer. If our concepts do not apply to God, then God will not have any of the properties Christians ascribe to this divine person. In fact, God will not have any of the properties for which we have concepts. God will not have such properties as self-identity or existence, these being properties for which we have concepts. The fact is God will not have any properties at all, because our concept of having at least one property does not apply to God. But how could there be such a thing? How could there be a being that did not exist, was not self-identical, and did not have any properties? Does this make even marginal sense?

I think not. It clearly makes no sense at all to say that there is such a being as God but that none of our concepts applies to God. We cannot coherently suppose that there is a being to which none of our concepts apply, because such a being would be neither wise nor nonwise, neither good nor nongood. Indeed, the concept of existence or "there-isness" would not apply to it, so that if there were such a being there would not be any such being. If we say God is such a being, our response to God should be incredulous puzzlement, rather than the Christian's reverence, awe, worship, trust, and gratitude. Why trust God, if the concept of being trustworthy does not apply? Why worship God, if God is not an adequate object of worship? In this view, the Christian life becomes a complete shambles. Of course, Kant also said other things that imply that some of our concepts *do* apply to God; that is part of his charm. But it is this agnostic, skeptical side of Kant's writings that has had the most influence. And about that side of his thought our verdict must be, I think, that Kant's detractors were right; his thought *is* inimical—deeply inimical—to religion, or any rate to any religion in which, as in Christianity, belief in God is essential.

Part Three

THE CONTEMPORARY CONTEXT

THE NINETEENTH century has been called the Age of Progress.[1] Although there were social upheavals—by 1848 there had been political uprisings in France, Germany, Austria, Italy, and Hungary—in general, people were optimistic. In England, especially, all was placid. Queen Victoria was on the throne. At midpoint in the century, in 1851, England held a Great Exhibition to display "the Works of Industry of All Nations." Its theme was "Progress." Inspired by the Queen's consort, Prince Albert, the exhibition was housed in a "Crystal Palace" of glass that enclosed nineteen acres of Hyde Park. The building itself illustrated the theme as one of the first examples of prefabrication and mass production. More than 6 million viewers passed through the exhibit hall to gaze at displays of raw materials, manufactured goods, and especially the great machines—locomotives, hydraulic presses, power looms.

At the beginning of the century, nearly two-thirds of all Europeans lived on farms. Sustenance came from the land. Tools were made by hand. Power came from wind and water and human effort. Travel was by horse or sail. By mid-century, machines were providing transport and power and manufacture. Population was shifting from the country to the city. The revolution that England celebrated in 1851 was the Industrial Revolution. Change, which had occurred so slowly for centuries, now suddenly accelerated. And it seemed all to the good.

Karl Marx sat in the British Museum Library researching and writing his critique of capitalism. And in Denmark Søren Kierkegaard deplored the conformity of most people to the dictates of the state and the church. But to most Victorians the future promised a continuity of progress.

Scientific Developments

Technological developments from 1851 until the outbreak of World War I in 1914 continued to change everyone's life-style. The telephone, the street light, the fountain pen, the box camera, and the wireless telegraph were all invented. Louis Pasteur, Joseph Lister, and the Curies were making discoveries that made surgery safer and more effective. Industrialists were perfecting ways to make steel, aluminum, and combustion engines as well as dynamite and machine guns. In 1903, Henry Ford established his first factory, and the Wright brothers made the first powered flight in an airplane.

Breakthroughs in scientific theory opened a new era in thought and application. In physics, Einstein introduced the special theory of relativity, and Max Planck formulated quantum mechanics. In mathematics, non-Euclidean approaches to geometry were being investigated, and attempts were made to found a universal algebra. Between 1910 and 1913, a three-volume work appeared, entitled *Principia Mathematica,* co-authored by Bertrand Russell and Alfred North Whitehead. It attempted to demonstrate that all mathematics could be deduced from a few principles of formal logic. It caused ferment in an area that had been fixed since Aristotle.

A scientific approach to the human and social sciences was blossoming in the second half of the nineteenth century. Sigmund Freud was born in 1856 and Emile Durkheim in 1858. Their names became synonymous with psychology and sociology. Anthropology as a systematic study of primitive human societies began. And archeologists unearthed evidence in Egypt, Crete, and Troy of the gradual emergence of civilization.

A positive attitude toward change was the new intellectual element in the nineteenth century. In 1867, British Prime Minister Benjamin Disraeli declared, "Change is inevitable. In a progressive country change is constant."[2] No idea was more responsible for that attitude than the theory of evolution. Charles Darwin published his *On the Origin of Species* in 1859. By the end of the century, nearly all scientists accepted some sort of evolutionary hypothesis. To some laypeople, the idea of evolution undermined the authority of the Bible and traditional morality. Others were more optimistic. They saw evolution as the guarantee of inevitable human progress. Developments in science, medicine, and technology gave powerful support to their conviction.

Philosophers of Progress

John Stuart Mill (1806–1873) was an influential philosopher in the English-speaking world during the nineteenth century. His social and political philosophy stressed the importance of individual freedom and the development of strong individual character. Mill was one of the first Englishmen to advocate the equality of women. Religiously, Mill concluded that skepticism was the proper religious attitude toward supernatural religion. But he maintained that it was appropriate to encourage religious hopes. He entertained the theory of a limited deity with whom humans could cooperate to bring about improvement in the world.

Other philosophers developed ideas of process and becoming. Herbert Spencer (1820–1903) popularized Darwin's views and applied them to society. Henri Bergson (1859–1941) wrote of a vital force that guided unceasing evolu-

tion and could be known by intuition and instinct. The poet William Words-
worth inspired people with a sense of humankind's continuity with nature.
These elements of empiricism and pragmatism were linked by the American
philosopher William James (1842–1910). John Dewey (1859–1952) continued
James's work and applied it especially to American education.

Twentieth-Century Disillusionment

The optimistic nineteenth century ended in 1914. During the next four
years, 30 nations, representing 1.4 billion people on six continents, were engaged in the most devastating conflict that humankind had ever seen. Science
and technology, which had symbolized the promise of inevitable progress, were
used to devise instruments of mass destruction. By the time of armistice in 1918,
10 million combatants were dead and another 20 million wounded. Another 10
million innocent lives were lost to disease and famine.

After a brief decade of economic recovery, humankind's faith in progress
was again stunned. The United States fell into an economic depression with the
collapse of the stock market in 1929. In the next few years, the depression
spread to the other industrialized nations of Europe. Factories shut down, banks
closed, and millions lost their jobs. Anxiety, hopelessness, and despair scarred
an entire generation.

In the bitter aftermath of war and depression, totalitarian movements arose
that regimented people and suppressed their individuality for the sake of achieving nationalistic dreams of conquest and expansion. Before the 1930s were over,
World War II had begun. This time, literally the whole world was involved.
Seventy million people fought in the war, and 30 million died, civilians as well
as soldiers. During the conflict, the Nazis attempted systematically to extermi-
nate Europe's Jewish population. Jews were herded into concentration camps,
where 6 million were murdered.

The conclusion of World War II marked the beginning of a new and more
ominous era—the Atomic Age. On August 6, 1945, an atomic bomb, secretly
prepared by European and American scientists, was dropped on Hiroshima, Ja-
pan. The single explosion was 2,000 times more powerful than any previous
bomb. It destroyed most of the city, killed 68,000 people, and left a radioactive
atmosphere that injured thousands more.

Existentialist Reaction

In the immediate aftermath of World War II, the dominant philosophy was
existentialism. It paralleled the earlier work of Kierkegaard, but it was decisively focused by the despair of a world in which all traditional cultural values
seemed to have collapsed. Jean-Paul Sartre (1905–1980) had worked in the
French underground movement resisting Nazism. He spoke for a generation
that believed that it had to order its own world and create its own values. A hu-

man being just existed and had to create its own essence. Sartre pessimistically proclaimed that a human being was "condemned to be free." He rejected God and anything that seemed to limit human freedom. For Sartre, "Hell is other people," and death was the final absurdity of existence.

Divisions After Kant

The major philosophical thinkers of the nineteenth and twentieth centuries responded to and exemplified the motifs of the cultures in which they lived. Philosophical trends, like cultural ones, exhibited the tension between (1) the rise of science and its attendant hope for human progress and (2) the perverse uses of science for destruction and the attendant human despair. The case studies of nineteenth- and twentieth-century philosophers that follow illustrate this dialectic tension.

Early in the nineteenth century the Kantian synthesis collapsed. Kant had combined elements of seventeenth-century rationalism and eighteenth-century empiricism. He had attempted to synthesize the felt reality of the free human spirit and the sensory evidence of the cause and effect controlled material world. Philosophers following Kant seized on one dimension of his synthesis and separated it from the other. We still struggle with the dichotomies between human values and scientific facts that were implicit in Kant and became explicit in the nineteenth and twentieth centuries. The problem of knowledge, epistemology, overshadowed all other concerns. Most philosophers felt that a comprehensive view of reality was impossible and contented themselves with a specialized focus on one problem or dimension of reality. Many rejected the possibility of metaphysics. Even Whitehead, who attempted philosophy on the grand scale, did so primarily from the premises of modern mathematics and physics.

The Nineteenth Century

Johann Gottlieb Fichte (1792–1814) rejected Kant's belief that things-in-themselves existed even though they were beyond the reach of human knowledge. For Fichte, only ideas were real. Human ideas and judgments were considered to be true if they formed a coherent system.

George Wilhelm Friedrich Hegel (1770–1831) sought to remove the restrictions that Kant had placed on reason. Hegel acknowledged that human understanding encountered apparent paradoxes. He boldly asserted, however, that reason could find a synthesis that would resolve the apparent contradictions between theses and their antitheses. His dialectical method enabled him to posit a continual progress of thought from a thesis to its antithesis to a new synthesis.

For Hegel, finally, only the whole was true. Ultimate reality was an "absolute spirit," or "mind," which came to expression through historical events. Extensions of the approach Hegel developed were classified as idealism.

Near the end of Hegel's career, and in the immediately ensuing years, his views became widely accepted. For right-wing Hegelians, the "absolute spirit" was realized in the state and church of their time and, of course, in Hegelian philosophy.

In Denmark, Søren Kierkegaard (1813–1855) reacted violently to what he considered an idolatrous conformity to merely human institutions and ideologies. Kierkegaard contended that the Christian story of God becoming a human being in Jesus Christ posed a paradox that human reason could never resolve. The infinite qualitative difference between God and humanity could never be absorbed into a higher synthesis.

For Kierkegaard, a person's own personal, subjective commitment alone was truth. Young Søren had been raised as the last child of an older-than-usual father. Søren had been initiated into intense introspection. He believed that his family suffered under a "curse." Kierkegaard could not live like others in conformity to society. He wished to be known only as "that individual." Kierkegaard sketched three differing attitudes toward life: the esthetic, which viewed life objectively, at a distance; the ethical, which lived life in conformity to rigid rules; and the existential, a life of passionate, subjective commitment. For Kierkegaard, only the existential approach to life lived in the risk of personal faith was authentically human. Thus, Kierkegaard laid the groundwork for subsequent philosophies of existentialism.

Another, different reaction to idealism was developed as dialectical materialism. Karl Marx (1818–1883) studied philosophy in Berlin five years after the death of Hegel. Marx fell in with a group of younger, left-wing Hegelians. They rejected the right-wing assumption that Hegel's thought represented the culmination of all thought and that the German state was the perfect form of institutional life. Rather, the left-wing Hegelians emphasized their master's concept of continuing dialectical development. This led these youthful radicals, including Marx, to espouse revolution in the church and state and rigorous transformation of traditional patterns of thought.

Because of his commitment to radical ideas and causes, Marx was a political refugee all of his life. He attempted to make a living as a journalist, but each newspaper and journal for which he worked was soon suppressed by the government. He was exiled from Germany, France, and Belgium and lived the last thirty years of his life in England. Marx was aided by his wife, Jenny, who shared his radical views. They lived in extreme poverty, which led to the early death of three of their children. Their financial support came primarily from gifts from Friedrich Engels, the son of a wealthy textile manufacturer. Together, Marx and Engels produced *The Communist Manifesto* in 1848.

Marx spent most of the last three decades of his life poring over economic data in the British Museum Library. His statistical and historical studies formed the basis for a massive analysis of capitalism, one volume of which was published in his lifetime. Marx did not view himself as a philosopher. He categorized his work as "scientific" research, free of philosophical, religious, or ethical speculations.

Karl Marx identified with the cause of the common laborer. He joined a British workingmen's association and served as a theoretician and propagandist for them. Marx's fundamental concept was a revolutionary one in philosophy. He declared: "The philosophers have only *interpreted* the world in various ways; the point is to *change* it."[3] This approach put *praxis,* active involvement in the struggle for justice, above theoretical thought. The fundamental reality was "labor," which common working people produced. Because of this, some people question whether Marx can be classed as a philosopher. Marx is usually identified as a dialectical materialist.

If the nineteenth century actually ended with the beginning of World War I in 1914, then William James (1842–1910) was a nineteenth-century person. His philosophy of pragmatism brought into singular focus another aspect of Kant's earlier synthesis; namely, the importance of the practical reason. James emphasized the freedom of human will and declared that truth was judged by its practical consequences. An idea was true if it made a difference in the world.

James graduated from Harvard Medical School in 1870. He soon returned to teach anatomy and physiology in 1873. By 1875, he was teaching psychology, and by 1879 he was lecturing in philosophy. For James, the progression was quite natural. He had always probed scientific questions for the more general, philosophical considerations that lay behind them.

In both psychology and philosophy, James was essentially self-taught. His wealthy father had reacted against his own earlier rigid indoctrination in religion and education by raising his children in a succession of schools so that they would continually question and think for themselves. William James's *Principles of Psychology* in 1890 established his reputation as an original mind. His later studies in religious phenomena and philosophy remain as an original, distinctively American, contribution. His pragmatic philosophy captured the optimistic, nineteenth-century spirit of a young nation in which all things seemed possible by the exertion of one's will.

The Twentieth Century

The two eminent twentieth-century philosophers whose cases we will study were both formed in a milieu that continued the nineteenth-century emphasis on scientific progress.

Alfred North Whitehead lived until nearly the middle of the twentieth century. He experienced two world wars, a great economic depression, and the development and destructive use of the atomic bomb. But throughout it all he never lost his faith in progress. Victor Lowe, one of Whitehead's students, and his biographer, concluded,

> The nineteenth century was a peaceful century, and sheltered the pursuit of thought. Whitehead was fifty-three years old at the beginning of the World War I. As a youth, he went to Cambridge during one of her great ages. Fortunate occasions arose, at various times for the exercise of his powers. . . . If it be also true that mathematics and metaphysics are naturally akin, then it is impossible to imagine a set of conditions more favorable for the creation of a philosophy. The man fitted the conditions perfectly. The philosophy of organism is the ultimate intellectual achievement of the nineteenth century.[4]

Whitehead's early training was in the British preparatory school tradition of Latin and Greek classics. After studying at Cambridge, he stayed on to teach mathematics for twenty-five years. At nearly fifty years of age, Whitehead suddenly moved to London where he studied and taught philosophy of science until near to retirement. At age sixty-two, Whitehead unexpectedly received an offer to teach philosophy at Harvard. Although Whitehead had never formally studied or taught philosophy, he became a professor in that field and during the next thirteen years did his most creative writing.

Whitehead's thought offers a dynamic and sometimes confusing blend of two dominant influences in his background: classical philosophy and contemporary science. Like the classical realists of Greece's Golden Age, Whitehead believed that there was a real world in which everything was interrelated and that the human task was to understand it. But the answers the Greeks had given in metaphysics and epistemology were no longer adequate. Modern science had changed the focus of philosophy. Reality was now understood not in terms of substances and essences. Reality in science was described in terms of relationships and processes. Physicists do not have to define what an atom is; they only need to understand how it acts. Psychologists no longer ask the question "What is a human?" The issues now are "How do humans behave?" and "How can they adjust to their environment?" Whitehead's philosophy took these changes of focus into account.

But in the end Whitehead was not a scientist, but a philosopher. The task of science is specialization and analysis. The task of philosophy is generalization and synthesis. "It follows that Philosophy is not a science," Whitehead declared.[5] Whitehead was a modern man, at home with the thought of Planck and Einstein. But Whitehead was also a classical metaphysician, equally comfortable with Plato and Aristotle.

Whitehead's process philosophy endeavored to unify all of human knowledge and experience. He attempted new ways to blend into organic relations traditional opposites: thought and feeling, spirit and matter, fact and value. His method was to understand these elements, not as essences but as relationships. In doing so, he took modern physics and philosophy since Kant with utter seriousness. A person perceiving was viewed as a natural organism both reacting to and a part of the environment being perceived. Whitehead repudiated the traditional dichotomies that had dominated from Aristotle to Hume: subject and predicate, substance and quality, particular and universal. For people trained to think in those terms, Whitehead is terribly difficult to understand. It remains to be seen whether future generations trained in new math, relativity physcis, and ecological biology will find Whitehead's way of thinking more comfortable to common sense.

Ludwig Wittgenstein was born into a wealthy family of brilliant, talented, and strong-willed parents and siblings. Two of Ludwig's elder brothers committed suicide when their father insisted that they follow him into the family steel industry rather than pursue artistic careers. Ludwig Wittgenstein thus was well acquainted with tragedy. Karl Wittgenstein, the father, died of cancer in 1913 when Ludwig was twenty-four years old. Another older brother committed suicide rather than be captured during World War I.

In his formal training, Wittgenstein pursued engineering. Informally, he read widely and was impressed with Kierkegaard and Tolstoy. Throughout his life, Wittgenstein felt the need for the personal purity and simplicity that Tolstoy advocated and lived with an intense individualism reminiscent of Kierkegaard.

Wittgenstein went to England to study aerodynamics. In 1911, he moved to Cambridge to study mathematics under Bertrand Russell. From math he moved to philosophy and was soon being treated as a peer by the Cambridge faculty.

Ludwig Wittgenstein became the founder of two, quite distinct schools of comtemporary philosophy: logical positivism and linguistic analysis. Both schools shared an antimetaphysical stance: philosophy is viewed as an activity, not a set of theories, the object of which is to remove confusions in our language.

After two years at Cambridge, Wittgenstein withdrew for a year to a remote cabin in Norway. In 1914, he enlisted in the Austrian army. The notebooks he kept while serving on the eastern front and in an Italian prison camp became his first book, *Tractatus Logico-Philosophicus*. The *Tractatus* declared that words are like pictures of things. When the referrents of these pictures are known and proper grammatical form is used, all problems are solved.

A group of philosophers of science called the Vienna Circle took up Wittgenstein's idea and developed them into the philosophy of logical positivism. They held that the only statements that could meaningfully be made were those which could be verified either by empirical science or by logic. All other statements, including metaphysical, religious, and ethical statements, were treated as nonsense.

After finishing the *Tractatus*, Wittgenstein felt that all of the essential philosophical questions had been answered. He gave away his inheritance and took a job teaching at a boy's school in an Austrian village. Listening to his students convinced Wittgenstein that ordinary human language was more complex than he previously had realized. In 1929, he returned to Cambridge where he was accepted as a faculty member on the basis of his *Tractatus*.

During the rest of his life, Wittgenstein lectured yearly at Cambridge, except for a period as a hospital orderly during World War II. He continually revised his former views but published only one article. His posthumously published volume *Philosophical Investigations* provided the basis for a new school of philosophy, linguistic analysis or "ordinary language philosophy."

The later Wittgenstein characterized language not as pictures, but as games. Wittgenstein felt that every statement had its own logic, which was established by listening to its use in ordinary language in a particular context, form of life, or language game. Metaphysical, religious, and ethical utterances were not nonsense. They were meaningful in the context of various forms of life that were not scientific or logical language games.

As he came to the end of his life, Wittgenstein was not satisfied that he had been successful in eliminating philosophical problems. He had, however, unintentionally fostered two vital and influential schools of contemporary philosophy.

Contemporary Philosophy and You

Three decades have passed since the deaths of Whitehead and Wittgenstein. Not only their thought, but also that of Kierkegaard, Marx, and James still have articulate and active adherents in the philosophical community. No other figures of their stature have yet risen to establish other alternate forms of doing philosophy in our time. Nor does any one school dominate philosophical reflection in North America at the moment. Part of the reality of our pluralistic era is that a variety of philosophical perspectives inform and energize theory and action in religion, politics, science, and the arts at present. Part of the benefit of studying the cases in our contemporary context will be a better understanding of the presuppositions that motivate contemporary movements. A further and even more valuable effect of interacting with these contemporary philosophers will be the stimulus to think for yourself, to propose alternate solutions to theirs, and to conceive of new questions that need to be asked.

NOTES

1. See, for example, C. S. Burchell et al, *Age of Progress*, Great Ages of Man (New York: Time-Life, 1966).
2. Richard L. Schoenwald, ed., *Nineteenth-Century Thought: The Discovery of Change* (Englewood Cliffs, N.J.: Prentice-Hall, 1965), p. 1.
3. Karl Marx, *Writings of the Young Marx on Philosophy and Society*, ed. and trans. L. Easton and K. Guddat (Garden City, N.J.: Doubleday, 1967), p. 402.
4. Victor Lowe, "The Development of Whitehead's Philosophy," in Paul Arthur Schilpp, ed., *The Philosophy of Alfred North Whitehead*, The Library of Living Philosophers, 2nd ed. (New York: Tudor, 1951), p. 124.
5. Alfred North Whitehead, "Mathematics and the Good," in Paul Arthur Schilpp, ed., *The Philosophy of Alfred North Whitehead*, The Library of Living Philosophers, 2nd ed. (New York: Tudor, 1951), p. 681.

CHAPTER 8

The Case of Kierkegaard

Must Love and Duty Conflict?

As EMIL BOESEN sat in the deserted restaurant, he reflected on the events of that evening in 1841. Søren Kierkegaard had met him at a theater in Copenhagen to inform him of his broken engagement with his fiancée. Was Kierkegaard really acting on the rationale he had worked out for breaking with Regine? Was he acting as a "knight of faith"? Or was he simply shackled to the past, the melancholy his father had inflicted on him? Could it be that, by giving up Regine, Kierkegaard thought that God would return her to him?

Nineteenth-Century Denmark

The first half of the nineteenth century in Denmark was a time of turmoil, reform, and nationalism. Denmark began the century with an absolute monarchy and a kingdom nearly large enough to rival major European powers. But by 1815, because of its collaboration with Napoleon, the country had been stripped of Norway as a possession. Denmark was thrown into a severe economic depression that lasted over a decade. Just as Denmark began to regain its economic strength, the nation's political life was threatened by the revolutions that took place in Germany in the 1830s. Aware of new forces that demanded a share in the government, King Frederick VI of Denmark and his successors responded with a series of practical reforms.

Denmark's catastrophic economic conditions and its altered political status following the Napoleonic Wars compelled the nation to discover a new source of spiritual strength. Neither orthodox Christianity nor the new rationalistic Deism seemed capable of providing a spiritual vision. Orthodox Christianity's historical reliability, apologetic value, and moral authority had been eroded by the Enlightenment. Deism, on the other hand, had been dealt a blow by the contentions of Hume and Kant that rationalistic proofs of God's existence were impossible. The deistic idea of a "watchmaker God" was collapsing.

Hegel

Denmark's intellectuals began to examine the new works of the German idealist, Georg Wilhelm Friedrich Hegel. Hegel was the foremost thinker in Germany at the time. His idealism proclaimed the existence of an objective truth (the Idea) that transcended and controlled the course of history. Hegel described the Idea as a dynamic force that moved history toward its conclusion through what he called a "dialectical development."

By "dialectical development," Hegel meant that there was a progressive manifestation of the Idea in history. This manifestation was progressive because the Idea was only partially manifested in any one historical period. Each partial manifestation of the Idea produced its own antithesis, or countermovement. This antithesis was a corrective thrust, which sought to overcome the deficiencies of the thesis, the original manifestation of the Idea. But this antithesis was also partial. Therefore it, too, had to be overcome. This movement, overcoming the inadequacies of the thesis and the antithesis, led to a synthesis, or the combination of what was strongest in the thesis and the antithesis. However, this new synthesis was also inadequate. Therefore it too had to be superseded. The synthesis became the new thesis, and a new antithesis and a new synthesis arose. This process Hegel called "dialectical development." Put into schematic form, "dialectical development" looked like this:

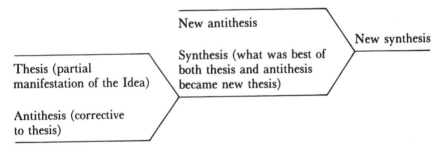

Thus Hegel saw an ongoing dialectical development in history in which each successive historical period was generated out of the tensions and shortcomings of the previous period. This movement would reach fulfillment only at the end of history.

According to Hegel, Christianity exemplified this process. Apostolic Christianity represented one stage in the expression of truth, while the heresies of the early church were the antithesis to that expression. The inadequacies of these two movements in turn gave rise to early medieval Catholicism, which was a synthesis of the partial truth contained in apostolic faith and the heresies of people like Marcion and Arius. Medieval Catholicism, in turn, became the new thesis. The Reformation became the new antithesis, and the Danish Lutheran Church was believed by many to be the new, and perhaps final, synthesis. Put schematically:

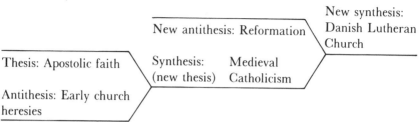

Hegel's theories had a special appeal for the church of Denmark. Hegelianism provided a sophisticated way of reconciling faith and reason. Hegel saw human reason as the self-manifestation of God actualizing his own essence throughout history. The bearers of this absolute Idea were nations and cultures, each of which constituted a necessary element in the Idea's progressive self-actualization. Because the Idea of God was thought to be actualized in the culture of nineteenth-century Denmark, the state church was believed to be the guardian and repository of true religion. To be faithful to the state and to the state church was to be faithful to God.

Kierkegaard's Early Life

Kierkegaard's father, Michael Pedersen Kierkegaard, was born in 1768. While still a young boy herding sheep as a serf in the bleak northern area of Jutland, Michael cursed God because of his wretched life. At age twenty-one, Michael was released from serfdom. With the help of an uncle, he became a cloth merchant in Copenhagen and soon became quite wealthy. At age twenty-six, he married the sister of a business associate, but she died after two years of marriage. Within the year, he married his wife's maid, Anne Lund, and five months later they had their first child. Five more children followed before Søren who was born in 1813, the child of middle-aged parents. By the time Søren was twenty-two, everyone in his family, save his father and one brother, had died.

Young Søren was raised in an atmosphere of deep personal faith and strong imagination coupled with anguish and melancholy. Michael Kierkegaard was committed to Moravian piety. The Moravians were a sectarian group that rejected the established religion and demanded a commitment beyond that of the state church. Michael was given to using his imagination to take young Søren on "trips of fantasy" while conversing with him in the family library. But coupled with this faith and imagination was a deep sense of anguish and personal guilt. Having cursed God as a boy and having slept with his deceased wife's maid before marrying her, he was convinced that God had damned him. As Søren's older brother, Peter, wrote of their father:

> The memory of this curse in his childhood never left the boy, the man, the patriarch—and seeing that God's grace from that very moment showered temporal bless-

ings upon him, so that instead of tasting the divine wrath he was overwhelmed with riches, marvellously gifted children, universal esteem—then solemn anxiousness and dread gripped his soul most deeply. God *did* exist, and *he* had cursed this God—was not this the sin against the Holy Ghost which never can be forgiven? It was for this reason the old man's soul continued in anxious dread, for this reason he beheld his children condemned to "the silent despair," for this reason he laid upon their shoulders in tender years the sternest requirements of Christianity—for this reason he was a prey to temptation and in constant conflict of soul.[1]

Søren Kierkegaard as a Young Man

Following the wishes of his father, Søren entered the university in 1831 and studied for a career in theology. But he soon lost all interest in a church vocation. As he wrote in his journal,

> In Christianity itself the contradictions are so great that, to say the least, they prevent a clear view. As you know, I grew up, so to speak, in orthodoxy, but as soon as I began to think for myself the tremendous colossus began to totter. . . . I am supposed to read for a theological degree, an occupation which does not interest me at all and so does not advance particularly quickly.[2]

His father and his older brother, Peter, who by this time was a respected Danish churchman, were disappointed and angered when they learned of Søren's change of interests. To make matters worse, Søren had begun to adopt the profligate life-style of a rich man's son. He frequented the fashionable theaters and cafes in Copenhagen and spent large amounts of money on clothes, liquor, and tobacco. Much of his time was spent in the company of a few friends who were part of Copenhagen's literary circles. He affected the life-style of a dilettante.

One night in 1836 Kierkegaard went out with some friends for a night on the town. He was in the habit of drinking quite a bit that year, and on this evening he became completely drunk. Seeing that he was in a drunken stupor, his friends drove him to a brothel in Copenhagen, where he awoke in bed the next morning. Precisely what happened late that night was a jealously guarded secret that Kierkegaard refused to divulge even to his journal. However, there were frequent references to guilt among the journal entries following this date, and they suggested the depth of his feelings.

The thought began to take shape in Søren Kierkegaard's mind that not only his father but his entire family lay under a divine curse. Because of his father's cursing of God, because of his own doubts about the Christian faith, because of his drunken night out, he concluded that perhaps he too was cursed by God. Despite his externally frivolous life-style, he became internally more and more serious. The thought of suicide was never far from his mind. A wry description entered in his journal in 1836 characterized this period of his life:

> I have just returned from a party of which I was the life and soul; wit poured from my lips, everyone laughed and admired me—but I went away—and the dash should be as long as the earth's orbit ————————————and wanted to shoot myself.[3]

Conversion

Against this background, Kierkegaard made an entry in his journal on May 19, 1838, that presented a startling contrast:

> *May 19.* Half-past ten in the morning. There is an indescribable joy which enkindles us as inexplicably as the apostle's outburst comes gratuitously: "Rejoice I say unto you, and again I say unto you rejoice"—Not a joy over this or that but the soul's mighty song "with tongue and mouth, from the bottom of the heart": "I rejoice through my joy, in, at, with, over, by, and with my joy"—a heavenly refrain, as it were, suddenly breaks off our other song; a joy which cools and refreshes us like a breath of wind, a wave of air, from the trade wind which blows from the plains of Mamre to the everlasting habitations.[4]

This entry marked the return of the prodigal. It was the most direct reference in all his writing to a conversion, but it was so cryptic that one could only guess at the nature of his experience. That this experience marked a turning point in his life, however, could not be doubted. Kierkegaard was reconciled to his father, who died shortly afterward. He then resumed his theological studies and completed them in 1839.

The Penitent

Kierkegaard's return to Christianity was marked by several important commitments. Certain ideas that he conceived during his "prodigal period" began to appear in his writing, and these ideas became the central points in his own psychological and intellectual development. The first point was Kierkegaard's conception of himself as a penitent. Certainly the doom that he believed lay over his family and the guilt feelings that he retained from his prodigal period contributed to this self-conception.

When Kierkegaard spoke of himself as a penitent, he was thinking primarily of one who could not live like people who went to church on Sunday and pursued the normal occupations of life the rest of the week. For him, to be a penitent was to renounce all claims on the world, to forget the possibility of living a normal life, and to be consumed by the task that God had set before him: to make people aware of true Christianity.

The Critic of Hegel

Kierkegaard also became committed to criticizing Hegel's philosophy and Hegel's influence on current Lutheran theology. Kierkegaard was very disconcerted by Hegel's system. In the first place, it failed to affirm the freedom of the individual. If each society, each period of history, was only one step in the progressive manifestation of the absolute Idea, then what was left for the individual? The individual was simply an insignificant part of a culture in which the Idea was partially manifested. Kierkegaard's contemporaries believed that to deviate from the latest historical expression of the Idea was not an act of freedom but an act of insanity, a flight from reason and truth.

Second, Kierkegaard objected that Hegel's system did not describe the world in which Kierkegaard lived. Although Hegel could look forward to the end of history when all the contradictions of history would be explained, Kierkegaard observed that the supposed end of history had little influence on the choices he had to make each day. It was one thing to affirm that all contradictions would be reconciled, all theses and antitheses joined into syntheses. It was another thing to live in a world that was full of contradictions and to have to make choices before the contradictions were resolved. Hegel's system, Kierkegaard maintained, was not very instructive for the business of living. Kierkegaard argued that the more one tried to become objective the more one lost touch with real life.

Then Kierkegaard conceived a thoroughly frightening idea. If it was true that at any one point in history one could not really know the truth—which was only to be revealed fully at the end of history—why should it be assumed that truth would be knowable or even desirable at the end? Suppose at the end of history the ultimate truth turned out to be ugly, cold, and merciless? There was nothing about the absolute Idea as Hegel conceived it that warranted people's affection and adoration.

Kierkegaard's fourth objection to Hegel was that his system was in fact antithetical to faith. When faith became natural and reasonable, it was in serious danger of ceasing to be faith. Kierkegaard expressed himself in a paragraph in his *Concluding Unscientific Postscript:*

> How strange is the way of the world! Once it was at the risk of his life that a man dared to profess himself a Christian; now it is to make oneself suspect to venture to doubt that one is a Christian. Especially when this doubt does not mean that the individual launches a violent attack against Christianity with a view to abolishing it; for in that case it would perhaps be admitted that there was something in it. But if a man were to say quite simply and unassumingly, that he was concerned for himself, lest perhaps he had no right to call himself a Christian, he would indeed not suffer persecution or be put to death, but he would be smothered in angry glances, and people would say: "How tiresome to make such a fuss about nothing at all; why can't he behave like the rest of us, who are all Christians? It is just as it is with F. F., who refuses to wear a hat on his head like others, but insists on dressing differently."[5]

The Opponent of a State Church

This last objection focused the third important theme that characterized Kierkegaard's newly discovered faith commitments. Kierkegaard objected to the entire concept of a state religion. Faith could become a completely external matter, completely lacking commitment, once Christianity became the official religion of the state. In an entry in his journal, Kierkegaard mused,

> Let us try a thought-experiment. If one could establish the fact that Christ had never existed, nor the Apostles either, that the whole thing was a poetical invention—in

case nothing was done on the part of the State or the congregations, no hint that they would suppress [the pastors] livings, I should like to see how many parsons would resign their posts.[6]

As Kierkegaard saw it, even the cows in Denmark deserved to be called Christian, because they had been born in a Christian country. So, Kierkegaard published a number of articles criticizing the Danish Lutheran Church for conspiring to produce faith without commitment.

Kierkegaard's Concept of Faith

In contrast to what he considered the sterile stance of the state church, Kierkegaard stressed the need for personal faith. First, faith had to be passionate. Kierkegaard deplored the idea that faith could be defined as the affirmation of an orthodox confession. Systematic theology held no interest for him. In his opinion the dominant Hegelian theological system actually undermined faith. The specific nature of Christian faith, as Kierkegaard understood it, was not determined by what it asked one to believe but by the act of faith it required of the believer.

Second, for Kierkegaard, this passion, faith, was a totally consuming one. It was not like the desire for pleasure, which could be turned off at will. It was like love, which seized a person, commanded his or her entire attention, and grew more consuming each day. Was this rational? Kierkegaard responded with an emphatic "No!" At the center of Christain faith was something that reason could not grasp—the incarnation. According to the Christian faith, the eternal God had become a limited, temporal creature. Being a Christian did not remove the paradox inherent in the incarnation. For Kierkegaard, faith was thus a passion rather than a process of thought because faith defied mere reason.

The Knight of Faith versus the Knight of Infinite Resignation

Kierkegaard illustrated this concept of faith in his work *Fear and Trembling*. In this work, the "knight of faith" was contrasted with the "knight of infinite resignation." The knight of infinite resignation was similar to the ancient Stoics or the more modern romantic heroes. He renounced everything in the world without any hope of getting it back. He completely gave up on the finite world and lived in the infinite. "The knights of infinite resignation are easily recognized; their gait is gliding and assured."[7] These were persons who could rise above the mundane world and seize life in its purest forms.

According to Kierkegaard, however, these knights of infinite resignation were not able to live in the finite world. In transcending the banal things of this world, they became strangers to the world. As he described them:

Whenever they fall down they are not able at once to assume the posture, they vacillate an instant, and this vacillation shows that after all they are strangers in the world. This is more or less strikingly evident in proportion to the art they possess, but even the most artistic knights cannot conceal this vacillation.[8]

In contrast to the knight of infinite resignation was the knight of faith. He, too,

> Has made and every instant is making the movements of infinity. With infinite resignation he has drained the cup of life's profound sadness, he knows the bliss of the infinite, he senses the pain of renouncing everything, the dearest things he possesses in the world, and yet finiteness tastes to him just as good as to one who never knew anything higher. . . . And yet, and yet the whole earthly form he exhibits is a new creation by virtue of the absurd. He resigned everything infinitely, and then he grasped everything again by virtue of the absurd. He constantly makes the movements of infinity, but he does this with such correctness and assurance that he constantly gets the finite out of it, and there is not a second when one has a notion of anything else.[9]

The knight of faith, then, gave up everything just as the knight of infinite resignation did. But "by virtue of the absurd" he believed that he would gain all that he had given up.[10] Believing this to be true, he continued to live in the finite. While the knight of infinite resignation was always "incommensurable" with everyday life, the knight of faith looked and acted "like a tax collector."[11] That is, the knight of faith looked and acted like anyone else.

In order better to explain the difference between the knight of infinite resignation and the knight of faith, Kierkegaard used two examples: Agamemnon and Abraham.

Agamemnon, the Knight of Infinite Resignation

Agamemnon, the Greek commander in the Trojan War, was becalmed at Aulis on the way to the battle at Troy. With the ship's provisions running low, Agamemnon was informed by a prophet that he had offended the gods, who were withholding the winds as a punishment. With the lives of his entire company at stake, he was told that the only way to appease the gods would be to sacrifice his daughter Iphigenia. Kierkegaard described Agamemnon's situation:

> When an undertaking in which a whole nation is concerned is hindered, when such an enterprise is brought to a standstill by the disfavor of heaven, when the angry deity sends a calm which mocks all efforts, when the seer performs his heavy task and proclaims that the deity demands a young maiden as a sacrifice—then will the father heroically make the sacrifice. He will magnanimously conceal his pain . . . yet soon the whole nation will be cognizant of his pain, but also cognizant of his exploit, that for the welfare of the whole he was willing to sacrifice her, his daughter, the lovely young maiden.[12]

Agamemnon was a tragic hero because he was caught between two conflicting ethical demands. He was Iphigenia's father, and he was the king of Mycenae. In this situation, he had to deny either his obligation to his daughter or his obligation to the state. He resolved the dilema by offering to sacrifice the individual for the greater good of the state. He resigned himself to the dictates of ethical reason.

Abraham, the Knight of Faith

Without his faith, his hope against hope, Abraham would simply have been, like Agamemnon, a figure of resigned obedience. Kierkegaard described the paradoxical nature of that faith:

> By faith Abraham received the promise that in his seed all the races of the world would be blessed. . . . Time passed, it became unreasonable, Abraham believed. . . . Then came the fulness of time. . . . Then there was joy in Abraham's house, when Sarah became a bride on the day of their golden wedding. But it was not to remain thus. . . . "And God tempted Abraham and said unto him, 'Take Issac, thine only son, whom thou lovest, and get thee into the land of Moriah, and offer him there for a burnt offering upon the mountain which I will show thee.' " So all was lost—more dreadfully than if it had never come to pass![13]

It looked as if God were only playing with Abraham. Having made the impossible take place, God would snatch Isaac away again. But in spite of the appearance,

> Abraham believed and did not doubt, he believed the preposterous. . . . And Abraham rose early in the morning. . . . He said nothing to Sarah, nothing to Eleazar. Indeed who could understand him? Had not the temptation by its very nature exacted of him an oath of silence? He cleft the wood, he bound Isaac, he lit the pyre, he drew the knife.[14]

Abraham's devotion to God had led him beyond the rational, beyond the limits of ethical reason:

> The ethical expression for what Abraham did is, that he would murder Isaac; the religious expression is, that he would sacrifice Isaac; but precisely in this contradiction consists the dread which can well make a man sleepless, and yet Abraham is not what he is without that dread.[15]

So Abraham was willing to sacrifice Isaac. But he was not simply resigned to killing Isaac, because he had faith:

> But what did Abraham do? . . . He mounted the ass, he rode slowly along the way. All that time he believed—he believed that God would not require Isaac of him, whereas he was willing nevertheless to sacrifice him if it was required. He believed by virtue of the absurd; for there could be no question of human calculation, and it was indeed the absurd that God who required it of him should the next instant recall the requirement. He climbed the mountain, even at the instant when the knife glittered he believed . . . that God would not require Isaac.[16]

Abraham's faith clung to the promise and to the impossible possibility that, having given up his loved one, he would nevertheless receive him back. Abraham believed that by "virtue of the absurd" he would get Isaac back.

Abraham differed from Agamemnon because he had faith, rather than Agamemnon's resignation. But there was another difference. Like Abraham, Agamemnon was called to sacrifice his child. But, unlike Abraham, Agamemnon's act remained within the boundaries of morality. His action was tragic but not immoral in his culture. But what higher principle was served by the sacrifice of Isaac? There was none. God was only testing Abraham's faith. In Abraham's case, the act of faith required a breach, or at least a suspension, of ethics.

The Engagement

In May 1837, Kierkegaard met a young girl of fourteen while attending a garden party in Fredricksberg. The young girl, Regine Olsen, later remembered that he "talked incessantly . . . his conversation welled up and was in the highest degree captivating."[17] Ironically, the subject of their first conversation concerned under what circumstances an engagement ought to be broken. Regine was not the only one captivated. Kierkegaard, recognizing his attraction to Regine, pursued a secretive and fantasized relationship with her by observing Regine from a coffee shop as she went to her music lessons.

Kierkegaard maintained this imaginary love affair until after he passed his theological examination in 1840. From that July until August, he vacationed in Jutland. On his return to Copenhagen, he decided to take positive action. On the eighth of September, he met Regine outside her house. After inviting himself inside the vacant house, he requested her, as he had so often in the past, to play the piano.

> She did so, and that wouldn't satisfy me. Then suddenly I took the music book, closed it not without a certain vehemence, threw it down on the piano and said, "O what do I care about music! It is you I want. I have wanted you for two years."[18]

Regine was speechless at the moment, but after a few days, on September tenth, she formally accepted his proposal of marriage.

The Break

Now, eleven months later, Emil Boesen sat pondering the events that had transpired since their engagement. Regine had given her being completely to Kierkegaard, who was truly in love with her. But from the beginning Kierkegaard had been apprehensive of his action. He had communicated to Emil a series of convincing rationalizations, all of which precluded the successful outcome of a marriage between himself and Regine.

Even before he asked her to marry him, Kierkegaard confided, he had gone about pregnant with ideas and had fallen in love with the ideal. Reality could not answer his burning desires. Emil remembered Kierkegaard wondering with the poets if "all love like all knowledge is remembrance."

Further, Kierkegaard confided, his penitence, his melancholy alienated him from Regine. His ghostly existence in a fundamentally spiritual world served as a barrier to the relationship. He could never initiate her into such terrible things as his melancholy, the dreadful night that brooded in the inmost depths, his wildness, lusts, and excesses. Kierkegaard's overwhelming concern with lust stemmed from his self-diagnosis as an uncommonly erotic individual. He suffered terribly from the guilt of visiting the brothel five years before. Kierkegaard's chosen role of the penitent was inconsistent with that of a husband.

Then there was the age difference. He was ten years her senior temporally, but existentially he saw himself as an eternity too old for her. Besides, his religious task would be endangered if he were to bind himself to anything on earth. His destiny to find truth made him a sacrifice for others, and if he were to pursue his task he must be sacrificed for others.

These ruminations on his shortcomings culminated in Kierkegaard's conception that a divine veto had been cast against his marriage to Regine. This concept of the divine veto was not a recent development, for as early as 1839 he had stated that his commitment to the role of a penitent would affect his personal relationships. Now he was sure that marriage conflicted with his definition of a penitent. He wrote in his journal,

> I saw that I had made a false step. A penitent such as I was, my *vita ante acta,* my melancholy, that was enough. I suffered unspeakably at that time. She seemed to notice nothing. On the contrary her spirits were so high that once she said she had accepted me out of pity. . . . She gave herself to me, almost worshipping me, asking me to love her, which moved me to such an extent that I was willing to risk all for her. How much I loved her is shown by the fact that I always tried to hide from myself how much she had moved me. . . . Had I not been a penitent, had I not had my *vita ante acta,* had I not been melancholy, my union with her would have made me happier than I had ever dreamed of being. But in so far as I was what, alas, I was, I had to say that I could be happier in my unhappiness without her. . . . There was a divine protest, that is how I understood it.[19]

The Decision

Boesen had watched as his friend wrestled with his predicament. Kierkegaard had left a short while before, crying remorsefully. Regine had left him a note begging him in the name of Christ and the memory of his deceased father not to leave her. He had been deeply disturbed by it and was in a quandary about what to do. Sitting in the deserted restaurant, Boesen reflected on Kierkegaard's predicament. Kierkegaard could still seek a rapprochement with Regine, but that would fly in the face of a divine veto. He could remain resolute in his decision despite Regine's pleadings, but Regine had sworn that if he abandoned her she would die of despair. Emil knew that Kierkegaard feared having Regine's death on his conscience.

Would Kierkegaard be able to break the shackles of his past and live in the existential fulfillment that he himself attributed to marriage, or would he remain eternally imprisoned within his father's melancholy? Was Kierkegaard truly a "knight of faith," or was his act one of infinite resignation? Or, could it be that, like Abraham, Kierkegaard thought he would gain Regine by renouncing her? Did Kierkegaard's love of Regine and his duty as a penitent have to conflict?

NOTES

1. Søren Kierkegaard, quoted in Walter Lowrie, *Kierkegaard* (London: Oxford University Press, 1938), p. 22.
2. Søren Kierkegaard, *The Journals of Søren Kierkegaard, A Selection*, ed. and trans. Alexander Dru (London: Oxford University Press, 1938), p. 8.
3. Ibid., p. 27.
4. Ibid., p. 59.
5. Søren Kierkegaard, *Concluding Unscientific Postscript*, trans. David Swenson and Walter Lowrie, with introduction and notes by Walter Lowrie (Princeton, N.J.: Princeton University Press, 1944), p. 49.
6. Lowrie, pp. 570–571.
7. Søren Kierkegaard, *Fear and Trembling*, trans. with introduction and notes by Walter Lowrie (Princeton, N.J.: Princeton University Press, 1945), pp. 51–52.
8. Ibid., p. 57.
9. Ibid., p. 55–56.
10. Ibid., p. 56.
11. Ibid., p. 53.
12. Ibid., pp. 84–85.
13. Ibid., pp. 21–23.
14. Ibid., pp. 26–27.
15. Ibid., p. 38.
16. Ibid., p. 47.
17. Lowrie, p. 197.
18. Kierkegaard, *Journals*, p. 92.
19. Ibid., pp. 92–93.

BIBLIOGRAPHY

Primary Source

Kierkegaard, Søren. *A Kierkegaard Anthology.* Edited by Robert Bretall. New York: Modern Library, 1936.

Biography

Lowrie, Walter. *Kierkegaard: A Life.* New York: Harper & Row, 1962. Two vols.

Interpretative Works

Barrett, William. *Irrational Man.* New York: Doubleday, 1958.
Carnell, Edward John. *The Burden of Søren Kierkegaard.* Grand Rapids, Mich.: Eerdmans, 1965.
Gill, Jerry H., ed. *Essays on Kierkegaard.* Minneapolis: Burgess, 1969.
Kaufmann, Walter. *From Shakespeare to Existentialism.* New York: Doubleday, 1960.
Thompson, Josiah. *Kierkegaard.* New York: Doubleday, 1972.

QUESTIONS FOR STUDY

1. Outline Hegel's dialectical understanding of history and indicate Kierke-gaard's reaction to it.

2. Both psychology and religion deal with guilt. How are these concepts and methods of dealing with guilt alike and different? Apply your findings to the case of Søren Kierkegaard and his father.

3. Describe the two differing models of faith that Kierkegaard offered in the persons of Abraham and Agamemnon.

4. To which of the preceding models of faith (or what combination of them) did Kierkegaard conform in his relationship to Regine Olsen?

5. Suggest an example from recent history of someone acting against the conventions of society in the name of religious convictions. Evaluate that event from the perspective of Kierkegaard's attitudes.

A Contemporary Response

HARRY A. NIELSEN

WHAT IS it that we, as students of philosophy, would want to know concerning Kierkegaard's broken engagement? The ethical soundness or unsoundness of his judgment? That could be well worth looking into. People today, too, have second thoughts after making a promise of marriage, and a change of mind, like a promise, can be made in ethically justifiable ways or ethically questionable ways. A parallel situation might some day turn up in our own lives. Probably for you or me, it would not be quite like the situation of Kierkegaard who, as the study shows, held a highly unusual combination of cards: a fearfully warped childhood, chronic melancholy, extraordinary intellectual gifts, a period of wild excesses followed by penitence as a way of life, hints that he had been marked as a sacrifice, and a task of some magnitude: "to make men aware of Christianity."

The Veto Against Marriage

First, as regards his actual decision to break off the engagement, it might help if we ask, "What does it mean to receive a divine veto against marrying?" On the face of it, this sounds decisive. God says, "No," which suggests that first the engagement was pledged, then God delivered his veto. This way of putting it suggests that God intervened by bringing a *new* factor, the veto, into the situation. But what form did the veto take? In other journal entries we find, "There was a divine protest, that is how I understood it" (p. 72)*; and, "If I had not believed that God had lodged a veto [Regine] would have been victorious" (p. 73). Such remarks suggest that Kierkegaard came to understand or believe or realize that something in the *past* amounted to a divine veto against his marrying. For example, immediately after the engagement (which, by the way, lasted a little

---

* Page references are to Søren Kierkegaard, *The Journals of Kierkegaard,* translated, selected, and with an introduction by Alexander Dru (New York: Harper Torchbook, 1959).

over a year) he experienced an uprush of misgivings that could have called to mind some very old vetoes in the biblical history. This would mean that the divine veto in this instance was not a sudden intervention of God, as for example when God commanded Abraham to sacrifice Isaac, or when an angel of the Lord, in a dream, overruled Joseph's plan to send Mary away in secret (Matt. 1:19–20).

As you can see, I am having trouble understanding the idea of a divine veto if we conceive it as something *new* thrust into the situation. How might the divine protest express itself, assuming it did not take the form of an intervention but rather of Kierkegaard's remembering something? Let us confine our discussion of this to just one of the factors already mentioned: his melancholy. In earlier times, the term *melancholy* stood for all forms of mental illness, including insanity. In this instance, it seems to be closest to what today we call *depression*. Kierkegaard writes often of his unhappiness, his anxiety, his dread, acute enough to keep him in a state of inner suffering that went far back into his childhood:

> From now on, humanly speaking, I must not only be said to be running into uncertainty but to be going to certain destruction—and, in confidence in God, that is victory. That is how I understood life when I was ten years old. [p. 116]

Can we put ourselves in the place of a man so unhappy that his greatest comfort lay in his ability to protect himself against shows of pity by concealing his pain? He mastered early in life the art of concealing his woe behind a jovial, witty exterior, a smiling mask, a masking smile.

What does this mean in relation now to marriage? In marriage masks come off or wear away. The glimpses add up, the parties become revealed to each other. Remarks such as the following may come in at this point: "I had to hide such a tremendous amount from her, had to base the whole thing on something untrue" (p. 72) and "If I had had to explain myself then I would have had to initiate her into terrible things—my relation to my father, his melancholy, the eternal darkness that broods deep within, my going astray, pleasures and excesses" (p. 87). An important side of his nature would have to be screened from Regine. He would have to watch his words for the whole of their lives together: "She also once said to me: that she would never ask me about anything if only she might remain with me" (p. 71). A wife who never asks about anything! How could he be happy play-acting a normal husbandly openness, yet sealed up? How could she be happy once it dawned on her that she would never really know him although they were supposed to be one flesh? Sorrows on both sides and unnatural silences lay in wait for them if he allowed this marriage to happen. For a brief time, love raced a pulsebeat ahead of reflection and prompted him to take a false step, but then reflection caught up, and he could step back, with much pain to everyone involved, but in time.

Even if we set aside the other singular or special features of Kierkegaard's life as described in the study, isn't there enough material in his melancholy for him to formulate the veto himself? Isn't there, in other words, a very old standing veto, as much human as divine against knowingly poisoning another's happiness?

Faith, Resignation, or Reflection?

Was Kierkegaard's decision the decision of a "knight of faith" along the lines of Abraham? "Had I had faith," he writes in retrospect, "I should have remained with Regine" (p. 88). But I do not want to pretend that a sentence taken in isolation can serve as a clincher. Faith was a factor in the total situation, and, as for renunciation, his tears speak for themselves. I cannot help thinking, though, that his decision is a lot closer to that of Agamemnon, the "knight of renunciation," than to that of Abraham. But here, too, there are differences. Like Agamemnon, Kierkegaard was caught between conflicting ethical demands, but his own reflection, rather than a sudden command from a higher being, seems to suffice as a basis for the decision. Can we speak also of a "knight of reflection," an individual who so binds himself (or herself) to the results of his own thinking—in this instance his second thoughts, misgivings and reflected memories—that he (or she) will obey its dictates to the letter, no matter how painful the going? Both Abraham and Agamemnon have their courses of action dictated by higher powers, but the term "knight of reflection" would apply to someone who really gives up a galaxy of immediate enjoyments—comfort, warmth, human love, the universal as here represented by marriage to the one he (or she) loves—because his own reflection, his own dialogue with himself, says it is the best thing to do. Here the model would be Socrates when he faced a choice between death and departure from Athens. If anyone could qualify as a "knight of reflection" in this sense, would it not be Socrates in the *Crito?*

The Task: To Unveil the Christian Faith

The case study speaks of Kierkegaard's "peculiar psychological development," which was connected with his melancholy and with his father's. To be robbed of one's childhood, whether by severe elders or some other turn of fate, is pretty certain to leave deep scars on a person's interior. If it does not break him or her outright, it means at least that he or she has no opportunity to strike up a slow, gradual, and balanced acquaintance with the dark side of human life. Instead, the dark side leaps out at him or her in the early, tender years. One possible consequence of this, and it seems to fit in with Kierkegaard's life story, is that the youthful imagination and intellect develop at an almost freakish rate as the person searches for some fixture he or she can lay hold of to provide stability. With Kierkegaard, the overdeveloped mind and imagination found a task to match. The essential demands of Christianity had been softened by custom, the shock of its first break-in had become muffled, and its core content was hard to tell apart from the kind of wisdom philosophers cook up. The task was to tear it loose from its human overlay so that people could see it as if for the first time.

Kierkegaard's handling of this task had an important impact on the history of philosophy and other regions of thought. *Philosophical Fragments* (1844), a small book that was followed a couple of years later by the much longer *Concluding Unscientific Postscript,* began the job of restoring Christianity to a distinctive place in the consciousness of philosophers. We have no room here for an extensive summary of these works, but together they attempt to remove certain veils from the ancient faith. Briefly, the *Fragments* examines two possible ways in which the individual might be related to the truth about his or her personal condition: the truth could be within one's reach, although forgotten (the Socratic position), or the individual could be alienated from the truth, cut off from it and attached to a rival position of one's own. In the latter situation, only by some kind of intervention into history from outside the world (the case study refers to this as the incarnation) could the individual have a chance to get his or her hands on that particular parcel of truth. The *Postscript* then explores the question of how an existing human being can bring him- or herself into relation with a historical intervention so as to take possession of the offered truth. As the case study points out, in these works and his authorship as a whole, Kierkegaard clearly felt he was doing a service to God and Christianity as well as to his fellow human beings. His journals express it in these words: "That my work has profited others, that God has approved it and helped me in every way is sure enough" (p. 127).

Melancholy and Christianity

But what of his abiding melancholy and whatever guilt went along with it? Much of his authorship developed under the shadow of this condition, and it is questionable whether someone could produce such works in so short a span of years unless his or her intellect and imagination had been stretched and deepened by suffering to dimensions far beyond the average. Yet a melancholy Christian is an odd combination, to say the least. As Kierkegaard remarks, "Christianity is certainly not melancholy, it is, on the contrary, glad tidings— for the melancholy" (p. 129). In the period between 1843 and 1847, still an unhappy man, he wrote more than a dozen books and many shorter pieces. As he describes his unhappiness in 1847, "It has until now lain deep down and the tremendous intellectual strain has helped to keep it down" (p. 127). How did he put together in his own mind Christianity and his secret melancholy? These journal comments from May 1847 are revealing:

> Of all sufferings none is perhaps so great as to be marked out as the object of compassion, none which tempts man so strongly to rebel against God. It is commonly thought that such a man is dull and of limited intellect, but it would not be difficult to show that this is the secret which lies behind the lives of some of the greatest minds in history. But it is kept hidden, and that can be done, for it is as though God were to say to a man, so long as he makes use of his outstanding gifts in the service of the good: I do not wish you to be thus humbled before men, to be abandoned in your unmerited misery, but where I am concerned it will help you to be conscious of your nothingness. [pp. 125–126]

That is one way to put together the seemingly incompatible elements of (1) accepting the glad tidings yet (2) existing in an underlying unhappiness. The person conceals the unhappiness from his or her fellows and turns his or her energies to serving the good. Still, this is far from an ideal situation, and in recognition of this Kierkegaard writes elsewhere in the same journal entry:

> But now God wishes things otherwise. Something is stirring in me which points to a metamorphosis. . . . I shall therefore remain quiet, in no way working too strenuously, hardly even strenuously, not begin on a new book, but try to understand myself, and *really think out the idea of my melancholy together with God here and now.* That is how I must get rid of my melancholy and bring Christianity closer to me. [p. 128]

The world has recognized Kierkegaard's contributions to philosophy and other areas of thought by giving him the fame it eventually bestows on original thinkers and by attending to the important distinctions and observations he brought to the scene. Over and above his influence on philosophy as an academic discipline, however, his writings have taught a great many how to philosophize, not so much about ancient and abstruse problems as about their individual lives. In his journals especially, he taught this in a highly Socratic manner—by example.

CHAPTER 9

The Case of Marx

Does Human Community Help or Hinder Social Change?

THE BALMY spring air of Paris gave no hint of the intense political drama taking place in 1871. After two short months of existence, the Paris Commune faced annihilation. Wild rumors of the Commune's revolutionary excesses were rampant. Condemnation was everywhere. Why had the International Working Men's Association not risen to their defense? Did the Commune embody what the workers had been striving for since the revolutions of 1848? Was this the next stage in the historical progression of the class struggle? Or was it simply a naive outburst, a spasm out of step with history and therefore doomed to set back the workers' cause? In London, Karl Marx pondered these questions as his friend Friedrich Engels strode into the room. The International's general council was growing exasperated—Engels could stall them no longer. Marx had to produce the council's communique on the Commune immediately.

Marx's Early Life

The Marx family lived in the ancient Rhineland town of Trier. In fact, Karl Marx's forefathers had been rabbis there for 200 years. Karl's father, Heschel, was an official in the Prussian government. Unlike his brother, who followed in the family tradition and became a rabbi, Heschel was not particularly interested in his Jewish heritage. When, in 1817, a wave of anti-Semitism was forcing Jewish bureaucrats to resign their posts, Heschel preserved his livelihood by changing his name to Heinrich and becoming a baptized Lutheran. A year later, on May 5, 1818, his son Karl was born.

Karl grew up in comfortable surroundings in Trier. The third of nine children, Karl became the eldest son when his brother Moritz died in 1818. Karl was a solid but undistinguished student in high school. Late in his career there, the mathematics and Hebrew instructors were both dismissed—the former as a materialist and atheist, and the latter as a revolutionary.

In October 1835, Karl embarked on the study of law at the University of Bonn. While there, he engaged fully in the rowdiness of student life. He was wounded in a duel; he once spent a night in jail for drunkenness. In addition to his general rowdiness, Karl had a problem that was to plague him all his life: his inability to manage money. His father complained, "As though we were made of gold my gentleman-son disposes of almost 700 thalers in a single year, in contravention of every agreement and every usage, whereas the richest spend no more than 500."[1] Hoping to curb his son's excesses, Heinrich decided that Karl should transfer to the University of Berlin in 1836.

Conversion to Hegel

On his arrival there, Marx found Berlin in the heyday of Hegelianism. Hegel had developed a philosophy based on the dialectical development of history. Now Hegelian philosophy was being used to explain virtually every field of study. There was Hegelian economics, Hegelian biology, and Hegelian history. Hegel's ideas were being applied everywhere.

At first Marx was put off by the rampant Hegelianism. He was more interested in the German romantic tradition than he was in rationalism. As a romantic, Marx was not interested in history or historical development. But because Hegel had died only five years before Marx went to Berlin and because Hegel's thought was so widely accepted, Marx had no choice but to "struggle with philosophy."

Marx soon became impressed with the Hegelian approach. He came to value the historical perspective Hegel brought to his ideas. He came to appreciate the way Hegel looked at situations holistically. Hegel's concept of an evolving history was especially appealing to Marx. The idea that the world was evolving, moving toward a greater realization of the Absolute Idea, was exciting. Hegel had a way of making one want to participate in life, of making one want to be a part of the process. Within a short period of time, Marx became a "convert" to Hegelianism. Marx formalized this "conversion" by joining the Young Hegelian Doctors' Club.

By the late 1830s, a split had developed among Hegel's followers. Hegel had seen history as the progressive actualization of the Absolute Idea, but he was somewhat ambiguous about the future. To some extent, he suggested that the Absolute Idea was fully realized: Christianity was the Absolute Religion, Hegelianism the Absolute Philosophy, and Prussia the Absolute State. The "Old Hegelians" endorsed this reactionary view—everything was to be kept just as it was. On the other hand, there was some reason to believe that Hegel saw the dialectic movement of history continuing: the current state of affairs would be superseded by even more adequate realizations of the Idea. The "Young Hegelians" endorsed this revolutionary aspect of the master's thought.

Initially, the key topic of discussion for the Young Hegelians was religion—primarily because politics was too dangerous. The first salvo of their attack on the orthodoxies of the day was thus David Strauss's *Life of Jesus* in 1835. But

the intimate connection between religious and political orthodoxy at that time
meant that the Young Hegelians could not avoid political criticism. The state
church and the state government were too closely linked to permit attacking one
without attacking the other. The task of political criticism was taken up in 1840
by Bruno Bauer's *The Christian State in Our Time.* Many suspected that it was
based largely on the ideas of Bauer's friend Karl Marx.

Marx's growing involvement with philosophy led him to consider an academic career. He thus began constructing a doctoral thesis on Democritus and
Epicurus, whose post-Aristotelian situation Marx saw as parallel to his own
post-Hegelian context. On the advice of Bauer, he sent his manuscript to the
University of Jena and was awarded his doctorate in absentia in 1841. Just as
Marx became ready to embark on a teaching career, however, the Prussian
minister of education decided to purge the unruly Young Hegelians. Marx's
friend Bauer was removed from his post, and Marx's own prospects were likewise eliminated.

Feuerbach and the Criticism of Hegel

After casting about for some time, Marx decided to pursue a career in journalism. During this same period, Marx began to deal with some problems he
saw in Hegel's thought. Despite his appreciation of the Hegelian process of dialectical development, Marx had some real problems with Hegel's notion of the
Absolute Idea. It seemed to Marx that Hegel was too idealistic and not realistic
enough. Marx came to believe that ideas reflected reality rather than shaped reality. There was not some Absolute Idea that caused the reality one saw around
oneself; rather, all ideas arose from a previous reality. Consciousness did not
shape existence; rather, existence shaped consciousness.

As Marx continued to deal with these inadequacies of Hegel's system, he
came across the works of Ludwig Feuerbach. In 1841, Feuerbach had written
the *Essence of Christianity,* a work that directly attacked the supernaturalist
idealism of Hegel.

Feuerbach claimed that Hegel's idealism led to a devaluation of humanity,
the senses, and the material world. Underneath Hegel's rationalism, Feuerbach
saw a religious, other-worldly longing. Feuerbach's critique involved purging
Hegelianism of this other-worldly impulse. Feuerbach held that the world of
ideas was generated by humanity and the material world, not vice versa. Feuerbach saw his own philosophy as

> Essentially distinguished from the systems hitherto prevalent, in that it corresponds
> to the real, complete nature of man; but for that reason it is antagonistic to minds
> perverted and crippled by a superhuman, i.e., anti-human, anti-natural religion and
> speculation. It does not . . . regard the *pen* as the only fit organ for the revelation of
> truth, but the eye and ear, the hand and foot . . . it recognizes as the true thing, not
> the thing as it is an object of the abstract reason, but as it is an object of the real,
> complete man.[2]

In place of Hegel's ideal, Feuerbach placed the human being. Often referring to his thought as "sensualism," Feuerbach stressed the reality of this world and the primacy of sense knowledge.

Marx saw Feuerbach as developing a kind of materialism, a focus on humanity and this world, that would overcome the problems of Hegelianism. Whereas history was for Hegel the history of Absolute Spirit, now it could be seen in the development of humanity and nature.

As Marx moved further and further away from Hegel's thought, he also moved further and further away from the Young Hegelians. It seemed to Marx that the Young Hegelians were too interested in ideas, speculating about revolution and not nearly interested enough in practical political action.

In April 1842, he produced his first article for the *Rheinische Zeitung*, a liberal newspaper in Cologne. In this setting, Marx began to focus on politics and, to some extent, economics. This practical engagement further distanced Marx from the speculative ideas of the Young Hegelians. Turning from their flashy but abstract slogans, Marx began his lifelong focus on practical political change.

Eventually, Marx became editor of the paper. His leadership was such that its circulation quickly doubled. In addition, political developments in the Rhineland led Marx increasingly to criticize the government. His January 1843 article on the poverty of the Mosel wine makers finally brought the censors down on his head, and the *Rheinische Zeitung* was suppressed in March.

Economics: Alienated Labor, Class Struggle, and Private Property

With the closing of the paper, Marx became free to accept the offer of his friend Arnold Ruge to become co-editor of a new journal. It was to be a review devoted to political action incorporating both theoretical and practical issues. Publishing in Germany was out of the question, so the decision was made to locate in Paris. With Marx's future given a new base of security, he finally felt free to marry his fiancée, Jenny von Westphalen.

Jenny von Westphalen was four years his senior, and a talented woman. A one-time Queen of the Ball in Trier, she had a quick mind and radical sympathies. Their marriage in June 1843 thus provided Marx with an intellectual partner of tremendous value. Jenny assisted Karl with most of his later publications.

After their honeymoon in Switzerland and an extended stay with Jenny's mother, the two of them headed for Paris. During this time, Marx continued his study of Feuerbach, his criticism of Hegel, and his preparation for the new journal. The first issue of *Deutsch-Französische Jahrbücher* came out in February 1844, but because of its poor reception and the growing estrangement between Ruge and Marx, Ruge discontinued publication.

With the demise of *Jahrbücher* and with the receipt of a large sum from the former shareholders of the *Rheinische Zeitung*, Marx was again free to throw himself wholly into economic and political studies. Particularly during the summer, while his wife and newborn daughter were away in Trier, Marx laid the foundations for his later economic and political theories.

In his study of "alienated labor," Marx saw that in a capitalist system

> The worker becomes a cheaper commodity the more commodities he produces. . . .
> All these consequences follow from the fact that the worker is related to the *product
> of his labor* as to an *alien* object. . . . The more the worker exerts himself, the more
> powerful becomes the alien objective world which he fashions against himself. . . . It
> is the same in religion. The more man attributes to God, the less he retains in him-
> self.[3]

The workers' labor was alien to them because it was not theirs. It belonged to
another. The workers' labor belonged to the capitalist, whose ownership of the
means of production was also ownership of the workers' labor. In return for the
workers' labor, the capitalist paid them a wage—a wage that Marx saw as always barely enough for subsistence. In this arrangement, the worker became
thoroughly alienated, for it "makes his life activity, his *essence,* only a means for
his existence."[4]

Over the years, human potential had been so minimized that no one was
able to produce the kind of life that was possible. Through alienation from their
labor, people became alienated from human existence. Those who were not
members of the working class were also alienated. They too were alienated from
fulfilling their potential. Although this individual alienation was important, it
was not nearly as important as the alienation people had as an economic class.
Workers, as a class, were alienated from those who owned the means of production. Those who owned the means of production were, in turn, alienated from
the workers.

This alienation gave rise to class struggle. The interests of one economic
class were always in opposition to the interests of other economic classes. These
differing interests led to conflict and struggle, class struggle. This was true of all
classes, not just the working classes.

According to Marx, the reason for this class conflict, as well as the reason
for the alienation that gave rise to it, was private property. It was because of
private property that some people were capitalists and others were workers. In
order to get rid of all the oppressive institutions that capitalism had developed
(which included religion, the state, the family structure, and so on), one must
first get rid of private property. As Marx explained it,

> Religion, family, state, law, morality, science, art, etc., are only *particular* forms of
> production and fall under its general law. The positive overcoming of *private proper-
> ty* as the appropriation of *human* life is thus the positive overcoming of all alienation
> and the return of man from religion, family, state, etc., to his *human,* that is, social
> existence.[5]

The overcoming of capitalism's alienation of labor by means of private property
was the key to attaining truly human existence.

To overcome alienation, to overcome private property, was, for Marx, the
meaning of communism. He criticized the "crude communists" of his time for
demanding "the reversion to the unnatural simplicity of the poor and wantless
man who has not gone beyond private property, has not yet even achieved it."[6]

At the same time, these "crude communists" advocated the community of women—which Marx saw simply as "communal lust"—and in fact the universalization of alienation, in the form of state capitalism. Against crude communism, Marx envisioned a true communism, a true overcoming of alienation. This would be "the riddle of history solved," the "true resolution of the conflict between existence and essence." Marx did not spell out his vision, but he affirmed it would have to be both postcapitalist (using the technology developed by capitalism) and nonalienating. In particular, because it would not rest on alienated labor, communism would not alienate people from each other. Rather, it would affirm the "species-being" or social integration of humanity. Marx felt that further detail on communism was unnecessary, because he saw that "communism is the necessary form and dynamic principle of the immediate future but not as such the goal of human development."[7]

Friendship with Engels

While Marx was intensely engaged in these economic and political studies, he formed what was to become the most important friendship of his life. Friedrich Engels had written an article on economics for the *Jahrbücher* which impressed Marx greatly. He was thus delighted to make Engel's acquaintance in August, 1844.

During their time together, Marx learned that Engels came from a large family of wealthy, textile industrialists. Since his birth in 1820, Engels had been immersed in the fundamentalist Lutheranism of Barmen in Prussia. Strauss's *Life of Jesus* had come to Engels as a breath of fresh air while working in his father's factory. Following its lead, he went to Berlin and joined the Young Hegelians. When his father sent him to work at the English branch of the family firm, in Manchester, he became a sharp and critical observer of workingclass life. It was in Manchester that Engels composed his *Outlines of a Critique of Political Economy*, which Marx had found very helpful. The two men immediately decided to spend ten days together discussing political economy, and planning a joint volume criticizing Bruno Bauer and the other Young Hegelians.

At the same time that Marx was pursuing his study of economics and his project with Engels, he was politically active among the expatriate German workers. He became a frequent contributor to their biweekly paper, *Vorwärts*. Late in the year, the Prussian government became so annoyed with the radical Parisian paper that it began to put diplomatic pressure on the French government. Consequently, in January 1845 *Vorwärts* was suppressed and Marx was expelled from Paris.

Historical Materialism, the Stages of Development, and Revolution

From Paris, Marx went to Brussels, then a haven for political refugees from all over Europe. Without a job, Marx was nonetheless financially secure. He had sold the family's belongings in Paris and had received an advance for the book he was writing on political economy. In addition, his Parisian associates sent him a gift in order to share "communistically" his expenses, and Engels gave him the royalties from his own *The Condition of the Working Classes in England.* This gift from Engels was the first in what would later become an extended and literally life-saving service.

When Engels arrived in Brussels in April, he found that Marx had already made substantial progress intellectually. According to Engels, by seeing that history had to be explained in terms of economics (rather than vice versa), Marx "had already advanced . . . to the main aspects of his materialist theory of history."[8]

The position toward which Marx was moving combined aspects of Hegel's idealism and Feuerbach's materialism. With Hegel, Marx agreed that history must be understood as a process. History was made up of various stages: each incomplete, each a necessary part of the process, each leading to the next stage. But Marx did not agree with Hegel's characterization of the Absolute Idea as that which guided and directed this process. For Marx, the various stages of history were not to be explained by some "other-worldly" idea. Furthermore, Marx held that the movement from one stage to another was not a gradual, slow, orderly process. Rather it was a sudden and often violently revolutionary change.

With Feuerbach, Marx agreed that the world must be understood in "this-worldly" terms. He agreed with Feuerbach that material forces shaped the world. But Marx felt that Feuerbach did not go far enough. While Feuerbach did criticize Hegel's emphasis on the Absolute Idea, an abstract and nonmaterial notion, he did not tie his criticism to historical development. Marx commented, "As far as Feuerbach is a materialist he does not deal with history, and as far as he considers history he is not a materialist."[9]

Combining what he thought best in Hegel and Feuerbach, Marx developed a view of history called "historical materialism." Most people in nineteenth-century Europe thought of history in political or personal terms. When strong leaders such as Napoleon came along, they altered history by changing the political structure. But Marx held that this view of history was mistaken. Such political changes were not the result of individual people. Rather, they were the result of the economic, material conditions in which people found themselves. In fact, most political changes were simply by-products of the "material conditions of life."

According to Marx, there were five stages in the development of history, five "modes of production" that "determine the social, political, and intellectual life processes." Each (except the last) of these five stages was incomplete. Each was a necessary part of the process, and each led inevitably (and sometimes violently) to the next stage.

The first stage was primitive communism. This was a society characterized by the absence of private property. With the advent of private property, the next three stages of development were introduced. After primitive communism came slavery, feudalism, and capitalism. Each of these stages was higher, more productive, more developed, and more efficient than the previous one. Each of these stages replaced what was becoming an inefficient and ineffective economic system. Each of these economic stages determined the way people thought and acted in that stage.

The final stage of the economic development of history was communism. There was no sixth stage, because private property ceased to exist at the level of communism. There was no longer any division in society between the haves and the have-nots. No longer were those who owned the means of production exploiting those who had no control over the means of production. So, after a transitionary period a society would be developed in which all people would be able to achieve the kind of skill, talent, and creativity that they were capable of achieving. People would no longer be restricted by the economic consequences of their actions. They would achieve such a high level of productiveness that all needs of the system could be met.

In response to the criticism that human nature would not allow this to happen, Marx argued that selfishness and greed were parts of any economic system based on private property. People were determined to be selfish and greedy by the "social production of their material lives." Change the mode of production (that is, eliminate private property), and the way people think and act would change too.

The stage Marx was particularly interested in was capitalism. Marx held that capitalism had served an important historical purpose. But it was now time for capitalism to give way to the next and final stage of development: communism. Furthermore, Marx felt that it was not enough simply to theorize about the overthrow of capitalism—one must commit oneself to bringing it about.

Marx gave an example of the practical difference resulting from his theory when he criticized Feuerbach's "communism." Abstracting himself from historical realities, Feuerbach thought communism was simply a particular way of looking at human life. Marx charged that Feuerbach wanted "merely to produce a correct consciousness about an *existing* fact; whereas for the real communist it is a question of overthrowing the existing state of things." [10]

Marx could not stop with ideas as Feuerbach had. Marx declared, "The philosophers have only *interpreted* the world in various ways; the point is, to *change* it." [11]

Marx's passage beyond the Young Hegelians and Feuerbach consisted of transferring the location of truth from the realm of abstract ideas and attitudes to the arena of historical action. For Marx, truth was not so much known as done. For this reason, Marx could not be romantic about the communist revolution. An ideal revolution needed only to capture the imagination, but a true revolution would have to be founded on the proper economic circumstances.

In the real world, Marx said, to be a communist was not simply to possess a certain attitude, but to be "the follower of a definite revolutionary party." [12] Marx made good on this statement in 1847 when the Communist League was formed. Although he was not an organizer of the League, Marx quickly joined it and was asked—together with Engels—to draft its platform or manifesto.

The *Communist Manifesto* in its finished form was almost entirely Marx's own work. His aims were to set out the party's foundation and program. The foundation was Marx's historical materialism. The program was class struggle and the abolition of private property.

Before the *Manifesto* was even off the presses, revolution had begun to sweep across Europe. When news of the revolution in Paris reached Brussels in late February 1848, the Belgian government expelled all suspect foreigners. After moving first to Paris, Marx continued on to Germany when revolution broke out in Berlin. Together with Engels, Marx quickly resurrected his old newspapaer as the *Neue Rheinische Zeitung.* Marx hoped the paper would become a focal point for radical politics throughout Germany. At first it took a relatively moderate line, seeking simply to deepen and consolidate what was in fact a very shallow revolutionary impulse. By the spring of 1849, however, it had sufficiently antagonized the recovered Prussian authorities so that they once again expelled Marx from the country.

Capital and the International

In mid-1849, Karl and his pregnant wife, Jenny, virtually destitute, arrived in London. Their condition was an accurate omen of their future, for the Marxes lived in a substandard existence in London for the next thirty years. At times their condition was so severe that survival was in doubt. Three of their children died due to lack of funds for doctors and medicines. Marx was able to acquire some funds through journalism, as correspondent for the *New York Tribune.* But their primary source of income was always Engels. Engels returned to work in his father's Manchester factory and devoted a large part of his income throughout the 1850s and 1860s to Marx's support.

Beyond his work for the *Tribune,* Marx's primary occupation for the rest of his life was the study of economics. His earlier work had developed the main outlines of his theory, but now this was sharpened and documented with an enormous wealth of data. Marx became a fixture in the reading room of the British Museum, where he pored over government records, histories, and the writings of other economists. He projected a work of enormous scope that would deal in detail with each of the first four economic stages. However he only completed the portion dealing with capitalism, called *Das Kapital,* or *Capital.*

In *Capital,* Marx set out the rules of capitalism. He explained how capitalism emerged from feudalism and how it must eventually give way to the final stage of development, communism.

The most stirring passages of *Capital* were Marx's documentation of the deprivations of the early Industrial Revolution. Although most of this material was simply objective, Marx did not avoid drama. He wrote,

> The historical movement which changes the producers into wage workers, appears, on the one hand, as their emancipation from serfdom and from the fetters of the guilds. . . . But, on the other hand, these new freedmen became sellers of themselves only after they had been robbed of all their own means of production, and of all the guarantees of existence afforded by the old feudal arrangements.[13]

Marx's historical materialism provided the key for understanding not only capitalism's past, but also its future.

> Along with the constantly diminishing number of the magnates of capital, who usurp and monopolize all advantages of this process of transformation, grows the mass of misery, oppression, slavery, degradation, exploitation; but with this too grows the revolt of the working class, a class always increasing in members, and disciplined, united, and organized by the very mechanism of the process of capitalist production itself. The monopoly of capital becomes a fetter upon the mode of production, which has sprung up and flourished along with, and under, it. Centralization of the means of production and socialization of labour at last reach a point where they become incompatible with ... capitalism. The death bell of capitalist private property sounds.[14]

Marx predicted that capitalist society would generate its own destruction. By bringing together a large labor force to work in the factories, the capitalists were organizing the workers. It would be only a matter of time before the workers would revolt against the capitalists and abolish private property. He asserted, as he had twenty years before, that with the abolition of private property a non-alienating (communist) society would be born.

At the same time that Marx was putting the finishing touches on *Capital,* he was again involved in workingclass politics. In 1864, a number of different workers' groups came together in London to form the International Working Men's Association. Marx was not one of the International's organizers but quickly ascended to its leadership, framing its inaugural address.

From the beginning, the International was a hodge-podge of people with various interests, bound together solely by their commitment to workers and their dissatisfaction with the status quo. It acted as the vanguard of working-class aspiration at the time. But Marx came to feel that while its prominence attracted many to the International, its effectiveness could only be maintained by reducing the internal conflict within the International. Consequently, an increasing amount of Marx's time after 1865 was devoted to conflict with rival factions in the International. In all of this, Marx's concern was with historical and therefore political effectiveness in the workingclass struggle.

The Commune

Not all the agitation in Europe during the late 1860s arose from the working classes. Bismarck, the "Iron Chancellor" of Prussia, had imperial plans for Germany. Consequently, France was provoked to war in July of 1870. First proclaimed by the Germans as a "war of defense," the Franco-Prussian war quickly took on the contours of territorial expansion. When the French emperor, Louis Bonaparte, was captured by the Prussians on September 4, the French government immediately reconstituted itself as a republic. It called itself the "Government of National Defense," but its aims quickly appeared to be otherwise. Working in the interests of the aristocracy and wealthy industrialists, the Republic sought a quick and favorable end to the Prussian disturbance.

Meanwhile, the Prussians advanced on Paris, laying siege to the city on September 18. The main body of Parisians had no relish for the Government of National Defense, because this group appeared more devoted to its own interests than to those of Paris. By January 28, 1871, the Republic had arranged an armistice with Prussia, but it still did not have the Parisians' confidence. The final bone of contention was the disarming of the city. The Republic called for it but the citizens refused.

On March 18, troops from the Republic sought to take away the city's cannons by stealth. They were soon discovered and, largely because of the women of Paris, their plan was foiled. In the momentum of the hour, the city's militia took the offensive and drove the forces of the Republic from the city. Almost by accident, the city was free. On March 28, the Paris Commune was proclaimed.

The Commune was a democratically organized coalition of forces administered by a ninety-two-member council. It had little coherent policy but drifted toward socialist lines. It acted against the city's oppressive rents, and at the request of the bakers it prevented employers from requiring night work. The Commune aided in the establishment of over forty-three workers' cooperatives, but launched no attacks on private property. The Paris branch of the International played a small role in the Commune, with seventeen of the ninety-two Council seats.

The Commune was quite disorganized. But to the rest of Europe it appeared as a threatening symbol. The Commune had few friends, for the ruling powers saw it as proof of the destructive chaos of worker militancy. On the other hand, many workers' groups saw it as a combination of fringe elements and typical Parisian chauvinism. The International had remained conspicuously silent. Now, as the troops of the Republic began advancing into the city and fighting grew more intense, the workers of Europe wanted to know: should they support the Commune?

The Decision

Marx agonized. If he threw the International onto the side of the Commune and it was crushed, the major political force of the European workers would be crushed along with it. But if he refused to stand with the workers of Paris, would not the International lose credibility with all workers?

Back in the fall, Marx had told the French workers,

Any attempt at upsetting the new government in the present crisis . . . would be a desperate folly. The French workers . . . must not allow themselves to be swayed by the national *souvenirs* of 1792. . . . Let them calmly and resolutely improve the opportunities of republican liberty, for the work of their own class organization. It will gift them with fresh herculean powers for the regeneration of France, and our common task—the emancipation of labor.[15]

Sensing that this advice would not be heeded by the Parisians, Engels predicted that a proletarian revolution in 1870 would be crushed, and would "set back another 20 years" the cause of the working class.

In March, two days after the Commune was proclaimed, Marx had written that it had no chance of success. It was not grounded in reality but in abstract ideas of justice and equality. Its foundation was not the historical development of the means of production but an historical accident. Marx exclaimed, "The decisive, unfavourable 'accident' this time is by no means to be found in the general condition of French society, but in the presence of the Prussians in France."[16] And yet the courage of the communards was striking. Marx cried out, "What elasticity, what historical initiative, what a capacity for sacrifice in these Parisians!"[17]

As he watched the struggle develop, Marx had second thoughts. Were the Communards out of touch with historical reality? Or were they moving forward in the development of history? Could the mixed forces of the Commune represent a new breakthrough by the working class? Or did they only represent themselves, another piece of Parisian delirium? Engels rose to leave. Marx had to make up his mind. Europe was waiting.

NOTES

1. Heinrich to Karl Marx, Karl Marx and Friedrich Engels, *Werke,* quoted in David McLellan, *Karl Marx: His Life and Thought* (New York: Harper & Row, 1973), p. 33.
2. Ludwig Feuerbach, *The Essence of Christianity,* trans. M. Evans, 2nd ed. (London: Kegan Paul, Trench, Trübner, 1890), pp. viii–ix.
3. Karl Marx, *Writings of the Young Marx on Philosophy and Society,* ed. and trans. L. Easton and K. Guddat (New York: Doubleday, 1967), pp. 289–290.
4. Ibid., p. 294.
5. Ibid., p. 305.
6. Ibid., p. 302.
7. Ibid., p. 314.
8. Engels, *Werke,* quoted in McLellan, *Karl Marx,* p. 140.
9. Karl Marx and Friedrich Engels, *The German Ideology,* ed. C. J. Arthur, (New York: International Publishers, 1970), p. 64.
10. Ibid., p. 60.
11. Marx, *Writings,* p. 402.
12. Marx, *German Ideology,* p. 60.
13. Karl Marx, *Capital,* ed. Friedrich Engels (Chicago: Encyclopaedia Britannica, Great Books of the Western World, 1952), p. 355.
14. Ibid., p. 378.
15. Karl Marx, *The Civil War in France* (New York: International Publishers, 1940), p. 34.
16. Ibid., p. 86.
17. Ibid., p. 85.

BIBLIOGRAPHY

Primary Sources

Marx, Karl. *Capital.* Edited by Friedrich Engels. Chicago: Encyclopaedia Britannica (Great Books of the Western World), 1952.

Marx, Karl, and Engels, Friedrich. *The Communist Manifesto*. New York: Appleton-Century-Crofts, 1955.

Biography

Berlin, Isaiah. *Karl Marx: His Life and Environment*. New York: Oxford University Press, 1959.

Interpretative Works

Hook, Sidney. *Towards the Understanding of Karl Marx*. New York: Day, 1933.
Kamenka, Eugene. *Marxism and Ethics*. New York: St. Martin's Press, 1969.
Lichtheim, George. *Marxism: An Historical and Critical Study*. New York: Praeger, 1961.
McLellan, David. *Karl Marx: His Life and Thought*. New York: Harper & Row, 1973.
Tucker, R. C. *Philosophy and Myth in Karl Marx*. New York: Cambridge University Press, 1961.

QUESTIONS FOR STUDY

1. Describe the political, economic, and religious environment in which Marx grew to maturity. Suggest factors in this environment that appear to have had a lasting influence on Marx.

2. How did Marx develop his philosophy by reacting against and incorporating elements of Hegelianism?

3. Outline Marx's theory of historical materialism. To what extent was he indebted to Feuerbach, and how did Marx go beyond Feuerbach?

4. Give reasons why Marx would want to support the Paris Commune and reasons why he would not. Which set of reasons do you think most closely coincides with his theory of historical materialism?

5. Evaluate the impact of Marx's thinking on present-day liberation movements in Africa, Latin America, Asia, and the United States.

A Contemporary Response

ROBERT C. WILLIAMS

ARE YOU so aware of yourself—your own needs, aspirations, problems, constraints, and dreams—that you cannot see how you interact with and are related to other people and social institutions? Do you care as much about the well-being and happiness of others as you do about your personal sense of fulfillment? Does your behavior in relation to your society or state consist more in other-regarding or in self-regarding actions?

These are vitally important and troubling questions for all of us. As members of a given cultural environment, each of us acquires a repertory of socially acceptable forms of behavior. These often generate in us alienation, frustration, and the fear that our full self-realization is being threatened. Moreover, these socially acquired and morally sanctioned styles of personal interaction determine how human beings become grafted into a community of purpose and social change.

Human communities, especially certain collective forms of modern industrial work and technology, too often create new forms of alienation and impediments to change, progress, and unity. Community is a universal social form among human beings and as such is affected by environment and change. In fact, change is one malleable component of the human social equation. Change gives us a choice between progress and decay.

Karl Marx was passionately concerned with these issues. He devoted his philosophical attention to them in his polemical writings (such as *Critique of Hegel's Philosophy of Law* and *The Communist Manifesto*), in his astute observations on alienation in politics and economics (*Economic and Philosophical Manuscripts* and *The German Ideology*), and in his systematic assessment of modern industrial communities and their conservative strategies of social change (*Capital,* Volumes 1 and 3).

Unlike many philosophers of his own era, Marx was not an idealist or intellectual romantic (a tendency he overcame after his encounter with the Hegelians). During his mature years, however, he did espouse a utopian vision of history and social existence based on politics and a realistic view of economics. He belongs to the company of those great thinkers (such as Plato, Augustine, Hobbes, Locke, and Mill) who boldly interpreted the structure and meaning of human life from a philosophical frame of reference. As a social critic and philosopher, his primary interest was history and its materialistic foundations. As an activist and engineer of sociopolitical change, he regarded the worker movement as a vanguard force in history. He sought to analyze the historical and political effectiveness of workers struggling for their own human and civil rights.

What, in Marx's terms, would help liberate workers and humanize social existence? Could such a step be achieved by organized force, ideology, or the politics of compromise? What would you do if today you were put in a position similar to that which Marx faced when asked to support the Paris Commune in a struggle against an imposing and brutal power? For Marx, the choice was force. But force and revolutionary power at what cost? He certainly did not want the International needlessly crushed or have it lose credibility with all workers. All philosophers encounter such moral dilemmas when reflective thought and social action are in conflict.

He hesitated, pondered, wavered. Finally, after the bloody suppression of the Commune, Marx prepared two draft statements about the Commune and its tenuous link to the International. The statement he finally submitted to the general council of the International read somewhat like an obituary.

The Commune was a courageous but defeated communal undertaking. Marx was unequivocally in favor of force as well as of those collective efforts and activities that would give impetus to needed change and a more humane social life. In his opinion, however, the leadership and organization of the Commune were too middle class and optimistic. The goals and strategies were incoherent. It was a loosely organized community that became an impediment to meaningful social change. If sheer communal force was to be used, it must not be an irresponsible or ill-timed exercise of revolutionary power.

However, Marx did not forget the moral significance of the Commune or the dedication of the Communards. Of the work and memory of the Commune and its specific association with the international workers' cause, he wrote,

> While European governments thus testify, before Paris, to the international character of class-rule, they cry down the International Working Men's Association . . . as the head fountain of all these disasters. . . . Our Association is, in fact, nothing but the international bond between the most advanced working men in the various countries of the civilized world. . . . The soil out of which it grows is modern society itself. . . . To stamp it out, the Governments would have to stamp out the despotism of capital over labor—the condition of their parasitical existence.
>
> Working men's Paris, with its Commune, will be forever celebrated as the glorious harbinger of a new society. The martyrs are enshrined in the great heart of the working class. Its exterminators history has already nailed to the eternal pillory from which all the prayers of their priests will not redeem them. . . . The working classes

know that they have to pass through different phases of class struggle. They know that superseding economical conditions of the slavery of labour by the conditons of free and associated labour can only be the progressive work of time. . . . But they know at the same time that great strides may be made at once through the Communal form of political organization and that the time has come to begin that movement for themselves and mankind.[1]

Marx's relevance for us today is perhaps best shown in his influence on the contemporary social movements and communities that insistently press for justice and a total restructuring of interpersonal relationships. By radical activity, individuals organized into groups can work to improve their condition and achieve freedom and justice. Oppressed individuals who work together for change constitute a community of their own creation. They are the agency, the social class, that creates new conditions for social existence and equality.[2] Blacks, women, and workers are three vocal communities that effectively agitate for renewal and change in contemporary societies. As such, they face decisions and actions similar to those Marx proposed in his program of revolution. In suggesting that organized groups can effectively work for the common good, Marx implied that communities can be useful change agents.

Black Americans perceive their oppression as grounded in the continuing exploitation by whites, who use them as instruments of labor and economic gain. Steeped in the reality of servitude and an oppression fostered by race hate, blacks have reacted with rage and bitterness. They want the autonomy and social well-being that the nation promises all citizens. To attain these goals, blacks have organized freedom movements, protests, and human rights struggles. These endeavors demand sacrifice and solidarity on the part of blacks.

Frederick Douglass, Marcus Garvey, Malcolm X, and Martin Luther King, Jr., have pointed blacks to the way out of their predicament. Nietzsche also showed the way, in his *Will to Power*. Today, blacks sense the need for stronger community ties and cooperation. Accordingly, black leaders know that substantial social change efforts must be built on a coherent and realistic interpretation of historical events and political power struggles. If American racism and economic exploitation are to be eliminated, blacks must work to strengthen their sense of community and collective social action.

The situation of oppression for black Africans is not unlike that which blacks face in America. Whereas in the past Africans have expressed their rage in myths and ancient rites, today they are using collective forms of armed struggle and violent resistance to achieve national liberation and social reformation. In calling his fellow Africans to a communal striving for change, Frantz Fanon reasoned,

> Comrades, have we not other work to do than to create a third Europe? . . . Europe has made her encroachments . . . she has justified her crimes and legitimized the slavery in which she holds four-fifths of humanity. . . . Come, brothers, we have far too much work to do for us to play the game of rearguard. . . . Humanity is waiting for something from us other than . . . an imitation of Europe.[3]

Do you think that black Americans are morally justified in their use of radical protest techniques (boycotts, strikes, urban violence, black studies programs, and so on)? Is the violence of revolutionary struggle on the continent of Africa acceptable to you? If you were put into the situation of black Americans or Africans, what forms of communal action would you be willing to employ to induce social change?

Men tend to see themselves as the necessary and superior other in the identity and reality of women. By seeing themselves, their sense of value and purpose, only through the reality and dominance of men, women have become passive in the midst of an imposed dehumanization and thingification of their being.

Some of the most vocal and radical forms of women's liberation are Marxist in both sentiment and intent. Women's support groups and communities are one collective means whereby women today are gaining economic, social, professional, and personal independence within male-dominated cultures. The liberation endeavor of women is a social force to be reckoned with. It is rising in both western and eastern, in developed and undeveloped, regions of the globe. Women worldwide, gathered in small groups and feminist communities, are willingly examining the new historical circumstances of the twentieth century in order to ferret out political positions and modes of sociological analysis that reflect the concerns and aspirations of women. These concerns and expectations are reflected in the struggles of women who seek to free themselves from oppressive female roles and traditional values.

Given Marx's perspective on workers and their right to collective struggle, do you feel that Marx would encourage women to come together as a social force in order to break the stranglehold of male dominance? Would Marx regard the women's liberation movement as a sufficiently viable social agent for change? What do you think?

Granted that the emancipation efforts of blacks and women are a force all over the world, is it not workers who are the direct heirs of Marx's legacy of revolutionary politics? Some people contend that the worker movement is outmoded in the developed communities of the West because of effective union organization. But inflation may have eroded almost all that organized workers have gained. And the devaluation of labor in developing countries puts organized labor in jeopardy.

The exploitation of the workers' labor is a social obstacle that blocks community and equality for all humanity. Labor is seen as a commodity in capitalism. Hence, if people relate to each other solely by means of the products of their labor, they are candidates for alienation, exploitation, and dehumanization. When the product to be consumed is valued above the laborer who produces it, the laborer is separated (alienated) from her or his purpose as a human being. The situation is made even more complex when labor becomes highly mechanized. When the value of human labor has been significantly diminished, the worker may have no choice but to see some form of organized revolutionary activity as the most reliable means of regaining justice and self-respect.

That the Marxist program for radical social change is important to the present-day worker movement is made evident by means of the serious manner in which Marx's name is invoked by workers and peasants who, in solidarity, struggle for change within the Third World. These movements represent the heritage of Marx's thought and program.

Students of Marx may either side with the early Marx, who was more humanistic and philosophical, or they may prefer to identify with the later Marx, who was more concerned about the evolving of economic and political realities. But whatever one's view of Marx, Marx is a philosophically and politically controversial thinker. The totality of his ideas about human nature, work, economics, history, community, and social change do not cohere into one systematic scheme, but they are still very much alive in the world today.

In the final analysis, Marx's social philosophy is both critical and constructive. It is critical of social reality,[4] and it is constructive in its militant call for radical change in human roles and relationships.[5]

Marx saw clearly that human beings are not born into ready-made or absolutely designed societies. Social reality is constructed and is affected by the force of change. And if human beings are affected by change so are communities. Some people and groups resist change, because of their vested interests and roles. Others press for change when they perceive that their interests will not be realized by existing social arrangements. Marx was not content simply to understand the fact that people and social institutions evolve, change, and decay. Such a view presupposed a mere passive role for philosophy, and Marx had come to the conclusion that philosophy could be a radically creative and humanizing force. Marx's view of philosophy in human affairs was that individuals and communities can function to change the world.

Perhaps the social stirrings engendered by activist groups in America, fights for Third World freedom, women's liberation endeavors, and grass-roots worker movements will be the concrete means by which we will see whether Marx's philosophical vision is applicable to our time and place. We may well decide that reflective thought and social action belong together. The heart of the matter is whether you and I believe that Marx has articulated a viable moral faith, even if his view of social institutions and change amounts to little more than poetry.

NOTES

1. Karl Marx, *Selected Writings,* ed. David McLellan (New York: Oxford University Press, 1977), pp. 550, 551, 557.
2. C. Gould, *Marx's Social Ontology* (Cambridge, Mass.: M.I.T. Press, 1979), p. 128.
3. Frantz Fanon, *The Wretched of the Earth,* trans. Constance Farrington (New York: Grove Press, 1963), pp. 313, 314, 315.
4. The stance taken by Marx in one of his early writings illustrates his preoccupation with the criti-

cal aspect of philosophical endeavor. "The criticism of heaven is transformed into the criticism of earth, the criticism of religion into the criticism of law, and the criticism of theology into the criticism of politics" (Karl Marx, *Selected Writings,* p. 64).

5. The constructive or positive features of Marx's thought are evidenced in many of his writings, but perhaps sections of the *Communist Manifesto* best exemplify this aspect of his thinking. "Let the ruling classes tremble at a Communist revolution. The proletarians have nothing to lose but their chains. They have a world to win. WORKING MEN OF ALL COUNTRIES, UNITE!" (Karl Marx, *Selected Writings,* p. 246).

CHAPTER 10

The Case of James

Can I Trust My Own Judgment?

WILLIAM JAMES sat in his study at Harvard University. It was spring, 1910, and he was tired. After a year of intense effort, his manuscript was almost ready. James knew that *The Meaning of Truth* was the sum of his career as a philosopher, and yet a nagging doubt remained. His theory of truth and his concept of free will ran counter to traditional scientific and religious ideas. He knew that. The book would be controversial, but that did not frighten him. The real issue, the fundamental one, James thought, was "Can I trust my own judgment? How can I know that I am right? Does my free choice, of an answer, or an action, really matter?"

His mind wandered restlessly back to another spring forty years before, to an entry scrawled in his journal.

> I think that yesterday was a crisis in my life. I finished Renouvier's second Essay and see no reason why his definition of free will—the sustaining of a thought because I choose to when I might have other thoughts—need be illusory. At any rate, I will assume for the present that it is no illusion. My first act of free will shall be to believe in free will.[1]

For James, the first conscious statement of free will had not been effortless. During the preceding two years at Harvard Medical School, he had been haunted by a sense of moral impotence, faced with the apparently inescapable dilemma of trying to maintain free will in the light of religious determinism on one side and scientific determinism on the other. He had rejected both the notion that all things were rigidly fixed by God's will and the concept that all reality was governed by fixed natural laws of cause and effect.

Now in 1910 as he wrote in his journal, James felt more and more certain that human effort had to count for something, that it must make a difference. He pondered the alternatives. Could God be all powerful and humans therefore powerless? Were humans mere outgrowths of the evolutionary process and all their efforts of no significance? Most crucial of all, had his own decision to act out of free will been rooted in reality or illusion? Was there really freedom to choose? Or was his need to believe in free will just a fabrication, a mental ploy to escape the crushing control of total determinism?

The James Dynasty

William James was born on January 11, 1842. The James family typified the energy, enterprise, and restlessness of a young and growing America.

William James's grandfather, William, came to Albany, New York, from Ireland in 1789 at the age of eighteen. Poor, but hardworking and thrifty, he parlayed his earnings through careful investments into a fortune of $3 million. He died in 1832, an eminent banker, trustee of Union College, staunch Calvinist, and father of eleven children.

His son Henry, Sr. (William James's father), became a respected theological writer and thinker in New York and New England. A restless man with a lively intellect, he was surprisingly active in spite of a leg amputated as a youth—the result of trying to stamp out a barn fire.

With this strict Calvinist background, religion was a family tradition. After graduating from Union College in 1830, Henry, Sr., began studying for the Presbyterian ministry. He attended Princeton Theological Seminary from 1835 to 1837 but became disenchanted with the absence of spirituality in what he called "professional religion." He left the seminary but continued to spend much of his spare time studying the Bible. At age thirty-three, he was preparing a paper on the book of Genesis. Then, one quiet afternoon following a cheerful meal, he was struck by a dreadful apparition:

> Fear came upon me, and trembling, which made all my bones shake. It was a perfectly insane and abject terror . . . some damned shape squatting, invisible to me within the room and raying out from his fetid personality influences fatal to life. The thing had not lasted ten seconds before I felt myself a wreck, reduced from a state of firm, vigorous manhood to almost helpless infancy.[2]

After a prolonged rest cure on the seacoast, he decided he no longer wanted to study the Bible. He put his notes and commentaries away and never looked at them again. At this point, his landlady introduced him to the mysticism of Emmanuel Swedenborg, and particularly the concept of purgation, regeneration, and illumination that Swedenborg called *vastation*. Henry, Sr. was convinced that his breakdown had been an instance of just such a vastationary change. He therefore renounced the God of strict Calvinism and became totally immersed in Swedenborgianism.

The Family Context

Henry, Sr., and his Scotch-Irish wife, Mary, encouraged cheerful anarchy as the norm in their family life. The James homes—and there were many, for the family constantly uprooted itself—were not noted for their peace or quiet. Their five children—William, Henry, Jr., Garth, Robertson, and Alice— "fought like cats and dogs." Meals were dominated by lively, often heated, debate in which the children were expected to expound and defend their own views, even when they ran counter to parental opinion. Guests at the Jameses' table included illustrious literary and political figures of the day: Ralph Waldo Emerson, Charles Dana, Felix Darley, William Thackeray, Washington Irving, Oliver Wendell Holmes, and James Russell Lowell.

Amid the chaos, Mary James, described by her son Henry as "soundless, sleepless, and selfless," presided as the calm eye of the hurricane, the "keystone of the family arch." She worshipped her husband, and he relied on her completely. He said that while she had not had intellectually speaking a liberal education, "she really did arouse my heart."[3]

Formal schooling for the James children was, as Henry, Jr., later said, "administered in small vague spasms." The family moved frequently, often several times a year, and often to Europe. Henry, Sr., cited the children's educations as the reason. Remembering his joyless Calvinist childhood, he was determined that his children not be subjected to dogma, pedantry, or rigidity in any form. His idea of intellectual freedom was to throw William and Henry, Jr., into as many schools as possible and let them formulate their own ideas.

London, Paris, New York, Geneva, Newport, Bonn, Albany—while most of the eastern United States pushed west toward new lands and gold, the Jameses restlessly wandered to Europe and back, staying only for brief periods in one place. William and Henry called themselves "hotel children." Both they and their brothers and sister experienced chronic ill health during these years of wandering.

William James's Development

In 1850 while living in Bonn, William decided to pursue the study of art. His father reacted violently, thinking William suited for science and engineering. Yet just a few months later Henry, Sr., wrote a friend announcing his decision to return to America so "William could study art." Apparently Henry, Sr., became amenable to this when he decided that none of the children seemed to be "cut out for intellectual labors."

The family moved to Newport, Rhode Island, where eighteen-year-old William studied painting with well-known artist William Hunt. A year's effort convinced him he would never be more than mediocre. Accordingly, he abandoned his brushes to enroll in Lawrence Scientific School.

By 1864, his interest in natural sciences led William to Harvard, where he studied under the eminent naturalist Louis Agassiz, accompanying him on an expedition to Brazil. It was in Brazil that William contracted a serious case of smallpox that undermined his health for the next fifteen years.

James traveled to Germany to study experimental physiology in 1867.

There he became interested in medicine and returned to Harvard Medical School, from which he received his degree in 1869. By 1873, he was a professor of physiology and anatomy, by 1878 of psychology, and in 1879 professor of philosophy. He later remarked,

> I originally studied medicine in order to be a physiologist, but I drifted into psychology and philosophy from a sort of fatality. I never had any philosophic instruction, and the first lecture on psychology I ever heard was the first one I ever gave.[4]

William and his brother Henry, born only sixteen months apart, had a relationship characterized by deep empathy and intense rivalry. Henry wrote short stories and novels using the European and American sites of their boyhood as settings. Both highly successful in their respective fields, they always felt a sense of their "inexhaustible brotherhood," as Henry put it. Henry felt outclassed and ignored by William, while William felt intimidated by Henry's impressive earnings as a young writer. Both experienced serious back problems that seemed to activate at the other's successes, as well as digestive disorders, nervousness, and eye problems.

Only when William married Alice Howe Gibbens in 1878 did his health improve. The chronic depressions and backaches ceased as he seemed to gain a new sense of purpose in life.

In 1890, William James published his first major work, The *Principles of Psychology*. It was an outgrowth of James's interest in the natural sciences, a descriptive work assembling facts and theories with the view that the world could only be known through pure experience. A two-volume work, *Principles* was one of the first attempts to treat psychology, not as superstition or philosophy, but as a legitimate, experimental science. *The Principles of Psychology* was soon viewed as the standard work in its field.

The Nature of Consciousness

Like Descartes, James was an interactionist who posited a psychic and mental chain of ideas interacting with a physical and material causal chain. Yet James was not a confirmed dualist. He had examined the mind-body solutions of other philosophers and rejected them all. For him, there was no separate "mind," but an organ called the *brain* capable of processing sensory data (thinking). As the brain acted, a thought occurred. What humans called *consciousness* was a series of isolated ideas associated by mental bonds, a continuum or stream of consciousness that flowed ceaselessly and changed constantly.

Each individual formed his or her own identity by selecting out of this stream of consciousness the parts that seemed biologically, esthetically, or morally useful. The mind worked on sensory data as a sculptor worked on stone. Each person's world was composed of the segments that ancestors and he or she selected or carved out from the mass of possible sensations.

According to James, consciousness was *personal*, or individualistic. It was always changing, a process rather than a static identity. It was sensibly *continu-*

ous: in spite of gaps, individual identity was always maintained. And it was *selective*, using the criteria of relevance and continuity.

In addition, consciousness was purposeful. Its function was to allow humans to make choices that would help them to adapt and survive.

Finally, consciousness could not be considered apart from the body. James felt that sensory processes expressed themselves as motor processes unless inhibited. Similarly, ideas, unless inhibited by other ideas, would lead to action. When asked for an example of this, James theorized that if one had problems arising in the morning all that was necessary was to picture the "getting up process" in the mind and at the same time to clear away all conflicting ideas. The result: that person would soon be standing up.[5]

Pragmatism

By the year 1896, James's intellectual priorities had shifted. Prior to this time, he had considered himself a psychologist with some interest in philosophical and theological problems. Now he began to consider philosophy his primary interest.

The seeds of James's philosophy had been planted in his approach to psychology. At the center was his theory of *pragmatism*, which stated that the validity of any knowledge had to be seen in terms of its consequences, value, or usefulness.

The term *pragmatism* was introduced in America in 1878 by mathematician and philosopher Charles S. Peirce, who had in turn borrowed it from Kant. James adopted it to describe his "method of settling metaphysical disputes" that otherwise might have been "interminable . . . and of interpreting each notion by tracing its respective consequences."[6]

For James, any statement that claimed to be true had to have practical consequences. It had to allow for the possibility of some future action and the formation of a willingness to act accordingly in all circumstances of the given kind. So, for any object to which a person would be prepared to apply an idea—such as "banana"—there were certain expected practical outcomes. One had to expect specific sense experiences from the object. And one had to be prepared to perform certain actions in response to it. This active element, this prospective, rather than retrospective, orientation was what set William James's empiricism apart from traditional British empiricism. James's view was characterized as *functionalism*. James said,

> The truth of a thing or idea is its meaning, or its destiny, that which grows out of it. This would be a doctrine reversing the opinion of the empiricists that the meaning of an idea is that which it has grown from.[7]

In addition to reorienting thought from past to future, James's radical empiricism implied a mind that actively participated. It actively operated on ideas in order to project them into the future; it selected ideas; it ordered and organized them. It acted on present ideas to create a guide to the future that would "seek to assure experiences which it desires and repress those it wishes to avoid."[8]

According to James, the mind was far from being the passive recipient of sensory impressions that it was in Locke's *tabula rasa*. For James, the mind was active, and ideas were "plans for action." The "meaning" of an idea lay in its implications for the future. "Truth" was a property exhibited by any idea that successfully dealt with life experience. Truth was what one could do with statements or ideas.

The Pragmatic Idea of Truth

Prior to James, philosophical idealists such as Berkeley had assumed that truth was a fixed relation. Once one discovered the truth about something, there was no further discussion. Nothing else had to follow that rational climax. Epistemologically, truth was a state of stable equilibrium.

James's pragmatism, on the other hand, took a different tack. He asked,

> Grant an idea or belief to be true, and what concrete difference will its being true make in experience? What would be different than the results if that belief were false? What, experientially speaking, is the truth's "cash value?"[9]

James answered his own question, saying that true ideas could be validated and verified. False ideas could not. The truth of an idea was established in its verification process, its test of functionalism. The idea literally became true in the process of verification as it exhibited satisfactory consequences. It was like a scientist who made a statement about a chemical. The importance of the statement would be magnified as the properties of the chemical were tested and verified.

James refused to go beyond his pragmatic definition of truth to a more idealistic definition that "unconditionally demands to be recognized." To do so, James felt, would be to subvert truth to arbitrariness and thereby deny its meaning.

The Deterministic Dilemma and the Will to Believe

By the mid-nineteenth century, the Calvinistic determinism that had pervaded much of American thought was beginning to retreat in the face of a widespread recognition that science taught that present reality was the result of complex development. The world was no longer seen as fixed forever but as in process of evolutionary change.

The unyielding predestinarian beliefs that had governed the life of William James's grandfather and terrified his father, burning the conviction of God's supernatural being into him "as with a red-hot iron,"[10] were giving way to a new spirit of exploration and investigation of geographical and intellectual frontiers. The pioneering spirit that swept the country reaffirmed people's roles in shaping their own destinies.

For James, the philosophical implications were inescapable. He intentionally placed himself in the center of the conflict.

Prior to Darwin, the reach of science had not been thought of as extending to human beings. All living organisms, and especially humans, were exempt from science's absolute laws of cause and effect. One of the most dramatic effects of Darwin's evolutionary theory was its overt challenge to the notion that humans were not subject to the laws of science. The work of Darwin, Pavlov, and Freud (who had just visited America) all supported the idea that scientific methodology could apply to life processes. Every organic event was controlled by its causes.

The question for James was one of freedom of will. Was human behavior *completely* determined by environmental forces and inherited structures? Or were humans free to act in ways not controlled by those forces?

James could not accept the human being as an impotent creature squirming under the thumb of an omnipotent God. Nor could he believe people to be helpless cogs in the evolutionary process, with no intrinsic significance beyond their biological function. If either were the case life would be a farce; there would be no reason to live, no will to believe. There had to be some freedom of will, some human power capable of determining the future. But how could it be proved?

The Subjective Mode

James admitted that freedom of will could not be proved objectively true, but he felt that it could subjectively be assumed. For example, people developed theories about the world and discussed them as a way of better understanding things. If there were two theories about the world and one seemed more rational, then a person would be entitled to feel that the more rational theory was the more true of the two.

> If a certain formula for expressing the nature of the world violates my own moral demand, I shall feel as free to throw it overboard—or at least to doubt it—as if it disappointed my scientific demand for uniformity of sequence; the one demand being, so far as I can see, quite as subjective and emotional as the other is.[11]

Free will could not be proved true or false by some external criterion. The alternative was to let one's subjective nature choose! One could pick the view one would like to have true, the view that would make the most sense, seem the most fitting and the most relevant. The test of a theory's success was always the degree to which it defined a universe consonant with one's active powers and provided a sense of familiarity in the world. In James's view, a world in which there were no tasks for the will to perform would not be rational. A world in which *anything* could happen would not be rational either. This "sentiment of rationality" worked with subjective feeling to enable one to make balanced choices. Whether one chose determinism or free will, the undeniable implication was that where choice was possible there must be freedom to choose, hence free will.

An unspoken corollary to the implication of free will was the fact that there was never any final truth. Whether in physics or in philosophy, truth was always in process. James wrote, "There can be no final truth until the last man has had his experience and said his say."[12] Each person experienced, interpreted, and chose individually: each sculptor carved a different statue.

Metaphysics

By the turn of the century, James's interests had become increasingly metaphysical. In 1902 he published *The Varieties of Religious Experience*, in 1907 *Pragmatism*, and in 1909 *A Pluralistic Universe*.

Throughout his career, he sought a midpoint between the dichotomous extremes he typified as "tough-minded" and "tender-minded." Was the universe supernatural—was there a being beyond the natural world of time and space? Or, was it natural, consisting of empirical reality only? William James had been born into a pre-Darwinian, supernaturalistic, Calvinistic world. His father, although not a Calvinist, was an adherent of supernatural Swedenborgian mysticism. Yet all of James's professional training was rational and scientific. He could deny the validity of neither the supernatural nor the natural. In attempting to resolve his dilemma, he focused on the problem of evil.

William James defined "good" as that which allowed a satisfactory life and "evil" as that which destroyed life or frustrated satisfaction. James believed that the world was not completely evil or completely good but was capable of being improved by human effort.

Because there were real possiblities for evil as well as for good James held that no good, all-powerful God could have created the world as we know it. If people were to be allowed any determinative powers at all, then God would have to be invested with correspondingly less power. The degree of human freedom of will dictated the degree of God's limits. Evil, in James's view, was something that God did not approve, but, nevertheless, could not prevent. God existed, but this God was not omnipotent. God was limited in power, or in knowledge, or perhaps both.

The Experiment

James put down his pen, pondering the implications of an indeterministic universe. Freedom of will meant that the human mind did not come on a world complete in itself. Was the character of the world given, or capable of being predetermined? Was the mind a passive spectator in existence or an active participant? Was reality changeless, or full of ever-changing possibilities that people could shape?

The human responsibility implied by such questions was immense. James realized that his views put him on the frontier of an uncertain future. But where else could he be? He could retreat back to the settled security of predestination or evolutionary rationalism, but that would be to deny human worth and significance. Would the alternative—publication of his ideas about truth and free will—be of any use? If the theory were wrong and free will did not exist, would life be worth living at all?

James looked at the manuscript. Even now in the bright spring of 1910, the memory of his decision to believe forty years before cast a shadow across his mind. Was the freedom to choose real or illusory? How could he know that he was right? Could he trust his own judgment?

NOTES

1. William James, quoted in Ralph Barton Perry, *The Thought and Character of William James* (New York: Braziller, 1954), p. 121.
2. William James, *The Literary Remains of the Late Henry James* (Boston: Osgood, 1885), pp. 59–60.
3. Leon J. Edel, *Henry James* (Philadelphia: Lippincott, 1953), p. 45.
4. Perry, p. 78.
5. Melvin Marx and William Hillix, *Systems and Theories of Psychology* (New York: McGraw-Hill, 1963), p. 146.
6. William James, *Essays in Pragmatism*, ed. Alburey Castell (New York: Hafner, 1955), p. 142.
7. William James, *Principles of Psychology*, vol. 2 (New York: Dover, 1950), p. 450.
8. Edward C. Moore, *William James* (New York: Washington Square Press, 1966), p. 80.
9. Ibid., p. 92.
10. Ibid., p. 7.
11. William James, *The Will to Believe and Other Essays in Popular Philosophy* (New York: Dover, 1956), pp. 146–147.
12. Moore, p. 61.

BIBLIOGRAPHY

Primary Sources

James, William. *Pragmatism*. London: Longmans, Green, 1928.
James, William. *Varieties of Religious Experience*. New York: University Books, 1963.

Biography

Perry, Ralph Barton. *The Thought and Character of William James*. New York: Braziller, 1954.

Interpretative Works

Davis, Stephen T. *Faith, Skepticism and Evidence*. Lewisburg, Pa.: Bucknell University Press, 1978.
Kuklick, Bruce. *The Rise of American Philosophy*. New Haven, Conn.: Yale University Press, 1977.
Roth, John K. *Freedom and the Moral Life: The Ethics of William James*. Philadelphia: Westminster Press, 1969.
Smith, John E. *Purpose and Thought: The Meaning of Pragmatism*. New Haven, Conn.: Yale University Press, 1978.
Wild, John. *The Radical Empiricism of William James*. New York: Doubleday, 1969.

QUESTIONS FOR STUDY

1. How did the experiences of William James's early life influence his concept of human freedom?

2. Describe the major changes that took place in American intellectual life in the last half of the nineteenth century. Assess their significance for the development of James's thought.

3. Explain the nature of consciousness according to James.

4. Trace the origin and define the meaning of the term *pragmatism* as used by James.

5. Discuss the subjective character of truth in science, as James saw it and as you understand it now.

6. Do you believe that you have genuine freedom to determine the course of your own life? How do you account for the influence of other potentially determining factors, such as heredity, environment, chance, and God?

A Contemporary Response

JOHN K. ROTH

WHY ARE you reading these words? One answer might be that you have to do so because they were assigned. Still, you do not have to read them. You are free to shut this book right now, aren't you? Try it and see—but don't forget to return.

Whatever you did in response to the preceding paragraph, its opening question remains. Why are you reading these words? Could you be doing something different in this very moment, or is your present activity inevitable, unavoidable, determined so that it could not be different?

Now expand the horizon and consider the newspaper you read this morning. Did the tornado reported on page 1 have to strike? How did that sordid murder happen? Why are current economic trends the way they are? Must there be conflict in the Middle East?

Such questions are not without answers. For example, as a psychologist, William James would understand that your reading of this page can be explained by reference to your being a student with certain motives and goals, some of which led you into a particular course where an assignment was made for you to carry out dutifully. James's knowledge of science and history, moreover, would make it clear that natural disasters and human dealings do not unfold in a vacuum. They are strands of an intricate web, and a conceptual framework of cause-and-effect relationships tells us much about why the individual strands and the web as a whole have one design and not another.

The Vise of Determinism

Our lives move into an unknown future, and they seem to follow a particular path partly because we make decisions freely. But, although we live forward, we understand backward; we know the present by means of the past. Although we may feel free, in retrospect we discover powerful forces and instincts that drive us from the inside as well as from the outside. So knowledge apparently requires us to affirm that what we are doing now is the effect of preceding causes, even if we do not grasp what all of the causes may be or exactly how they combine to produce what is happening now.

Far from eliminating James's puzzlement, such analysis intensified it. Indeed, James believed that hardly anyone escapes a struggle with the basic issue: Are we free agents or puppets on a string? To the extent that one takes cause-and-effect relationships to mean that the present is simply the product of the past, it seemed to James that all experience and reality become "the dull rattling off of a chain that was forged innumerable ages ago." Nothing can be other than it is. Real possibilities vanish. The commonsense conviction that present choices produce a genuinely new result because they are free—not beyond the influence of environment and previous events, but not totally controlled by them either—turns into self-deception. The vise of determinism squeezes freedom and significance out of existence.

Increasingly, James detested the *feeling* of that squeeze. Granted, feeling cannot be trusted completely as an avenue to truth. It needs to be interpreted and tested by thinking. But James believed that gut-level feeling should be taken seriously. Looking for a match between the two, James stuck by this intuition: When feeling and thinking do not jibe, the first step is *not* to scrap feeling but to see whether thinking ought to be revised. That principle focused his confrontation with determinism.

The result of that confrontation was James's philosophy of *meliorism*, the belief that the world can be made better by human effort. James underscored the openness of experience, the significance of choice making, hope within history, and belief that salvation for humankind is possible. Exploring how James developed these four strands of his philosophy will reveal how his mind worked and help us to decide whether his outlook is sound.

Sense and Nonsense

Some philosophers, James believed, thought that determinism was required to make sense of existence. That is, unless it was possible to develop cause-and-effect accounts in which the past could always explain the present completely, knowledge and especially science fell by the way. As scientist and as philosopher, not to say as an individual human person, James found such assumptions unnecessary and unconvincing. Far from making existence intelligible, determinism turned meaning into nonsense. To make his case, James chose the example of a senseless killing in Brockton, Massachusetts.

Savage murder, James argued, rightly creates feelings of abhorrence and regret. The meaning of such feelings is that an actual happening, in this case the killing, ought not to have occurred. The meaning of that "ought," in turn, is that the killing was avoidable. If determinism is valid, such feelings of abhorrence and regret cannot be other than they are, but neither is it possible in any meaningful sense to say that the murder could not have been. It was the unavoidable next link in a chain already forged. If determinism makes sense, James could find precious little of it in this scenario. That fact was evidence enough for him to assert that determinism offers people a promissory note on which it can never make good.

Note James's strategy. He gave no proof for freedom or indeterminism, nor did he claim that determinism was conclusively wrong. Determinism might be true, but the issue is whether it is incumbent on us, or even desirable, to believe that it is. James thought not, because determinism needlessly makes common sense nonsensical. As for the lingering charge that any nondeterministic approach would render scientific knowledge impossible, James argued that the indictment was sound only if science actually required a deterministic base. Another alternative exists, and it has the greater validity.

Scientific knowledge, James believed, was best understood as the result of tested hypotheses. Such knowledge was obtained by seeing and judging what happens. The seeing and judging are always fallible. They can result in inferences about causes and effects, laws of nature, and fundamental principles, but these interpretations can be made without assuming determinism and thus science itself can never prove that determinism is real. In fact, James urged, a view of reality much more in tune with what scientists actually do, not to mention what people feel in response to brutal death, is one that finds existence in process, moving into an open future. Freedom, not determinism, is the hypothesis that best fits the sense of human experience.

The Strenuous Mood

William James was keenly interested in good education. He advised teachers that their responsibility was not only "to generate . . . a large stock of ideas," but also "to build up a *character* in your pupils" (James's italics). James's point is that a good person is one who lives with care and passion directed toward development of talents and toward service that relieves suffering and injustice. Such ingredients form what he calls the *strenuous mood.*

Human beings are purposeful and value oriented. James's approval of the strenuous mood reflects and advances that estimate. Circumstances, however, do not always cooperate. They can rob life of meaning, make it unbearable—so much so that suicide becomes an option. Troubled by that fact, James set himself the task of reflecting on what he could say to convince a potential suicide that life is worth living.

In some cases, despair may have tipped the scales irrevocably. Rational discussion and persuasion may not have the power to check self-destruction. Nonetheless, as James reflected on suicide he would not give up the conviction that it was an *option* and not a fixed necessity. Suicide was unthinkable without choice making, and in James's estimate choice making entailed more than one possibility.

James thought that human freedom was centered in our capacity to *pay attention.* We can choose to focus this way or that, and our decisions make a practical difference. Suicide, therefore, is at least in part a function of how one's attention is placed. By redirecting attention, suicide may also be avoided. An appeal to the strenuous mood could serve that purpose, especially because it stresses refusal to give up, rebellion against despair, and courage that says, "Be not afraid of life. Believe that life *is* worth living, and your belief will help create the fact."

Such counsel, James recognized, could be no more than that. The most important lesson he drew from his reflections on suicide was that ultimately all of us must—and therefore can—appraise the world of life for ourselves. Whether life is worth living depends on what we decide and do. No fortunes are told in advance in James's world of freedom, but the collision of the strenuous and suicidal moods offers striking circumstantial evidence that the freedom of choice making is not to be overlooked.

Either/Or

William James did not live to see the twentieth century rip itself apart with world wars, death camps, and nuclear threats. His world contained no volatile oil shortages. He did work, however, in an era when the biology of Charles Darwin had been turned into a social theory. Some adherents of Social Darwinism, as the view came to be known, claimed not only that the fittest survive but also that human history is the testing ground in which conflict between nations, cultures, and even races, is inevitable. James protested this outlook, not least because it fueled the fires of imperialism. He offered instead his conviction that there could be a moral equivalent of war.

James was realistic. Pacifism was one of his ideals, but he recognized that people did not flock to its banner. The reason, James believed, was that in spite of, or even because of, war's horrors, a militaristically oriented life-style can provide meaningful challenges that require and elicit courage, discipline, communal spirit, and endurance. A nation must possess such qualities to assure its health, but the issue that James wanted to clarify was whether such effects necessarily required a militaristic stance.

Part of James's answer was yes. Some quality of meaningful struggle, with real gains and losses yet to be decided, does seem to be crucial for drawing out essential virtues. But part of James's answer was also no. There is ample opportunity for high ideals to be cultivated not by means of bombs and bullets but by doing battle against poverty, disease, and injustice.

Such problems would not eliminate themselves. Only hard work could do the job, but in that premise James took hope. Life, he believed, offers us "mutually exclusive alternatives of which only one can be true at once; so that we must choose, and in choosing murder one possibility. The wrench is absolute: 'Either—or!' " War *or* the moral equivalent of war—in that live option James found freedom and a reason to trust that human power might work for good.

Healthy Minds and Sick Souls

None of James's books is more widely read than *The Varieties of Religious Experience.* In that classic study he distinguishes between healthy minds and sick souls. The difference involves attitudes toward evil, the wasting of human life.

A healthy-minded approach to evil tends to see tragedy and misfortune as instrumental. Life's losses are part of a larger picture in which evil is either a means to some greater good or at least overcome by happy endings. James's study of religion indicated that such healthy-minded views often go hand-in-glove with versions of determinism. Such outlooks have a clear-cut asset. If accepted, they provide comfort by assuring that everything will work out well.

James chose not to embrace this healthy-minded religion, and the rejection of determinism figured in his disposition. If a deterministic religious perspective offered comfort, James found the price for that bargain so high as to make it no bargain at all. Determinism might guarantee some final outcome, but it would also necessitate all the evils along the way. It would legitimate evil and thereby encourage not the strenuous mood but the "don't care mood" of indifference. James would not veneer an essentially pessimistic attitude toward the details of existence with a gloss of optimism about the totality.

Unable to accept the claim that all evil is instrumental, James's sick soul had difficulties of its own. By refusing to embrace any philosophy that left existence determined fully by God, the laws of nature, or the forces of history, James won back the possibility that nothing has to be just as it is. Evil is all too real, he asserted, but it is also unnecessary and deserving of no apologies. The tradeoff, however, was that our sense of the future now lacked insurance to underwrite complete and everlasting joy.

True, James did retain a concept of God in his philosophy, but for the sake of freedom James's God was limited in power. For goodness to prevail, God and humankind would have to work together. The odds might be too great for all of us. Probably some losses would be final, but James was willing to take that risk if freedom required it. "For the practical life at any rate," he concluded, "the *chance* of salvation is enough. No fact in human nature is more characteristic than its willingness to live on a chance." For William James, it meant more to engage in a real battle against evil than to be assured of a sham victory because the means and ends had been programmed in advance.

The Faith-Ladder

On August 26, 1910, after hiking in the New Hampshire mountains, William James died. Left incomplete was an introductory textbook for his philosophy students. James's plan was to dedicate the book to Charles Renouvier, the French writer who forty years earlier had started him toward a philosophy of freedom. This unfinished work, *Some Problems of Philosophy,* was published posthumously. Its concluding pages contain some fragments that James intended to elaborate, and among them is an outline for a reasoning process called the "faith-ladder." It climbs this way:

1. There is nothing absurd in a certain view of the world being true, nothing self-contradictory.

2. It *might* have been true under certain conditions.
3. It *may* be true, even now.
4. It is *fit* to be true.
5. It *ought* to be true.
6. It *must* be true.
7. It *shall* be true, at any rate true for *me*.

That line of reasoning, parts of which are illustrated in what has gone before, summarizes James's way of arguing for freedom and against determinism. James understood the logic of freedom. It would not make good sense to expect that freedom's reality could be finally demonstrated or that real freedom could be consistent with one's being determined to believe that freedom is real. Freedom, including belief in freedom, rightly involves risk and choice.

James thought about those facts for a long time. At the end of his life, perhaps he was still uncertain whether the freedom to choose was genuine or illusory. If so, he must have known that such an outcome was fitting even as he affirmed freedom yet again. I choose to think—freely, I presume—that William James was correct on both counts. Do you?

CHAPTER 11

The Case of Whitehead

Will Modern Science Support a Vision of God?

LUCIEN PRICE, editorial writer for the *Boston Globe,* sat at his typewriter. It was November 12, 1947. On the previous day, he had taken advantage of the Armistice Day holiday to visit his friend, the retired Harvard philosopher Alfred North Whitehead. Now he was recording the conversation from memory, as he had done following their regular visits over the past fifteen years. Price felt that it was perhaps their last visit. Whitehead was eighty-six years old and failing in health. Yet Whitehead's mind and conversation had been lucid as always.

Price thought of publishing the conversations after Whitehead was gone. Whitehead had given permission. But what would be the reaction of the public? In the aftermath of a world war, people were suspicious of science and sure of the sinfulness of humanity. In philosophy, the existentialists with their pessimistic individualism were popular. And in theology the crisis theologians were dominant with their doctrine of a God totally other than and above humankind. How would people respond to this gentle philosopher with his liberal views, and his sense of adventure, and his hope for the future? Could they be interested in a philosophy in harmony with modern science that saw all of reality in a state of continually changing process? And how would they react to Whitehead's vision of God as involved with humankind and interacting with the world? Price looked at Whitehead's words as he had just typed them and wondered.

Whitehead's Early Life

Alfred North Whitehead was born on February 15, 1861, in the English village of Ramsgate, Kent. His grandfather and father had been successively headmaster of the same private school in the village. A year before Alfred was born, his father was ordained a clergyman in the Church of England and later gave up his school post to serve a rural parish in the area. Whitehead later commented,

I watched the history of England by my vision of grandfather, father, Archbishop Tait of Canterbury . . . and others. When the Baptist minister in the parish was dying, it was my father who read the Bible to him. Such was England in those days, guided by local men with strong mutual antagonisms and intimate community of feeling. This vision was one source of my interest in history, and in education.[1]

Whitehead's personality was also influenced by the surrounding land. "Geography," he said, "is half of character."[2] Roman forts and Norman churches marked the area. Near Whitehead's home had stood the oak under which the Saxon King Ethelbert had been converted to Christianity by St. Augustine in the sixth century. Young Alfred enjoyed regular trips to Canterbury Cathedral sixteen miles away. He knew the spot where Becket fell in A.D. 1170 and gazed at the tomb of Edward, the Black Prince, who died in A.D. 1376. Whitehead later reflected on the influence of his environment and said, "It shows how historical tradition is handed down by the direct experience of physical surroundings."[3]

Alfred was a frail child. he was taught at home by his father and encouraged to spend much time outdoors in the company of an old gardener. Each year in the late spring he visited his grandmother in London. From her windows overlooking Green Park he often saw Queen Victoria ride by in her carriage, a little figure in black, belonging, for him, to the unquestioned order of the universe.

At the age of fourteen, Alfred went away to Sherborne in Dorsetshire, one of England's oldest schools. There, too, he was surrounded by history. He later remarked,

> We had plenty of evidence that things had been going on for a long time. It never entered into anybody's mind to regard six thousand years seriously as the age of mankind—not because we took up with revolutionary ideas, but because our continuity with nature was a patent, visible fact. . . . There were incredible quantities of fossils about . . . the stones were built out of fossils, welded together.[4]

His education was classical. The boys at the school read Greek and Roman history and imbibed classical ideals. The prayer which each boy successively had to read daily in chapel stated that they were being trained to serve God in Church and State. Roman and especially Greek political philosophies were sufficient for that purpose for boys who were comparatively ignorant of the problems of modern industrial society. Their religion as well came in Greek. Whitehead remembered,

> Thus we read the New Testament in Greek. At school—except in chapel, which did not count—I never heard of anyone reading it in English. It would suggest an uncultivated religious state of mind. We were very religious, but with that moderation natural to people who take their religion in Greek.[5]

In addition to the classics, young Whitehead enjoyed reading poetry and studying mathematics, which was the best taught of the subjects. Sports also played a large part in the school's program. Having overcome his earlier frailty, Whitehead captained the football and cricket teams. These experiences made a deep impression:

Being tackled at Rugby, there is the Real. Nobody who hasn't been knocked down has the slightest notion of what the Real is. . . . They used to hack at your shins to make you surrender the ball. . . . but the question was how you took it—your own self-creation. Freedom lies in summoning up a mentality which transforms the situations, as against letting organic reactions take their course.[6]

After five years at Sherborne, Whitehead was offered a scholarship to Trinity College, Cambridge, in either classics or mathematics. He chose mathematics, and during his whole undergraduate period he studied only mathematics, pure and applied, and never went inside another lecture room. This intensely narrow concentration in class was complemented by continual conversation with friends, faculty, and alumni every evening after dinner. These discussions covered politics, religion, philosophy, and literature. Although he never formally studied philosophy, Whitehead later noted that by the end of his five years as an undergraduate he nearly knew by heart parts of Kant's *Critique of Pure Reason*.

Whitehead's Career, Phase 1: Cambridge

In 1885, Alfred North Whitehead was given a fellowship at Trinity and a teaching post. He remained there for twenty-five years. It was a period of great personal stability and equally great intellectual stimulation. Darwin's published work was only two decades old. Non-Euclidean approaches to geometry were beginning to be discussed, along with new approaches to logic and attempts at a universal mathematics. And, most challenging of all, were new discoveries in physics. Whitehead's reaction was

We supposed that nearly everything of importance about physics was known. . . . But . . . the whole science blew up, and the Newtonian physics, which had been supposed to be fixed as the Everlasting Seat, were gone. Oh, they were and still are useful as a way of looking at things, but regarded as a final description of reality, no longer valid. Certitude was gone.[7]

In 1890, Whitehead married Evelyn Willoughby Wade, an Irish girl who had been educated in France and only come to live in England at the age of seventeen. They were devoted to each other, and Whitehead freely acknowledged his wife's influence on his thought.

The effect of my wife upon my outlook on the world has been so fundamental, that it must be mentioned as an essential factor in my philosophic output. Her vivid life has taught me that beauty, moral and aesthetic, is the aim of existence; and that kindness, and love, and artistic satisfaction are among its modes of attainment.[8]

The years of 1891 to 1898 were formative in many ways for the Whiteheads. Four children were born to them. One died at birth. Later, all three children exemplified the family sense of duty, serving during World War I. The youngest son, Eric, was killed when his plane was shot down over France in March 1918.

Also during this period, the Whiteheads were both somewhat disaffected with Anglicanism. They made a serious and intensive study of the literature of Roman Catholicism, but at the end of seven years of study, no conversion occurred. Whitehead took all his theology books to a local bookstore and sold them.

In 1898, Whitehead's first book was published, *A Treatise on Universal Algebra*. In the next few years, he was deeply involved in community affairs. He argued for the equality of women in a losing debate at the university. And he spoke for the Liberal party at local meetings in the country villages of his district.

Whitehead's Career, Phase 2: London

In 1910, a second period of Whitehead's life abruptly began. At nearly fifty years of age, and with three children, Whitehead and his wife left Cambridge and moved to London. Having no teaching position there Whitehead took a bottle-washing job at London University. In 1911, he began teaching at University College. After four years, he was made a professor at the Imperial College of Science and Technology. During the next dozen years, he became first dean of the faculty of science and then president of the senate of the University of London.

During this period, Whitehead was deeply involved in the technical problems of mathematics and philosophy of science, as well as in the general questions of university education and administration. Regarding mathematics, he pondered two kinds of questions: "Which formal theory best fits the facts of nature?" and "How can mathematics be made understandable to the general public?" He published an extremely technical and innovative three-volume work, *Principia Mathematica,* co-authored with his former student Bertrand Russell, during 1910–1913. In 1911, he issued his elementary and very readable *Introduction to Mathematics.* He produced several books in the philosophy of science including *The Concept of Nature* (1920). In 1922, he published *The Principle of Relativity with Applications to Physical Science* to introduce an alternative mathematical formulation to that of Einstein's theory of relativity.

Whitehead's Career, Phase 3: Harvard

In 1924, Whitehead was sixty-three years old. He faced mandatory retirement as a civil servant in two years. As a complete surprise to him, he received an invitation to join the faculty of Harvard University in the philosophy department. His wife handed him the letter on a dismal London afternoon. After they had both read it, she asked him, "What do you think of it?" To her great surprise he replied, "I would rather do that than anything in the world."[9]

The original offer from Harvard was for a five-year appointment. After two years, Whitehead was asked to stay as long as he was able. During his thirteen-year tenure at Harvard, Whitehead wrote eight books and numerous articles. He also lectured three times a week and gave himself generously to students in conference. He declined to teach students the thoughts of others but used the classroom to develop his own ideas.

Whitehead continually and eagerly learned from others. He offered a joint seminar with the philosopher W. E. Hocking, one of the first examples of "team teaching" in the United States. And he felt that he learned from his students. He said, "It is all nonsense to suppose that the old cannot learn from the young."[10] During all his years at Harvard, the Whiteheads held open house to students one night a week. The fare was hot chocolate, cake, and conversation with both the Whiteheads. Alfred once remarked, "By myself I am only one more professor, but with Evelyn I am first-rate."[11]

While at Harvard, Whitehead's interest in nature led him further to the question of human nature and that, in turn, led him to investigate the nature of all reality. He began to create a new metaphysic, a comprehensive theory of reality. For Whitehead, that meant dealing with the nature of God. *In Science and the Modern World,* Whitehead challenged "scientific materialism" as being an inadequate description of the richness of reality as we experience it. He wrote, "The only way of mitigating mechanism is by the discovery that it is not mechanism."[12] At the same time, Whitehead confronted static notions of religion. He said, "Religion will not regain its old power until it can face change in the same spirit as does science."[13] The book was immediately hailed by many American thinkers, among them John Dewey, as providing a more adequate framework for relating both scientific facts and personal values.

The next year Whitehead gave four lectures at King's Chapel in Boston, published as *Religion in the Making* (1926). He argued that religion embodied humanity's deepest vision of reality. Whitehead contrasted Buddhism as a metaphysic generating a religion, with Christianity, as a religion seeking a metaphysic. He asserted, "The Buddha gave his doctrine to enlighten the world: Christ gave his life. It is for Christians to discern the doctrine."[14] Whitehead devoted himself to developing that metaphysic.

Process Thought: Metaphysics

The metaphysic that Whitehead developed was one of process. He sometimes called it a "philosophy of organism." According to Whitehead, there were three notions that made up the "category of the ultimate." The first of these notions was *creativity*. The other two notions were the *many* and the *one*. Creativity was central to his understanding of process. It was the ongoing process by which a novel one came into being from the many and then perished back into the many again.

At any moment, the universe consists of a diversity—the many. But, according to Whitehead, "it lies in the nature of things that the many enter into complex unity."[15] The unique *one* that resulted from this moment of unification (which Whitehead called a *concrescence*) was an *actual entity*. This unity differed from a traditional substance, however, in that it was temporary and was interrelated with all other actual entities. These actual entities were drops of experience, complex and interdependent. They were microcosmic entities like atoms, groups of which, called *societies,* formed the macrocosmic things of everyday experience—rocks, plants, and people. To call these realities of which the world was made up "drops of experience" was not to imply that they all had consciousness. Consciousness only emerged in very sophisticated societies of entities like the society we call the human brain.

Nor did these actual entities have an enduring or continuous existence. Whitehead defined an actual entity as the unity to be attributed to a particular instance of concrescence. A concrescence was a growing together of remnants of the perishing past into a unique, immediate unity. The process by which entities related to other entities was called *prehending* (grasping) or *feeling* (sympathizing). This was the process by which actual entities incorporated the data of other objects into themselves. That growing together of the separate *feelings* of diverse entities from the past into one unity of feeling Whitehead termed the *satisfaction* of the actual entity. In the moment of attaining its satisfaction, an actual entity *perished.* It now had an *objective immortality* in that it could become a datum for new instances of concrescence.

Actual entities were not things that had enduring substances, but activities that occurred in a moment and then became a part of the past. Yet, for Whitehead, this was a meaningful description of life:

> Now as a first approximation the notion of life implies a certain absoluteness of self-enjoyment. This must mean a certain immediate individuality, which is a complex process of appropriating into a unity of existence the many data presented as relevant by the physical processes of nature. Life implies the absolute, individual self-enjoyment arising out of this process of appropriation. I have, in my recent writings, used the word "prehension" to express this process of appropriation. Also, I have termed each individual act of immediate self-enjoyment an "occasion of experience." I hold that these unities of existence, these occasions of experience, are the really real things which in their collective unity compose the evolving universe, even plunging into the creative advance.[16]

Process Thought: God

How did God fit into this process? God was not a person, but for Whitehead, God was a conscious, personal reality. Whitehead had written,

> God is an actual entity, and so is the most trivial puff of existence in far-off empty space. But, though there are gradations of importance, and diversities of function, yet in the principles which actuality exemplifies all are on the same level.[17]

Whitehead was a thoroughgoing empiricist. He accepted only what could be grounded in experience. He said, "God is not to be treated as an exception to all metaphysical principles, invoked to save their collapse. He is their chief exemplification."[18] God, for Whitehead, was the entity in which all others existed, and God was the persuasive power that related entities to each other and guided the whole process toward fulfillment. Whitehead declared, "Everything must be somewhere; and here 'somewhere' is the nontemporal actual entity . . . the primordial mind of God."[19]

God had not one nature but two: a dipolar nature. God's *primordial* nature was a nontemporal actual entity conceptually valuing the timeless realm of eternal objects. But God's *consequent* nature physically *prehended*, or incorporated into itself, and preserved the actual entities of the temporal world. God related entities to each other on a grand order as God integrated the physical feelings of God's consequent nature with the conceptual feelings of God's primordial nature. Whitehead wrote of God,

> He saves the world as it passes into the immediacy of his own life. It is the judgment of a tenderness which loses nothing that can be saved. It is also the judgment of a wisdom which uses what in the temporal world is mere wreckage.[20]

God was not *before* all creation, rather, but was *with* all creation. According to Whitehead, God was "that factor in the universe whereby there is importance, value, and ideal beyond the actual."[21] God set before each actual entity an initial *subjective aim*, a vision of what it might become. This initial subjective aim offered an ideal growth on the part of the entity that would result in the kind of world filled with novelty and yet order that would provide a maximum intensity of satisfaction for God. For Whitehead, "all order is therefore aesthetic order, and the aesthetic order is derived from the immanence of God."[22]

Process Thought: Evil

What of instability, disorder, and evil? How could he reconcile his understanding of God with the evil in the world? Whitehead recognized that evil was a fact in the world. He wrote, "Now evil is exhibited in physical suffering, mental suffering, and loss of the higher experience in favour of the lower experience."[23] Things that we call evil might be good in themselves but had the character of destructive agents among things greater than themselves. Whitehead responded to the problem of evil by claiming that God could not prevent the occurrence of evil because God was not all powerful. God was good and persuasive and sought to bring order from instability and constructive outcomes from evil. But God did not exercise coercive control over reality. According to Whitehead, "God has in his nature the knowledge of evil, of pain, and of degradation, but it is there as overcome with what is good."[24] This overcoming of evil by good within God's nature was what Whitehead called the "kingdom of heaven." However, God's concepts of goodness and morality were necessarily different from those of human beings. According to Whitehead, God as creative and persuasive love was a "little oblivious" as to morals. What was good from God's perspective did not always seem good to persons. According to Whitehead's vision of God: "He does not create the world, he saves it; or, more accurately, he is the poet of the world, with tender patience leading it by his vision of truth, beauty, and goodness."[25] For Whitehead, therefore, "The power of God is the worship He inspires."[26] We perceive God in the world not in the image of a ruling Caesar, or a moral absolutist, nor an unmoved mover, but in that "brief Galilean vision of humility" that "dwells upon the tender elements in the world, which slowly and in quietness operate by love."[27]

Reflection

Lucien Price looked up from his typewriter and paused. Whitehead's health was failing and he probably would not live much longer. The time for publishing their conversations might be coming soon. Price mused over the meaning of possibly his last conversation with Whitehead.

> It was a mistake, as the Hebrews tried, to conceive of God as creating the world from the outside, at one go. An all-foreseeing Creator, who could have made the world as we find it now—what could we think of such a being? Foreseeing everything and yet putting into it all sorts of imperfections to redeem which it was necessary to send his only son into the world to suffer torture and hideous death; outrageous ideas. The Hellenic religion was a better approach; the Greeks conceived of creation as going on everywhere all the time *within* the universe. . . .
>
> God is *in* the world, or nowhere, creating continually in us and around us. This creative principle is everywhere, in animate and so-called inanimate matter, in the ether, water, earth, human hearts. But this creation is a continuing process, and "the process is itself the actuality," since no sooner do you arrive than you start on a fresh journey. In so far as man partakes of this creative process does he partake of the divine, of God, and that participation is his immortality, reducing the question of whether his individuality survives death of the body to an estate of irrelevancy. His true destiny as co-creator in the universe is his dignity and his grandeur.[28]

How would people in a post-war world respond to Whitehead's adventurous vision? Would they affirm Whitehead's philosophy of science, which held that all of reality was in a constant process of becoming and perishing? Could they accept the idea of a patient and persuasive God in process of intimate interaction with people and the world? Price wondered as he pulled the paper from his typewriter.

NOTES

1. Alfred North Whitehead, *Essays in Science and Philosophy* (New York: Philosophical Library, 1947), p. 4, hereafter cited as *Essays*.
2. Nathaniel Lawrence, *Alfred North Whitehead: A Primer of His Philosophy* (New York: Twayne, 1974), pp. 13–14.
3. Whitehead, *Essays*, p. 5.
4. Ibid., p. 32.
5. Ibid., p. 37.
6. Quoted in Lawrence, p. 17.
7. Lucien Price, *Dialogues of Alfred North Whitehead* (Boston: Little, Brown, 1954), pp. 6–7.
8. Whitehead, *Essays*, pp. 8–9.
9. Price, p. 10.
10. Ibid., p. 11.

11. Ibid., p. 11.
12. Alfred North Whitehead, *Science and the Modern World* (New York: Macmillan, 1925), p. 111, hereafter cited as *Science*. See Victor Lowe, *Understanding Whitehead* (Baltimore: Johns Hopkins University Press, 1962), p. 13.
13. Whitehead, *Science*, p. 270.
14. Alfred North Whitehead, *Religion in the Making* (Cleveland: World, 1960), p. 55, hereafter cited as *Religion*.
15. Alfred North Whitehead, *Process and Reality* (New York: Macmillan, 1929), p. 31, hereafter cited as *Process*, quoted in Donald W. Sherburne, ed., *A Key to Whitehead's Process and Reality* (New York: Macmillan, 1966), p. 218. We are indebted to Sherburne's careful work for the analysis of this term and others that follow. Words underlined are technical terms in Whitehead's thought.
16. Alfred North Whitehead, *Modes of Thought* (New York: Macmillan, 1938), pp. 205–206, hereafter cited as *Modes*. See the helpful glossary of terms in F. S. C. Northrop and Mason W. Gross, eds., *Alfred North Whitehead: An Anthology* (New York: Macmillan, 1961), pp. 925–928.
17. Whitehead, *Process*, p. 28, quoted in Sherburne, p. 225.
18. Whitehead, *Process*, p. 521, quoted in Sherburne, pp. 225–226. It is clear that Whitehead did not believe that God was a male, nor even a person. However, in accordance with the conventions of his time, Whitehead regularly refers to God with the masculine pronoun.
19. Whitehead, *Process*, p. 73, quoted in Sherburne, p. 226.
20. Whitehead, *Process*, p. 525, quoted in Randolph Crump Miller, *The American Spirit in Theology* (Philadelphia: United Church Press, 1974), p. 154.
21. Whitehead, *Modes*, p. 140. See Northrop and Gross, p. 926.
22. Whitehead, *Religion*, p. 105. See the helpful treatment in Miller, p. 155.
23. Ibid., p. 92.
24. Ibid., p. 149. See Miller, p. 155.
25. Whitehead, *Process*, p. 526, quoted in Miller, p. 156.
26. Whitehead, *Science*, p. 276.
27. Whitehead, *Process*, p. 520, quoted in Sherburne, p. 244.
28. Price, pp. 370–371. See the treatment of this passage in Norman Pittenger, *Alfred North Whitehead* (Richmond, Va.: John Knox Press, 1969), pp. ix–xi, and also David Ray Griffin, *God, Power and Evil* (Philadelphia: Westminster Press, 1976).

BIBLIOGRAPHY

Primary Sources

Whitehead, Alfred North. *Essays in Science and Philosophy.* New York: Philosophical Library, 1947.
Whitehead, Alfred North. *Process and Reality.* New York: Macmillan, 1929.

Biography and Autobiography

Lawrence, Nathaniel. *Alfred North Whitehead: A Primer of His Philosophy.* New York: Twayne, 1974.
Schilpp, Paul Arthur, ed. *The Philosophy of Alfred North Whitehead.* The Library of Living Philosophers. New York: Tudor, 1941.

Interpretative Works

Cobb, John B., Jr., and Griffen, David Ray. *Process Theology: An Introductory Exposition.* Philadelphia: Westminster Press, 1976.

Leclerc, Ivor. *Whitehead's Metaphysics.* New York: Macmillan, 1958.
Lowe, Victor. *Understanding Whitehead.* Baltimore: Johns Hopkins University Press, 1962.
Mays, W. *The Philosophy of Whitehead.* New York: Crowell-Collier, 1962.
Price, Lucien. *Dialogues of Alfred North Whitehead.* Boston: Little, Brown, 1954.
Sherburne, Donald W., ed. *A Key to Whitehead's* Process and Reality. New York: Macmillan, 1966.

QUESTIONS FOR STUDY

1. How did Whitehead deal with the problem of change? Compare his views with those of the following early Greek philosophers:
   a. The pre-Socratics
   b. Plato
   c. Aristotle

2. To what extent was Whitehead's thought rooted in his life experience?
   a. Select central elements of his philosophy and show evidence from his life experience that helps to explain them.
   Or
   b. Pick significant experiences in his life and seek embodiments of those experiences in his philosophy.

3. Outline Whitehead's metaphysical system. Be sure to define terms such as
   a. Actual entity
   b. Creativity
   c. Prehending
   d. Satisfaction
   e. Objective immortality

4. Describe Whitehead's concept of a dipolar God and God's relationship to the world.

5. What role did esthetics play in Whitehead's philosophy?

6. Discuss Whitehead's response to the problem of evil. Consider the following issues:
   a. In what ways does Whitehead's response solve traditional problems?
   b. What traditional needs does Whitehead's view leave unmet?
   c. What is your own solution to the problem of evil? Argue for its adequacy.

A Contemporary Response

MARJORIE SUCHOCKI

How is there any credibility in a philosophy that speaks of hope when our experience in the world increasingly speaks of disillusionment and despair? The problem is particularly critical when that philosophy claims to be an applied philosophy that describes reality. Is hope truly consistent with the reality of our experience?

If Price wondered about the credibility of Whitehead's view in the disillusionment of a post-World War II world, the question is even more acute in this latter part of the twentieth century. For the first time in the world's long history, the world itself is threatened with destruction through the power of its chief inhabitants, humankind. We possess the power to destroy the world not simply in the most obvious way of nuclear destruction but also in the more invidious ways of pollution of the environment and an inability to control our own zooming population growth. The image of the lemmings rushing into the sea is evoked with increasing frequency as these triple threats to existence continue to gain in power. Now, however, the horror of the image is that we must envisage not simply the community of the lemmings going blindly, impetuously toward their own destruction. Rather, the image takes on surrealistic overtones, for the creatures pull the surface of the earth with them as they go; as they drop over the cliff into the waiting sea all life falls with them; earthscape is turned to moonscape. Whether we read the problems in apocalyptic terms or in muted tones, the questions posed by Price remain: "What is the credibility of a philosophy of hope in the midst of such a world? How does such a philosophy speak to experience? How, indeed, can it claim to be based on experience?"

The problem is compounded, of course, inasmuch as Whitehead's account of the creative advance of nature is interwoven with an account of a God who is continuously at work with us in creative activity. Whitehead suggests that God, as well as the world, is formed through this activity. If this is so, what if the restless fear of the destruction of the world is realized—is God, too, affected by such destruction? If the world is in some sense the creation of God, is the destruction of the world the destruction or lessening of God as well? How could a God affected by the world be a source of hope? Is not such a "God" pitiable, being at the mercy of a world dancing with ultimate death? To phrase the question like this, of course, leads to the final issue posed in Price's dilemma: "Where is the power of the 'poet of the world' to deal with radical evil? How does 'tender patience' respond adequately to violent destruction?" If such a God cannot deal with evil, we return again to the basic issue: How is there any credibility to this philosophy of hope in a world where disillusionment and despair constantly threaten to undo us?

The problem is more important than an exercise in critical thinking. The difficulty is that the danger of despair rests in its paralyzing effect on action. If in fact the problems facing our society are now out of hand, if in fact the image of the lemmings is all too appropriate to our condition, if in fact we have passed the point of no return—then what is the sense of trying to change our self-contrived fate? Society is larger than the individual; why should we as individuals try to change society? Shall we not instead create island communities in the dark sea of the world, and in these communities do our best to live our private lives in what happiness we still can wrest from existence? Withdrawal from public issues in an attempt to create private meaning would seem to be the counsel of disillusionment and despair. "Why bother?" becomes the unanswerable question if there is no credibility to hope. But in such a situation, the absence of action is the most devastating form of action, for it leaves unchecked the momentum of forces unleashed. Nonaction has a negative power to create the very reality it fears, so that our "island communities of private meaning" are no more effective than a picket fence built to keep out the sea.

Hope, on the contrary, has a catalytic force. Hope speaks of an open future rather than a closed future, of realizable alternatives rather than one predetermined course of events. If in fact there are many possible futures, then *which* future comes about depends on present action. To be convinced that a number of alternatives are consistent with reality, and that there is a power threading its way throughout existence toward optimum modes of richness, is to dare action even against formidable odds. Therefore, if the situation in the world is as dire as we have presented it, then now above all times we cannot afford the false luxury of cynicism, disillusionment, or despair. Investigating the credibility of hope can itself become a means toward hope and therefore toward constructive action as well.

How does Whitehead's philosophy bespeak the reality of hope? Hope, to *be* hope, must be grounded in reality. If a vision of hope is to activate us, it must be consistent with the world we experience. The key to investigating the credibility of hope in Whitehead's vision lies in understanding what he means by experience. As seen in the case study presentation, Whitehead analyzes experience in terms of the most irreducible component of existence, which he calls the "actual entity" or "actual occasion." It is as if all of the elements of the past were impulses of energy, forcing an account of that energy; the emerging actual occasion *is* that accounting. All of the past is incorporated, brought together, "interpreted," in each moment of the present. This "interpretive bringing together" is the existent reality. No sooner does it complete its becoming than that completion itself becomes an energy force demanding a further accounting, pushing another present into existence. The present moment is thus related to both a past (the data at the actual occasion's disposal) and the future (the new present that it will force into being). Every moment of present experience must be understood in relation to a past—how far does that past extend? Every moment of present experience must be understood in relation to a future—how far is the future? Answering these questions becomes a route to investigating the credibility of hope.

The account of Whitehead's own history indicates an answer to the first question—how far does that past extend? In the references to Whitehead's youth, the case study speaks of Roman forts, of an historic tree, of cathedrals, and tombs. These material things, made from the stuff of earth, communicate the human past to Whitehead. Nature mediates history; the natural world and the human world together enter the experience of the present. As they do so, they provide the parameters of their own interpretation. A particular people built these walls; King Ethelberg was converted beneath the tree; Becket was in this cathedral; Edward in that tomb. Stories are told, and spots are marked, and the places themselves become the stories mutely but powerfully told. The young boy incorporates the history into his own experience, interpreting himself in its light. The past that becomes a part of Whitehead's identity, then, is not simply the immediate past of his family and friends, but the more distant past, which is yet made present to him through history and nature.

His past, however, extends yet further into the reaches of earth's time: "there were incredible quantities of fossils about . . . the stones were built out of fossils, welded together." To hold a fossil is to touch antiquity, and that past, too, enters into our experience, adding its own data to our self-understanding. But what are its data? And how do simple stones, however old, add to our self-understanding, much less bespeak the credibility of hope?

Fossils tell a silent story that would amaze us if we were not so accustomed to it. They tell of the progression of the world from simplicity toward complexity, from the inorganic to organic. The progression moves steadily through eons of time, relentlessly yielding ever deeper modes of complexity. Each stage of development supports the next, but is transcended by the next, as if the world responds to a call always pulling it beyond one achievement to yet another of increasing complexity. The movement is not without casualty: the wreckage along the way is vast, and whole lines of complex forms reach an end and are lost. The history is harsh—yet it is nevertheless a history of movement, of gradual attainment of successively greater forms of complexity and life. In humanity, the world of nature comes to expression; it wakens to consciousness, looks at itself, wonders, questions, speaks. A further stage is reached, one that Teilhard de Chardin, another process thinker, referred to as that in which evolution became conscious of itself.

The introduction of self-consciousness into this story of movement first told by the fossils creates a qualitatively different factor in the story. Self-consciousness adds an element of control to the direction of the movement. One could use the image of a river for evolution, and the movement within evolution toward complexity is like a current pulling whatever is in that river along. But the current is strong, and sometimes dangerous; sometimes the material in the river disintegrates, or breaks on rocks, or is cast ashore. When a degree of consciousness is achieved by those who are in the river, then it is possible not simply to drift with the current, but to swim with it—or against it. Whether one continued in the stream or whether one ends up adrift is partially the decision of oneself, for the power of consciousness tends toward the power of control to direct the movement of life. The danger, of course, is that the power also allows the destruction of life.

To see ourselves in light of this long past might contribute to our affirming the wonder of the world and of ourselves; we might also feel awe at that "current" or "call" that seems to pull the evolution of things beyond present achievements. But we have not yet provided a ground for hope precisely because (1) there is no guarantee that any one complex species shall propagate itself forever—on the contrary!—and (2) given the complexity of consciousness, we have as much ability to direct our own movement in destructive ways as in constructive ways. Despair and hope appear to be relatively equal options.

Only by taking the future into account does Whitehead weigh the options toward hope. That is, he must account for that "call," or "current." Why is there a transcendence of the past? Why not simple repetition of the past? Each actual occasion, unifying its past, goes beyond it to some extent. If this "going beyond" were always totally explainable in terms of the past, then there would be no problem. However, the fossils insist—and our own experience insists—that this is not the case. Not only is the present more than the simple repetition of the past, but with significant frequency the present introduces a novelty that transforms the past. Whitehead gives a good example of such transformative novelty in his statement concerning physics quoted in the case study: "We supposed that nearly everything of importance about physics was known. . . . But . . . the whole science blew up, and the Newtonian physics, which had been supposed to be fixed as the Everlasting Seat, were gone." Novelty, whether in nature or in human history, transforms the past. Why?

Whitehead takes as axiomatic the principle that everything that happens has its reason either within itself, or in some other actuality. At issue here is the refusal to allow power to that which is not actual: power is located in actuality. If, however, we consider the phenomenon of novelty, how do we account for its power? Prior to actualization, the novelty is only possible—it is the future, relative to everything that exists. The power of novelty cannot be reduced to the power the becoming actuality has to envision the possibility of the future, for the possibilities must exist prior to the envisioning of them. That is, the very grasp of a future possibility presupposes the power exerted by that possibility.

To illustrate this in part through the case study, consider Whitehead's invitation from Harvard University to join the philosophy faculty. Whitehead was sixty-three, with a career in physics and mathematics behind him; his future, following on that career, seemed sure. Suddenly and surprisingly, the invitation comes, and a new possibility for the future emerges for him. "Freedom," he had said earlier, "lies in summoning up a mentality which transforms the situation, as against letting organic reactions take their course." Given the new possibility, Whitehead transformed his past, using it now as the basis for developing a new metaphysical vision. The transformation depended on the gift of the possibility and on Whitehead's response.

We could trace the locus of the possibility to a series of interconnecting events and coincidences, but at some point in the chain the possibility of Whitehead being invited to Harvard emerges as a totally new idea in the world. At that point, the question again must be raised: "How do possibilities have power?" The power must be mediated through actuality, according to the axiom, but no actuality in the world provides the ground for novel possibilities. Further, Whitehead needed to account for the power of *all* possibilities, and not simply those which we see as radically new. Also, a study of the problem of possibilities would yield further complexities: the requirement ultimately was for an actuality that could ground all possibilities, order these possibilities into value, and account for the provision of relevant possibilities to the becoming world. In short, Whitehead needed a ground for what we call the future in order to account for the power of possibilities exerted in the present, pulling existence into novel modes in the direction of complex and increasingly rich forms of existence. Whitehead needed God.

To construct a notion of God that would answer the philosophical problem of the locus and power of possibilities, Whitehead had to remain consistent with his analysis of the dynamics of existence. That is, possibilities, to have power, must be rooted in actuality; actuality has been defined as a relational response to a past with an effect on the future. Further, this effect is understood as the result of the actualization of a possibility that is to some degree novel. That is, the becoming of the new actuality is potentially transformative both in its interpretation of the past and its effects on the future. How can God be understood as actual in keeping with these dynamics and still provide the needed account of possibilities? If God is precisely the same as all other entities, does not God, too, require a source for possibility? But if God is not to be understood through the dynamics of actuality, then is there not a basic incoherence and arbitrariness with respect to the concept of God?

Whitehead resolves the dilemma by applying the dynamics of existence to God in a reverse manner. That is, while he understands finite existence as beginning with feelings of the past and unifying those feelings in terms of a possibility, he considers the reality of God as beginning with a unification of all possibilities, which then affects the divine feelings of the world. The categories are the same, but the manner of application is different. The reversal escapes the charge of arbitrariness, because the effect of the reversal renders the power of possibilities coherent. By understanding God through the reversed dynamics,

Whitehead can posit an understanding of the world that gives a rational account of all our experience, including the power of possibilities.

Briefly, the reversal would indicate the following: God feels all possibilities primordially, unifying them in an ordered vision of harmony. God also feels the world in every moment of its many occurrences. These feelings of the world-as-it-is are integrated with God's own nature, according to God's self-creative ordering of all possibilities. This means that the world-as-it-is is felt in terms of the world-as-it-might-be. Therefore, through the integration of the world into God's nature, new possibilities are felt as relevant for the world. These possibilities gain their relevance both through God's knowledge of the actuality of the world, and through God's own nature toward the optimum harmony of all reality. Thus the possibilities are always transformative in terms of deepening modes of harmony.

We might provide an analogy to illustrate this. Imagine a situation in which Joan, Stephen, and Fran are classmates; Joan knows Stephen well, having been his friend since childhood, whereas Fran knows Stephen only in the context of the class. Stephen is notified that his father has had a serious heart attack. Then, just as he is getting ready to leave college to be with his father in the hospital, word comes that his father has died. Who can best help Stephen through his grief, Joan or Fran? Precisely through her long empathetic understanding of Stephen, Joan will be able to respond to him more appropriately. Likewise, the fullness and precision of God's knowledge of the world through its effect on the divine nature becomes the basis of God's appropriate response to the world. Returning to the analogy, we would expect Joan's response to Stephen to be conditioned not only by her knowledge of him, but also through her own character. Her actions will be consistent with who she is, and her actions will also be a reinforcement or a deepening of who she is. Likewise, God's primordially self-created character governs God's responses toward the world in terms of the world's good. In the analogy, Stephen is responsible for how he deals with Joan's aid; likewise, the world is responsible for whether it moves with or against the transformative possibilities made available to it by God through the divine responsiveness to the world.

The sense in which the analogy is not sufficient is that the analogy presupposes the power of transformation through new possibilities for action. In the metaphysics provided by Whitehead, such possibilities are not accepted without an account of why possibilities should be so effective in the first place. God is the source and ground of possibilities, the "current" that moves within and with the world, luring it in directions of complexity and richness of value. Whether or not these directions are actualized depends on the response of the world.

The basis of hope in Whitehead's philosophy is that he does indeed identify a "current," a source of transformative goodness beyond the world, yet at work within the world. The hope is tempered, because the actualization of the good depends on ourselves: we can work against it as well as with it. But if in fact God is truly responsive to the world in ways that are unfailingly consistent with the divine nature as well as with the needs of the world, then our hope is reinforced by the sense that what we do affects the kinds of possibilities God can realistically offer to the world. It is *our* action to which God responds transformatively; if our actions are in keeping with the good of the world, then the relevant possibilities for the world, in keeping with the divine faithfulness, will be accordingly richer than if we fail to act toward the good. In a process view, our actions matter: God uses them in providing transformative possibilities for the world. Thus the hope that Whitehead's philosophy inspires is a catalyst for responsible action in the midst of the world's problems, not through withdrawal into privacy, but through involvement where it is most needed and where we are most suited for action.

Price must face one further problem: If Price himself is convinced of the credibility of hope in Whitehead's thought, he nevertheless must ask the question of its communicability. Do we explain metaphysical arguments in order to increase hope and therefore action in the world? Whitehead's understanding of existence in terms of the relatedness of things offers pragmatic counsel. In a world of relativity, what we do or do not do affects everything else, necessarily, to a greater or lesser degree. We are, then, responsible for action. By acting in accordance with hope, we invite responses in accordance with hope. The actions themselves become a concrete way to share the vision of hope. In a world of relativity, everything and everyone matters. And the lemmings need not reach the sea.

CHAPTER 12

The Case of Wittgenstein

Can Language Clarify Our Problems, or Does It Confuse Us?

WITTGENSTEIN was enraged! How dare a journal accuse him of keeping his work a secret! Since 1930, for seventeen years, he had given lectures almost every year at Cambridge. Surely that was not the behavior of a man trying to keep a secret! It was true that his *Tractatus Logico–Philosophicus* was the only thing he had ever published. But he had never felt satisfied with any of his later work.

Showing the accusing article to some of his friends, Wittgenstein asked them to publish a reply. When they refused, saying they did not know how to answer the criticism, Wittgenstein became even more angry. Feeling forsaken and unfairly attacked, he considered having the manuscripts of the *Philosophical Investigations* published. That would prove that he was not trying to hide anything. But was he really ready for that? Having rejected his earlier "picture" theory of language, how could he retain the distinction between factual language and religious and ethical language? How could he keep religious and ethical language safe from analysis? Given these reservations, Wittgenstein wondered whether or not he should publish.

Austria-Hungary

In the nineteenth century, Austria-Hungary was one of the most powerful countries in the world. Its solid constitution, history of stability, and large territory made it one of the leaders of Europe. Its music and art were unrivaled throughout the world. Its industrial might was second only to that of the British Empire.

But as the nineteenth century came to an end and the twentieth century began, Vienna, the capital city of Austria-Hungary, was faced with serious problems. The constitution that had remained solid throughout the nationalist struggles of the Czechs, Rumanians, and Slavs now proved inflexible. Rapid economic growth and continued racial turmoil shook the nation. A series of scandals left the population without trust in their leaders. The values of the past century were being discarded with nothing left to replace them. In music, people such as Arnold Schönberg were discarding the musical forms of the past. In art and architecture, conventional ornamentation was being replaced by bizarre decoration. In ethics, there was no recognized common ground for the discussion of personal or social morality.

Early Life

It was into this period of decline that Wittgenstein was born in 1889. Wittgenstein's family was, in many ways, a reflection of the Austro-Hungarian society. His father, Karl Wittgenstein, was a stern, unbending man who had become a millionaire in the Austro-Hungarian steel industry. In addition to his keen business sense, Karl also had a deep love and appreciation for music. Johannes Brahms, Gustaf Mahler, and Pablo Casals were frequent house guests of the Wittgensteins.

Despite his love of music, Karl insisted that his five sons follow him into the business world. When his eldest son, Hans, asked that he be allowed to pursue a career in music, Karl refused. Following a prolonged argument over the matter, Hans fled to North America and finally killed himself. Karl's second son, Rudi, made a similar request; and receiving the same answer, he too committed suicide.

In 1913, Karl died of cancer. His third son, Kurt, took his own life in World War I, preferring death to capture. Karl's fourth son, Paul, despite losing his right arm, became a successful concert pianist. Maurice Ravel's famous "Concerto for the Left Hand" was written specifically for Paul.

The women in the Wittgenstein family were equally as gifted (and equally as strong-willed) as the men. Ludwig's mother, Leopoldine, was an accomplished pianist. His eldest sister, Hermine, was an excellent painter. The youngest of his three sisters, Margarete, was the rebel of the family. A close friend of Sigmund Freud, she helped Freud escape from Austria when Hitler took over.[1]

The Wittgenstein family, with all its talents and conflicts, had an especially strong influence on the young Ludwig. Because Karl was a firm believer in private tutoring, Ludwig was educated at home. It was not until he was fourteen years of age that Ludwig spent much time away from the family residence.

Having shown great promise in the field of engineering (at age ten, he built a working sewing machine out of match sticks), Wittgenstein was enrolled in the Linz *Realschule* in 1904. He arrived at the school at about the same time that another Austro-Hungarian was leaving: Adolf Hitler. Although he primarily studied engineering, Wittgenstein's course of study led him into philosophical and ethical questions. In the Austria-Hungary of that time, many educated people discussed philosophy as it related to their own particular fields.

Wittgenstein did not have any "formal training" in the classical problems of philosophy, although he was very impressed with the writing of Søren Kierke-gaard. But the culture in which he lived provided him with a set of problems and a conception of philosophy which he continued to explore for the rest of his life.

After leaving Linz in 1906, Wittgenstein spent two years studying in Berlin. In 1908, he went to the University of Manchester in England to study aerody-namics.

While designing a propeller, Wittgenstein became interested in mathematics and eventually went to Cambridge in 1911 to study the subject under Bertrand Russell. Russell recalled one of his early encounters with Wittgenstein:

> At the end of his first term at Cambridge he came to me and said, "Will you please tell me whether I am a complete idiot or not?" I replied, "My dear fellow, I don't know. Why are you asking me?" He said, "Because if I am a complete idiot, I shall become an aeronaut; but, if not, I shall become a philosopher." I told him to write me something during the vacation on some philosophical subject and I would then tell him whether he was a complete idiot or not. At the beginning of the following term he brought me the fulfillment of this suggestion. After reading only one sen-tence, I said to him, "No, you must not become an aeronaut."[2]

Following two years at Cambridge, Wittgenstein went to a remote region of Norway. He remained there, living in isolation until 1914 when war broke out. He enlisted as a volunteer in the Austrian artillery. While serving on the east-ern front, he kept notebooks on various philosophical issues. These notebooks formed the basis for the *Tractatus Logico-Philosophicus*. Following his capture by the Italian army in 1917, Wittgenstein managed to complete the work. While still a prisoner of war, he had a copy of the *Tractatus* sent to Russell, who received it enthusiastically. The work was finally published in 1921.

Tractatus: Theory of Language

In the *Tractatus,* Wittgenstein portrayed philosophy as an activity, not a set of theories. In the nineteenth century, philosophers such as Kant and Hegel had tried to present systems that would account for all of reality. But these systems were often contradictory and antiscientific. According to Wittgenstein, most of the problems of philosophy could be traced to a misuse of language. As he put it in one of his early notebooks, "Philosophy gives no pictures of reality and can neither confirm nor confute scientific investigations. Philosophy teaches us the logical form of propositions: that is its fundamental task."[3]

Throughout his life, Wittgenstein continued to hold to this conception of philosophy. Thirty years later he wrote, "Philosophy is a battle against the be-witchment of our intelligence by means of language."[4]

Because most problems in philosophy were related to language, the greater part of the *Tractatus* was devoted to language; its nature and relation to the world. Wittgenstein presented this relationship in terms of a "picture theory of meaning." According to Wittgenstein, language consisted of statements or prop-ositions that picture the world. Just as a picture had something in common with that which it pictured, language had a logical form in common with the world it pictured. This logical form was obscured by ordinary language. The job of philosophy was to clear up this obscure language and ultimately to develop a language that more perfectly pictured the world.

This "clearing up" of ordinary language was done by analysis. Propositions were made up of names (which stand for objects) and a logical form. Together, these names and the logical form created a picture. This picture was the meaning of the proposition. The job of analysis was to find these names and clearly show the logical form. So, for example, the proper way to analyze the proposition "John is going to the store" was to discover what objects the names *John* and *the store* stood for and clearly show the logical form of "_____is going to_____."

Tractatus: **Religious and Ethical Language**

This method of analysis allowed Wittgenstein to make a sharp distinction between factual language, on the one hand, and religious and ethical language, on the other. Factual propositions were those which could be analyzed, because they "pictured" a state of affairs in the world. Religious propositions, however, did *not* "picture" anything in the world. Terms such as *God* or *Being* were not really names. They did not point to anything. Wittgenstein explained that "God does not reveal himself *in* the world."[5] Similarly, ethical assertions could not be analyzed. "The nature of the Good has nothing to do with the facts, and so cannot be explained by any propositions,"[6] Wittgenstein wrote.

The separation of religious and ethical issues from philosophical analysis was fundamental for Wittgenstein. Living in a culture where values were constantly being attacked, he felt the need to remove values from the realm of criticism. Following in the footsteps of Kierkegaard, he made religion and ethics a matter of "wordless faith."[7] No longer were religious and ethical concerns subject to analysis. According to Wittgenstein, one could not even ask religious or ethical questions about the problems of life. As he stated near the end of the *Tractatus,*

> When the answer cannot be put into words, neither can the question be put into words. The *riddle* does not exist. . . . The solution of the problem of life is seen in the vanishing of the question.[8]

But what about the propositions in the *Tractatus* itself? The book claimed that one could not use language to talk about the nature of reality. But to say that was to make a statement about the nature of reality! Wittgenstein was aware of this problem. He said,

> My propositions serve as elucidations in the following way: anyone who understands me eventually recognizes them as nonsensical, when he has used them—as steps—to climb up beyond them.[9]

He likened his work to a "ladder" that was discarded or kicked away once it had been used to climb to a correct picture of the world. Still, Wittgenstein felt that his book presented "on all essential points, the final solution of the problems."[10] However, he also felt that these solutions did not accomplish much. As he put it, "The value of this work consists [in showing] how little is achieved when these problems are solved."[11]

In 1919, following the war, Wittgenstein gave up philosophy, gave away his inheritance, and went to work teaching children in Upper Austria. Having given the "final solution" to the problems of philosophy, he believed that his philosophical work was completed.

Logical Positivism

By the end of World War I, the Austro–Hungarian empire was destroyed. The only remaining vestige of its former greatness was its music, art, and learning. In this period of political and social anarchy, a group of scientists and philosophers began to hold regular discussions. Later known as the "Vienna Circle" the group sought an account of science that would include both mathematics and sensory experience. Ernst Mach, Moritz Schlick, Rudolf Carnap, Kurt Gödel, and Friedrich Waismann were all members of the group.

The Vienna Circle developed a philosophy called "logical positivism" based on the thinking of David Hume and Ludwig Wittgenstein. The positivists began by using Hume's "empirical criterion of meaning." Hume had said that ideas only had meaning if they were copies of sense impressions. The positivists took this criterion and, using Wittgenstein, modified it slightly, developing the "verification criterion of meaning."

The positivists claimed that the "meaning of a proposition is its method of verification." To find the meaning of the proposition "That cow is brown," one had to discover how to verify it. Presumably one could verify it by going out into the pasture and looking to see if the cow was, in fact, brown. The proposition, then, meant something about physical cows and the color, brown. The appropriate kind of scientist should then verify the truth of the statement. The philosopher's task was simply to identify whether the proposition was meaningful; that is, whether there was a means by which it could be verified.

According to the positivists, there were two general types of propositions that were meaningful: propositions such as "That cow is brown," which could be verified empirically, and propositions such as "All unmarried men are bachelors," which were logically necessary. This was similar to Wittgenstein's picture theory of meaning. Like Wittgenstein, the logical positivists looked for names and logical form. They attempted to develop a perfect language that would clearly reflect the world. They also excluded religious and ethical propositions, maintaining that propositions about God, being, the good, and so on were meaningless because they were neither logically necessary nor empirically verifiable.

The logical positivists were similar to Wittgenstein in another way, as well. Like the propositions in the *Tractatus,* the propositions the logical positivists used to describe their philosophy did not meet their own criterion. Their basic assumption, "All meaningful statements must be either empirically verifiable or logically necessary," was itself neither "empirically verifiable" nor "logically necessary." The standard that they set up for meaningful propositions was not itself a meaningful proposition.

The Return to Philosophy

While working as a schoolteacher, Wiggenstein discovered that the ordinary language of his students was more rich and complex than he had previously realized. Without knowing anything about the logical form of propositions, his students were quite capable of communicating clearly.

Following six years as a schoolteacher, Wittgenstein resumed his studies in philosophy. In 1926, while working on a house that he had designed for his sister he attended the meetings of the Vienna Circle. New questions about language began to fascinate him. In 1929, he returned to Cambridge and, after submitting the already famous *Tractatus* as a doctoral dissertation, he became a research fellow.

For the rest of his life, Wittgenstein gave lectures almost yearly at Cambridge. One of his students gave the following account of those lectures:

> He nearly always held them in his own room or in the college rooms of a friend. He had no manuscript of notes. He *thought* before the class. The impression was of tremendous concentration. The exposition usually led to a question, to which the audience was supposed to suggest an answer. The answers in turn became starting points for new thoughts leading to new questions. It depended on the audience, to a great extent, whether the discussion became fruitful and whether the connecting thread was kept in sight from beginning to end of a lecture and from one lecture to another.[12]

After these intense sessions, Wittgenstein would often go to the movies. He insisted that Westerns were the only movies worth seeing because they portrayed the struggle of good versus evil in such a clear and simple way. He also enjoyed reading detective stories. Once he remarked that he could not understand how anyone who enjoyed detective stories could stand to read the philosophical journal *Mind*.

In general, Wittgenstein disliked professional philosophy. He once said to a friend,

> What is the use of studying philosophy if all that it does for you is to enable you to talk with some plausibility about some abstruse questions of logic, etc., and if it does not improve your thinking about the important questions of everyday life.[13]

During the early 1930s, Wittgenstein wrote much but did not publish. By this time, he had ceased to believe in a picture theory of language and was no longer interested in finding a perfect language hidden in the obscurity of ordinary usage. In place of thinking about language and pictures, he began to explore the relationship between language and games. In 1935, he returned to Norway and lived in isolation while working on the *Philosophical Investigations*.

Philosophical Investigations: Theory of Language

The basic thesis of the *Investigations* was that meaningful language occurred in the life of human beings as they did the things that human beings do. The meaning of a given word was no longer to be found by showing how it was a part of a proposition that pictured the world. Rather, "the meaning of a word is its use in the language."[14]

The various situations of "forms of life" in which human beings use language provided the context for what Wittgenstein called "language games." Just as there was no one characteristic that was common to all games, so also there was no theory that could explain all the uses of language. Wittgenstein explained,

> Instead of producing something common to all that we call language, I am saying that these phenomena have no one thing in common which makes us use the same word for all, but that they are *related* to one another in many different ways. And it is because of this relationship, or these relationships, that we call them all "language."
>
> Consider for example the procedings that we call "games." I mean board-games, card-games, ball-games, Olympic games, and so on. What is common to them all?— Don't say: "There had to be something in common, or they would not be called 'games' "—but *look and see* whether there is anything common to all. For if you look at them you will not see something that is common to *all,* but similarities, relationships and a whole series of them at that.[15]

For example, the proposition "That cow is brown" must be analyzed in its context. Was the proposition intended to make a scientific observation, or was it simply being used to distinguish one cow from the next? In the first case, what might be called the "language game of twentieth century zoology," there was a need for precision and accuracy not necessary in the second case, "the language game of farming." Although the proposition remained formally (structurally) the same in both cases, and the means of verifying the proposition were the same, it was clear that the zoologist meant something quite different from the farmhand. The two uses of the proposition arose out of different contexts, different "forms of life."

Wittgenstein also maintained in the *Investigations* that there was no need for a "perfect" language. Rather than trying to sift out the names and logical form of language, one should examine the forms of life out of which language arose. All language was suited to the particular needs it served, so no sifting or perfecting process was needed, ordinary language was already perfectly suited to express the ideas people wanted to express. Wittgenstein declared,

> We are not *striving after* an ideal, as if our ordinary vague sentences had not yet got a quite unexceptionable sense, and a perfect language awaited construction by us. On the other hand it seems clear that where there is sense there must be perfect order. So there must be perfect order even in the vaguest sentence.[16]

The only time problems arose was when propositions were taken out of their particular language game and applied to a context for which they were not intended. For instance, when mathematical precision was called for in history or sociology, problems were bound to arise. Mathematical precision was part of the language game of the natural sciences and not of the liberal arts or social sciences. This was not to say that the liberal arts could not be precise, but rather that they could not be judged by the standards of another language game. The rules of basketball could not be judged by the rules of chess, yet both were valid games with proper rules.

Philosophical Investigations: Religious and Ethical Language

The "game" theory of language left Wittgenstein with a major problem. The "picture" theory of the *Tractatus* had made a complete distinction between religious and ethical language on the one hand and factual language on the other hand. Because religious and ethical words did not picture anything in the world, they were without meaning. They were outside the world of facts, and hence, outside the world of analysis and critique.

But what happened to this distinction in the "game" theory of the *Philosophical Investigations?* The fact that at least some people apparently understood the use of words such as *God* and *good* seemed to indicate that they were a meaningful part of language. Such words seemed to belong to the "language games" of religion and ethics. Religious and ethical terms did not need to be "purged" in order to form a more perfect language.

What then was to become of the original absolute distinction? Wittgenstein attempted to deal with this problem by claiming that religious and ethical propositions were usually taken out of their contexts. In fact, religious and ethical propositions were usually so far removed from their respective contexts or language games that they were meaningless. As Wittgenstein explained,

> Suppose someone said: "What do you believe, Wittgenstein? Are you a sceptic? Do you know whether you will survive death?" I would really, this is a fact, say, "I can't say. I don't know," because I haven't any clear idea what I'm saying when I'm saying "I don't cease to exist," etc.[17]

(For a comparison of the basic ideas of the *Tractatus* and the *Investigations*, see the table on p. 208.)

The Return to Cambridge

Wittgenstein returned to Cambridge in 1937 and was appointed a full professor in 1939. But before he could begin teaching World War II began. Wittgenstein volunteered to work as an hospital orderly in London and later in Newcastle-upon-Tyne.

Following the war, Wittgenstein returned to his teaching post. He soon became depressed over his students' continual misunderstanding of his lectures. When he taught that words were to be understood in their context apart from "fixed" meanings, many students took it as an excuse for sloppiness in their own thinking. Furthermore, Wittgenstein was distressed about the *Philosophical Investigations*. Although he was close to completion, he still pondered the use of religious and ethical language. As he wrote to a friend in 1945, "My book is gradually nearing its final form . . . and the truth is: It's pretty lousy. (Not that I could improve on it essentially if I tried for another 100 years.)"[18]

The Decision

In the winter of 1947, a literary and critical journal published an article giving a popular account of current British philosophers. In the article, Wittgenstein's later work was said to be basically unknown.

The insinuation that he kept his work a secret angered Wittgenstein. He considered his yearly lectures to be a kind of publication. As he reread the article, Wittgenstein considered the possible responses. He could immediately publish his *Philosophical Investigations*, but the problems of religious and ethical language still bothered him. He could continue to work on the manuscript and ignore the article, but would more time really help? What should he do?

Comparison of Wittgenstein's Early and Later Work

1. Similarities
   a. Philosophy is an activity, not a set of theories.
   b. Object of philosophy is to remove problems.
   c. Primary interest is with the nature of language and its relation to philosophy.
   d. Philosophy is concerned to show the separation between religious and ethical language on the one hand and factual language on the other.

2. Differences

	Tractatus (early) (1918–approx. 1930)	*Investigations* (later) (approx. 1930–1951)
a. Ultimate data	Names (which stand for objects) and logical forms	Forms of life in which language games are embedded
b. Meaningful propositions	Only those which picture a state of affairs in the world	Those which arise out of the ordinary uses of words
c. Religious and ethical propositions	Meaningless because they are not pictures of states	Not completely clear: apparently to be understood in the context in which they are used

NOTES

1. For more information on Austria-Hungary and the Wittgenstein family, see Allen Janik and Stephen Toulmin, *Wittgenstein's Vienna* (New York: Simon & Schuster, 1973).
2. Bertrand Russell, *Portraits from Memory* (London: Allen & Unwin, 1957), pp. 26–27.
3. Ludwig Wittgenstein, *Notebooks 1914–1916* (London: Basil Blackwell, 1961), p. 93.
4. Ludwig Wittgenstein, *Philosophical Investigations* (New York: Macmillan, 1958), no. 109, p. 47.
5. Ludwig Wittgenstein, *Tractatus Logico-Philosophicus* (London: Routledge & Kegan Paul, 1922), 6.432, p. 149.
6. From Friedrich Waismann, *Ludwig Wittgenstein und der Wiener Kreis*, p. 115, cited in Janik and Toulmin, p. 233.
7. Janik and Toulmin, *Wittgenstein*, p. 24.
8. *Tractatus*, 6.5–6.521, p. 149.
9. Ibid., 6.54, p. 151.
10. Ibid., preface, p. 5.
11. Ibid.
12. Norman Malcolm, *Ludwig Wittgenstein: A Memoir* (London: Oxford University Press, 1958), pp. 16–17.
13. Malcolm, p. 39.
14. Wittgenstein, *Investigations*, no. 43, p. 20.
15. Ibid., nos. 65–66, p. 31.
16. Ibid., no. 98, p. 45.
17. Ludwig Wittgenstein, *Lectures and Conversations*, edited by Cyril Barrett (Berkeley: University of California Press, n.d.), p. 70.
18. Malcolm, pp. 42–43.

BIBLIOGRAPHY

Primary Sources

Wittgenstein, Ludwig. *Tractatus Logico-Philosophicus*. London: Routledge & Kegan Paul, 1922.
Wittgenstein, Ludwig. *Philosophical Investigations*. New York: Macmillan, 1958.

Biography

Janik, Allen, and Toulmin, Stephen. *Wittgenstein's Vienna*. New York: Simon & Schuster, 1973.

Interpretative Works

Fann, K. T. *Wittgenstein's Conception of Philosophy*. Berkeley: University of California Press, 1969.
Kenny, Anthony. *Wittgenstein*. Cambridge, Mass.: Harvard University Press, 1973.
Malcolm, Norman. *Ludwig Wittgenstein: A Memoir*. London: Oxford University Press, 1958.
Pears, David. *Ludwig Wittgenstein*. New York: Penguin, 1969.
Pitcher, G. *The Philosophy of Wittgenstein*. Englewood Cliffs, N.J.: Prentice-Hall, 1964.

QUESTIONS FOR STUDY

1. Trace the development of Wittgenstein's views of language to his life situation and relationship with people. Illustrate with data from the case.

2. Outline the main principles contained in Wittgenstein's *Tractatus Logico-Philosophicus* and contrast them with Wittgenstein's later ideas concerning language found in *Philosophical Investigations*.

3. Discuss Wittgenstein's attitude toward metaphysics in both his earlier and later work.

4. What is the meaning of the word *game*? Give examples. Divide the class into two teams and have one team define *game* according to the *Tractatus* and the other team defend the view of *game* found in *Philosophical Investigations*.

5. Put yourself in the place of a logical positivist who has gone into a church and hears a minister preach that "God is love." How would the positivist react? Do the same simulation using a linguistic analyst as the hearer. How do you personally respond when you hear such proclamations as "God is love"?

A Contemporary Response

JERRY H. GILL

THREE MAIN issues arise from a consideration of Wittgenstein's case, issues that both illuminate the unique character of his philosophy and illustrate its applicability to nonphilosophical but important areas of concern. The three issues are (1) the function of philosophy, (2) the nature of language, and (3) the status of religious and ethical judgments. A brief treatment of these issues will give some indication as to how Wittgenstein might have fruitfully faced the decision that confronted him in the winter of 1947.

The Function of Philosophy

Without too much oversimplification, it can be said that traditionally philosophers have viewed philosophical problems as having definite answers, and thus, as being capable of being *solved*. The history of philosophy is often seen as the history of the various answers offered by philosophers as solutions to philosophical problems. At the beginning of the twentieth century, the picture of the function of philosophy underwent a rather radical change. Some thinkers, such as Bertrand Russell, still maintained that philosophical problems must be solved—although Russell did argue for a new method of arriving at solutions, namely the method of mathematical logic—but many other thinkers, represented by both A. J. Ayer and the young Wittgenstein, came to regard philosophical problems as "pseudo-problems" that could not be solved, but only *dissolved*. The only problems capable of solution, according to such logical empiricists, were those which lay in the domains of the various sciences. Philosophy's function was simply to distinguish between the "real problems" (scientific and logical ones) and the "pseudo-problems."

It is often thought—even among people who should surely know better— that the later Wittgenstein shared this view that philosophical problems and/or metaphysical problems were not to be solved, but only dissolved. Although he did direct many of his remarks against the views of traditional philosophers and

Russell, a careful reading of the *Philosophical Investigations* should make it clear that Wittgenstein did *not* maintain that philosophical problems were pseudo-problems only capable of being dissolved. My own suggestion is that a more profitable way to characterize his view of philosophical problems is to say that, rather than maintaining either that they are to be solved or that they are to be dissolved, Wittgenstein contends that philosophical problems are to be *re-solved*. The point of putting it this way is threefold: first, the resolution of a problem, unlike the dissolution of a problem, implies that the problem is (or was) real; second, this way of speaking still distinguishes philosophical problems from scientific ones that have specific answers; and third, the term *resolution* suggests the sort of conceptual and linguistic disentanglement that characterizes Wittgenstein's actual procedure. Knots are untied (solved), fake knots are exposed (dissolved), but tangles are disentangled (resolved).

> The problems are solved, not by giving new information, but by arranging what we have always known. Philosophy is a battle against the bewitchment of our intelligence by means of language.[1]

Consider now Paragraph 133, in which Wittgenstein focused most directly on the question of the aim of philosophy:

> It is not our aim to refine or complete the system of rules for the use of our words in unheard-of ways.
>
> For the clarity that we are aiming at is indeed *complete* clarity. But this simply means that the philosophical problems should completely disappear.
>
> The real discovery is the one that makes me capable of stopping doing philosophy when I want to.—The one that gives philosophy peace, so that it is no longer tormented by questions which bring *itself* in question.—Instead, we now demonstrate a method, by examples; and the series of examples can be broken off.—Problems are solved (difficulties eliminated), but not a *single* problem.
>
> There is not *a* philosophical method, though there are indeed methods, like different therapies.[2]

The type of completeness Wittgenstein had in mind does away with the specific philosophical problem in question—by resolving it—but it does not do away with all philosophical problems in one fell swoop. Although he subscribed to the latter position in his *Tractatus,* in the *Investigations* Wittgenstein was content to take up specific problems and deal with them one by one. Such a procedure is one that in one sense will never be completed, but that in another sense can be completed at any time—namely, when a given difficulty has been resolved. This view of the function of philosophy provides peace because one is no longer driven by the unrealizable goal of arriving at an exhaustive and final system of truth about reality. The use of the continuous present tense ("stopping doing philosophy") brings this point out clearly. On the other hand, there is always plenty of philosophical work to be done—the problems have not been put aside as pseudo-problems. Thus, specific difficulties can be dealt with by means of examples and clear vision, without resorting to philosophical dogmatism of either the traditional or the positivist type.

The Nature of Language

Perhaps the best way to get at Wittgenstein's understanding of the nature of language is by drawing a contrast between the root metaphors of his early and later works.

In the *Tractatus,* Wittgenstein sought to ground linguistic meaning in the formal, abstract structure of language. Through an analysis of the logical relationships among words, conceived of as an interlocking network of arbitrary symbols, he claimed to have explained both the nature of language per se and the nature of its relationship to the world. The root metaphor on which this account of language and reality was based was "logical space." In essence, this is a mathematical model, arising most likely from Wittgenstein's early training in engineering and his work with Russell in the foundations of mathematics.

In the *Investigations,* language is spoken of in *organic* metaphors. Speech is seen as a dynamic phenomenon that is alive, in the sense that it is always changing; parts of it die off and new parts grow on. Thus language is alive both internally, in terms of its developing nature, and externally, in terms of its *functional* relation to the world. Language is not viewed as a static reflection of reality, but rather as an instrument by means of which reality is dealt with and altered. Moreover, it is "open-textured," in the sense that it is both flexible and evolving.

In fact, this dynamic, interactive emphasis of the *Investigations* is carried over into its very form and structure. Its central stylistic characteristic is that of dialogical development, not in the heavy-handed fashion of Plato, but in the sense of honest wrestling with ideas and potential opponents, a kind of "thinking-out-loud." Here the metaphor of a labyrinth is especially important. The difference between a series of points located in logical space and the crisscrossing, overlapping, mazelike character of a labyrinth is not simply that of order and precision versus nonuniformity and ambiguity. Equally as important is the fact that one is on the outside looking in with respect to the former, while one is inside the latter. This represents a crucial change in standpoint from the early work of Wittgenstein to the later. The external position gives one the delusion of objectivity, that total order and precision are possible, while the internal standpoint forces one to see that such goals are both unattainable and unnecessary.

One final aspect of this organic, functional view needs to be mentioned, and that is its social dimension. In the *Investigations,* language is portrayed as part of the social, public fabric of human existence, not as existing independently of life, nor as the result of a single, objective thinker's dream. Language is a *community* enterprise, arising out of and finding its meaning in the social matrix of interpersonal and institutional interaction. Here, too, the placement of language *in* the world, and of speakers within language, completely avoids the kind of subjective and skeptical muddles generated by the approach of the *Tractatus.* It does so by choosing a different starting point and arguing that the traditional philosophical muddles are abstractions that themselves stand in need of justification in terms of concrete human speech, and not vice versa.

The Status of Religious and Ethical Judgments

I should like now to explore briefly the implications of Wittgenstein's insights for the problem of the meaning of religious and ethical discourse. More specifically, I want to engage the current discussion of what has been called "Wittgensteinian fideism" (or belief on the basis of faith alone). In response to the challenge of logical empiricism, that expressions of religious beliefs are cognitively insignificant (not subject to being judged true or false), certain thinkers have put forth the view that religious and ethical beliefs are totally independent and unique and are thus not subject to the usual standards of cognitive significance. For the most part, they have drawn on the later Wittgenstein's concept of diverse language games for support of their view—hence the term "Wittgensteinian fideism" (or faithism). Simply put, this point of view maintains that the language used to express religious and ethical beliefs is indigenous to a given community of faith and need only conform to the intramural criteria of that community to be meaningful.

There are three criticisms I wish to bring against this whole approach. The first pertains to the fact that in spite of the necessity of being on the "inside" of a religious tradition or community in order to understand it, such a necessity does not preclude the possibility and value of raising questions about the meaning and/or truth of the utterances made within the language-game in question. To do so would be to consign almost all of us to a kind of schizophrenia, because we each participate in many different language-games. Moreover, such a position completely overlooks the possibility of a person's conversion or change of commitment from one community to another, which is a rather common occurrence.

Second, Wittgensteinian fideism is not, in the final analysis, Wittgensteinian at all. Nowhere in the *Philosophical Investigations* does Wittgenstein maintain that all language games are independent of one another. In fact, his dominant model is that of crisscrossing, overlapping paths forming a kind of labyrinth. Moreover, there is a difference between language games and forms of life. A case can be made for interpreting religious belief and expression as a language game, but it is most difficult indeed to view them as comprising a distinct form of life. Wittgenstein invariably speaks of life forms as involving beliefs and behavior patterns that are not taken on or left off in the way religion frequently is. This points to a commonality of life form among human beings that underlies differences of language games and renders them open to consideration and appraisal by all those participating in it.

Thirdly, it is not the case that forms of life, embedded in bedrock beliefs, are irrational and/or beyond all justification. Wittgenstein presses this point quite strongly by grounding rationality in *persuasion*. The crucial point is that, apart from some underlying commonality, even persuasion would be both powerless and meaningless. It is when we have reached the bedrock level that the logic of persuasion is seen to be that of tacit, or intuitive, knowing. At this level, those certainties that made all others possible—and that cannot be said—manifest themselves in the patterns of our common humanity. If basic religious beliefs are of this kind, and I believe they are, then their meaning and truth must be revealed *within* our common human existence, not *independent* of it. Wittgenstein's line of argument grounds all beliefs and forms of reasoning, even persuasion, in commonality of life form, not in mutual independence.

Thus I do not think that Wittgenstein's later work can be used to support this particular interpretation of religious and ethical belief. Rather, I believe that it suggests the possibility of a more radical, all-inclusive understanding of value judgments as a form of tacit knowledge that, although it cannot be rendered entirely explicit, can be expected to reveal itself in the warp and woof of human existence. Although it cannot be "said," it will "show" itself.

In conclusion, then, my own suggestion would be that Wittgenstein's later work already contained, at least implicitly, the answer to his dilemma. The nature of his approach to philosophy, as an *activity* rather than a *system* of thought, gave rise to the suspicion that he was keeping something a secret. The notion that philosophical problems, while both inevitable and real, can be resolved but not solved makes a straightforward presentation, in standard book form, difficult if not impossible. Nevertheless, his "open-textured" understanding of language, as a contextual, social activity grounded in the everyday tasks of the human form of life, is as valuable as it is revolutionary and thus deserves to be known. Moreover, this approach to language provides a way of thinking of religious and ethical discourse that allows for meaning while avoiding the difficulties of both reductionism (explaining intangible reality completely in terms of the tangible) and isolationism. This solution goes a long way toward undermining the insidious dichotomy between fact and value that characterizes so much of our contemporary experience.

Fortunately, even though Wittgenstein did not publish a reply to the indictment leveled against him, his *Philosophical Investigations* were published two years after his death in 1951. Philosophy has not been, and never will be, the same again.

NOTES

1. Ludwig Wittgenstein, *Philosophical Investigations* (New York: Macmillan, 1958), no. 109, p. 47.
2. Ibid., no. 133, p. 51.

General Bibliography

Reference Books and Histories of Philosophy Used in Preparing These Cases and for Further Study

Allen, E. L. *From Plato to Nietzsche: Ideas That Shape Our Lives.* New York: Association Press, 1959.

Bertman, Martin A. *Research Guide in Philosophy.* Morristown, N.J.: General Learning Press, 1974.

Brehier, E. *The History of Philosophy.* Translated by Wade Baskin. Chicago: University of Chicago Press, 1965–1969. Seven vols.

Copleston, Frederick. *History of Philosophy.* New York: Doubleday, 1961–1965. Seven vols.

Edwards, Paul, ed. *Encyclopedia of Philosophy.* New York: Macmillan, 1967. Eight vols.

Jones, W. T. *A History of Western Philosophy.* New York: Harcourt, Brace and World, 1952. Five vols.

Stumpf, Samuel E. *Socrates to Sartre: A History of Philosophy.* New York: McGraw-Hill, 1966.

About the Contributors

MARILYN McCORD ADAMS is professor of philosophy at the University of California in Los Angeles. She studied at the University of Illinois and at Cornell University, where she earned her doctorate. She has published articles on William of Ockham and with Norman Kratzmann has published a translation of Ockham's treatise on predestination, *God's Foreknowledge and Future Contingents.*

STEPHEN T. DAVIS is associate professor of philosophy and religion at Claremont Men's College in Claremont, California. He has degrees from Whitworth College and Princeton Theological Seminary and a doctorate in philosophy from Claremont Graduate School. He is the author of *The Debate About the Bible: Inerrancy versus Infallibility; Skepticism, Evidence, and Faith: An Essay in Religious Epistemology;* and *Logic and the Nature of God.* He edited *Confronting Evil: Live Options in Theodicy.*

JERRY H. GILL is professor of Christianity and culture at Eastern College in St. Davids, Pennsylvania. He has degrees from Westmont College, the University of Washington, and New York Theological Seminary, and received a doctorate from Duke University. He is the author of *Ingmar Bergman and the Search for Meaning, The Possibility of Religious Knowledge,* and *Ian Ramsey: To Speak Responsibly of God,* and was the editor of a series of yearly collections of articles entitled *Philosophy Today.*

ROBERT C. LEVIS is associate professor of philosophy at Pasadena City College in Pasadena, California. He has a degree in mathematics from the University of Delaware and master's degrees in philosophy of religion from Union Theological Seminary in New York City and in philosophy from Columbia University. He has taught French and algebra as well as philosophy. He recently returned from a year of research and teaching in France.

ARTHUR F. HOLMES is professor of philosophy and chairman of that department at Wheaton College in Wheaton, Illinois. A native of England, he has bachelor's and master's degrees from Wheaton and a doctorate from Northwestern University. He is the author of *Philosophy: A Christian Perspective, Faith Seeks Understanding, The Idea of a Christian College,* and *All Truth is God's Truth.* In addition he has written the article, "Christian Philosophy," in the *Encyclopedia Britannica* (thirteenth edition).

RALPH McINERNY is professor of philosophy at the University of Notre Dame in Indiana and director of The Medieval Institute. He has degrees from St. Paul Seminary and the University of Minnesota, and a doctorate from Laval University. He is the author of a two-volume *History of Western Philosophy, Thomism in an Age of Renewal,* and *St. Thomas Aquinas*. In addition, he has written novels, short stories, poems, and a series of Father Dowling mysteries.

GEORGE I. MAVRODES is professor of philosophy at the University of Michigan. He has degrees from Oregon State College, Western Baptist Theological Seminary, and the University of Michigan, where he earned his doctorate. He has served on the program committee of the American Philosophical Association and is a member of the board of editorial consultants of the *American Philosophical Quarterly*. In addition to numerous journal articles, he has published a book, *Belief in God*.

HARRY A. NIELSEN is professor of philosophy at the University of Windsor in Windsor, Ontario, Canada. He has degrees from Rutgers University and the University of Connecticut, and has a doctorate from the University of Nebraska. He is the author of *Methods of Natural Science: An Introduction, The Visages of Adam: Philosophical Readings on the Nature of Man,* and *The Inch: Diary of a White Christian*. In addition, he has published poetry, a short story, and a children's book entitled *Olaf and the Frump*.

ALVIN PLANTINGA is professor of philosophy at Calvin College. He has degrees from Calvin College, the University of Michigan, and Yale University, where he earned his doctorate. He has been a visiting lecturer at many American universities and in 1980 gave the Freemantle Lectures at Oxford University. Among his publications are *God and Other Minds; The Nature of Necessity; God, Freedom and Evil;* and *Does God Have a Nature?* He was chosen vice-president of the American Philosophical Association, 1980–1981.

JOHN K. ROTH is Russell K. Pitzer Professor of Philosophy at Claremont Men's College, Claremont, California, and is on the faculty of the Claremont Graduate School. He has a bachelor's degree from Pomona College and a master's degree and doctorate in philosophy from Yale University. He is the author of *Freedom and the Moral Life: The Ethics of William James* and has edited two volumes of James's writings. Among his most recent works are *American Dreams: Meditations on Life in the United States* and *A Consuming Fire: Encounters with Elie Wiesel and the Holocaust*.

MARJORIE SUCHOCKI is associate professor of theology at Pittsburgh Theological Seminary. She holds degrees from Pomona College and the Claremont Graduate School, where she earned her doctorate. She has written articles on theology and the feminist experience. She is writing a book on process theology for laypeople entitled *A Vision of Reality*.

ROBERT C. WILLIAMS is associate professor of philosophy at Vanderbilt University in Nashville, Tennessee. He studied at Oakwood College, Louisville Presbyterian Theological Seminary, and Union Theological Seminary in New York City. He received his doctorate from Columbia University in New York City. He has published extensively in the area of black religion and African philosophy. During 1979–80, he was visiting faculty scholar in philosophy at Harvard University. In the 1980–81 academic year, he served as assistant director of intercultural research at the National Endowment for the Humanities.

Index